A VICIOUS CYCLE

Escaping the Beast Within

David Valenti Maurice Kennedy

Published by:
Light Switch Press
PO Box 272847
Fort Collins, CO 80527
www.lightswitchpress.com

ISBN: 978-1-939828-02-6
Printed in the United States of America

Baby Boy

He's truly a blessing. God thanks for baby boy. He's innocent and pure as
sugar, and my heart fills with love and joy.
At infancy you surrounded him with Angels and like a
book his mind is open and ready to explore.
You've filled him with your knowledge and wisdom,
and his gifts are what people can't ignore.
Once encountered by his beauty the absence of his
presence keeps people wanting more.
Please God limit his sufferings because with your blessings
there's nothing he can't endure.
I'll plant the seeds of your will, and I promise that I will enjoy,
His triumphs into manhood but until then he'll always be my baby boy...

David V.M. Kennedy

1

It was an unseasonably warm spring day in the city of York, Pennsylvania during March of 1976. The temperature was hovering around 82 degrees, and the children of Hope Avenue, (Hope Alley is what the locals called it) played as if a vile stench didn't even exist in the atmosphere. There was trash everywhere and not just from the routine waste management pick up either. The smell lingering in the air was as if someone spray painted each house with an odor that smelled like the inside toe jam of a person infected with athlete's foot. This was no ordinary avenue of the typical inner city norm. The houses were somewhat run down but they still looked stable enough for habitation. In what looked like one of the local neighbor's yard appeared to be what looked like a mini junk yard. The yard had a section about 30 feet from the home that had an old rusty Volkswagen Beetle parked inside of what looked like a garage of weeds. Old pieces of lumber were scattered throughout the yard, and there was also a pile of wood that looked like it was stacked in a formation that was ready for someone to have a bon fire.

Most of the neighborhood kids played in the street as they looked out for cars that rarely traveled down Hope Avenue. The children's ages ranged from elementary to middle school aged kids, and sitting on the stoop of one of the homes was a little boy. He appeared to be in the first grade, and he sat alone holding a red rubber kick ball. This simple red rubber ball appeared to be more to him than a simple toy. He gripped and caressed the ball with a passionate and desirable look on his face. Unlike the other children this kid stood out as if a saguaro cactus was in the middle of a farm during a Pennsylvanian snow storm. While wearing a shirt with multiple stripes that had the color sequence of red, white, and blue the six year old child was neat from head to toe. His hair was in the style of an Afro, but he did not appear to have the look of a "typical" full blooded African American child.

Even though the child looked like he had mixed features it was his hair that was the most noticeable one. It appeared to be larger than his entire body, and it looked like soft pure cotton that was dipped in jet black ink. His baby pot belly could not even overwhelm the presence of his hair. Although it was playtime in a rundown neighborhood, this kid had the look of a young model on the verge of instant stardom. With so many children to play with on the block the question was why did this particular child play alone?

Inside the little boy's house was the boy's mother who was a young woman in her early twenties preparing dinner. She just finished washing her dishes and as she sprayed the remaining suds in the sink she yelled for her son to come inside.

"Devon!" his mom yelled repeatedly.

"Yes mommy," he replied.

"Didn't you hear me calling you boy?"

"I'm sorry mommy, but I was exploring my imagination," he said with an intellectual response.

"Exploring your imagination? Get in this house," she said with a chuckle.

"Aw mom can I please play for a little while longer?"

"Go ahead but you stay where I can see you!"

"Ok, I will, has daddy arrived home yet?"

"No he has not, why?"

"Well he said that we were going to construct my model car."

"He's going to construct your model car?"

"Why, yes mother, I plan on enhancing my room with the décor of toy models," Devon said as he tried to keep from laughing.

"Boy you are a trip! You don't even know what the heck you just said. But then again I'm sure you do!"

"I do now Mom, I looked it up in the dictionary!"

"Well good for you Devon!"

"Thanks Mom, do you wanna see my fort?"

"I will sweetie, but now because I'm getting ready to watch the Ms. America Beauty Pageant."

"What's a beauty pageant? Oh, I know! Is that when they wear those diamond made dresses? Why don't you have a diamond dress Mom? You're beautiful."

"Well thank you son but those are called sequence dresses; they are not diamonds at all!"

"Well when I get rich Mom, I'm gonna by you a diamond dress!"

The little boy's mother laughed as she headed toward the house, and the woman in her early twenties was simply amazed at the conversations that her little six years old carried. She had to remind herself that this was the same kid who began reading at the age of three.

As the young mother reached for her apron from the handle of her white oven door, she began staring out the window into the neighborhood. She placed her forearms on the sink as she daydreamed about her life. The young mother was only twenty two years old and her name was Marsha Chance. She had her son at the tender age of fifteen one month prior to her sixteenth birthday. She named him Devon Soriano Piccolo Chance. Instead of taking on his father's last name she gave her son Soriano as one of his middle names due to the fact that Devon's father carried a name that wasn't his birthright. The name Soriano came from his biological grandfather who passed away before Devon was even thought of. Even though Marsha gave birth as a teen, she had a young life that was full of experience, and she had no choice but to be prepared for motherhood.

Although Marsha was a teenage mother who had to grow up extremely fast, and in spite of being adopted at the tender age of four, she was raised by a strong Christian based family who provided her with a stable religious upbringing. Marsha knew who her biological mother was but she never developed a true mother daughter relationship due to her mother's selfish ways. Her mother wanted nothing to do with Marsha or her younger sister Sicily. Both sisters grew up referring to their biological mother as Becky Ann rather than calling her mom.

Even though it is disrespectful for a child to call their parents by their first name Marsha had a very good reason to not respect her biological mother. Becky Ann had children during a time period where everyone was behaving in a promiscuous behavior. She put herself first and her children on the back burner while she took a ride through York on the "keep it on the down low train". This promiscuity caused Marsha not to know who her real father was thus causing a chain reaction that was surely to make the ugly seeds of the beast within to sprawl through the children of each generation to come.

Even though Becky Ann could have been a warm and nurturing mother, her selfishness interrupted what could have been a beautiful motherhood. One could argue that Marsha's mother was a product of her environment. York, Pennsylvania was a small city of about 70,000 people, and it was a three ring circus for promiscuity. Many secrets were kept from one another as each rider of the "keep it on the down low train" made stops at many different stations! As the conductor of the "keep it on the down low train" yelled, "All aboard!" there was one thing that these passengers during this time period lost sight of and that was the "luggage" that they left behind. Many children in the future suffered due to their behavior and Devon was one of them. Devon's mother and father were both raised in a dysfunctional environment and they were prime examples of the "luggage" that went unclaimed at Grand Sexual Station.

Although Becky Ann's ignorance forced Marsha and her younger sister Sicily into adoption, they were taken in by their cousin Eva Promise and her husband Sal. The Promises were morally cognizant and they gave Marsha a stable spiritual upbringing. Regardless of how happy the home was Marsha rebelled like the average teenager usually does and she became pregnant with Devon at the age of fifteen.

In spite of Marsha's adoptive parents not condoning her pregnancy they still loved her as if she was their own daughter. They forgave her for her "sin" and yet she moved in with Devon's father whose name was Devon Piccolo. Like Marsha, big Devon was also an orphan who was adopted. Big Devon was adopted when he was two years old by an elderly Italian-American man who took him in as a favor for his biological father whose name was Arthur

Soriano. Similar to Marsha's mother big Devon's father was also a "victim" of the times. Arthur Soriano was the epitome of a young black martyr during the civil rights movement and he could care less about how people viewed him. Although he was a multi-talented young man who etched his family's name in the "stone of everlasting respect," his selfish behavior and promiscuity became the seeds that fertilized the eggs of the beast within.

Even though interracial relationships were not accepted in the 1950s in York this did not stop Arthur from womanizing outside his racial profile. Although Arthur indulged in immoral behavior, this was normal mannerism during this time period. After World War II Arthur took on a job as a window washer and he held his job for eight years until his death. After the war Arthur met Big Devon's mother who was a Sicilian woman who came to America with her father who bootlegged liquor for the mob. Her name was Rosa Petrino, and secretly she had a relationship with Arthur until she gave birth to Big Devon and his sister Sarah whom she raised until she discovered Arthur was married. Rosa's secret came out and she immediately had pressure from her family for dating a black man and as soon as the harsh reality of not being Arthur's one and only set in, she abandoned her children.

In spite of having years of window washing experience, Arthur had mysteriously fallen to his death from a twenty story building. Arthur was a longtime friend of Mr. Piccolo and when he died Mr. Piccolo swore to look after Big Devon. Big Devon was labeled a "bastard" because of the fact that his father had impregnated his mother out of wedlock while he was married to another woman, and he was taken in by a caring couple after his mother abandoned him and his sister Sarah. Big Devon Piccolo was now 24 yrs. old and he was only three months shy of his eighteenth birthday when little Devon was born.

Even though Big Devon was seventeen at the time of junior's birth, he truly felt like he was in love, and he believed that Marsha was his soul mate and the one true love of his life. Big Devon stood about five feet nine inches tall and he wore a full beard with his long silky black hair that was braided into corn rolls. Everyone around the block new big Devon as Chippy, and he seldom went by the name Devon. Chippy was a short and stocky African-Italian mixed young man who commanded respect throughout the neighborhood and not just because of his toughness but by his biological Soriano bloodline alone.

Chippy met Marsha at a track meet when they were in high school. Marsha held the fastest time in the 100 yard dash in the state, and not only did she have athleticism, but she had the look of an ebony goddess. She had a sweet light caramel complexion with slightly slanted eyes and a smile so radiant it could replace the moon in the sky on a crisp clear winter evening. Although Marsha was blessed with this feminine prowess, don't mistake her beauty for her weakness. Around the block Marsha was known to hold her own because she had the reputation of "that chick that knocked that dude out".

In the kitchen Marsha's daydream was interrupted by a loud pulsating ring of her telephone.

"Hello?"

"Girl, what you doing? I got some scoop for you," said a woman excitedly.

"What's up Valerie? How you doin' girl?"

"Ain't nuthin' guess what I heard?"

"Valerie I'm trying to cook! I ain't got time to hear no gossip!"

"Um Umm, girl you wanna hear this you dig?! Marsha, I told you Seth likes you right?"

"Uh, hello? I have a kid to Chippy. How long have you known me?"

"Girl I know but ain't like you married or nothing besides Seth got mad dough! Girl it's 1979 and this fool got a 1980 Corvette!!!"

"And..."

"And when I was getting my hair done I heard this fool was trying to find out where you hung out so he could get your number!"

"Really, well you right about that, a fool! I have a man thank you and that fool better hope Chippy don't find out that he's looking for my number!"

"I mean Marsha, Chippy's my boy and all but he ain't got no money!"

"Valerie, money ain't everything girl! Besides Chippy is in trade school and… hold on Valerie, I think I hear Devon."

Marsha set down the sharp butcher knife she'd been using to tenderize her meat, and she grabbed the phone from between her ear and shoulder and placed it next to her red salad bowl. She stepped out the back screen door which had a slight tear in the bottom screen, and as she went outside she saw Devon sprinting around the corner. "Mom!!!" he screamed. Devon showed the world class speed his mother was blessed with as he ran from Darryl a 12year old kid who chased Devon on a daily basis.

"Come here you little curly head punk!" Darryl yelled.

"No! Leave me alone!"

"I'm gonna knock your little head off when I catch you!"

"Mommy help, please help me Mom!"

Marsha hopped off the three step stoop that was in the back yard, and as Devon ran he looked behind himself not realizing what was in front of him, and at that moment Marsha belted "Devon!!!" By then it was too late, and inside their yard was a pole which had a rusty thin wiry fence attached to it which looked like a prison fence that only appeared to be missing the barbed wires. It was as if the yard was incased in a mini prison yard, and the pole had a screw protruding out which was about the six years old eye level. Before Devon could heed his mother's warning he found himself flat on his back screaming in agony as blood spewed everywhere. Devon's face looked as if he had a blood geyser attached to his head. Marsha rushed to her baby's side while frantically screaming for someone to call for the paramedics.

"Sweet Jesus somebody help me!!! Call 911! Somebody please call 911!" Marsha knelt down next Devon as she grabbed a dish towel from her left apron pocket. The white towel with yellow butterflies was still moist from wiping the counter after she finished the dishes.

"It's gonna be ok baby, Mommy's here. Mommy's here." Devon screamed as the blood began to drench his brand new looking shirt, and he cried more at the sight of the blood then the actual pain to his eye.

"Ow, Mommy, ow, it hurts! It hurts!"

The screw in the pole had just missed lodging into his eye by a mere half inch. It made a gash so deep that it sliced his right eyebrow just above the ridge of his eye.

As Devon lay in his mother's arms he heard the sound of an ambulance siren getting louder as it came down Hope Avenue. The paramedics arrived in a red and white ambulance that had yellow letters painted on it. The ambulance had a picture of a white rose on it and the word ORK was painted in yellow. By looking closer one would see the faded outline of the letter Y in front of ORK. Devon was placed into the White Rose ambulance, and he was rushed to the hospital while the paramedics soothed him as they put pressure and gauze on his eye to stop the blood.

The ambulanced rushed Devon to the York Hospital, and it drove for what seemed an eternity and Devon began to calm down while his mother soothed him.

"Are you ok baby?"

"Um hmm," he sobbed.

"It's ok baby Mommy got you, Mommy got you," she said as she rocked him back and forth.

"Hmm (sniff) hmm Mommy (sniff) hmm Mommy," Devon murmured as his mother held him closer. As Marsha held tighter she thought his cries which sounded like tiny growls were from the pain, but it wasn't. Devon was envisioning what he was going to do to Darryl!

Devon took his right hand that had dried up blood on it and wiped the snot off of his nose. He then wiped his snotty hand onto his red, white, and blue shirt. He had a look of disgust because his favorite shirt had blood on it, and to him the snot was supposed to somewhat wash the blood away. As they arrived to the emergency room Devon was taken out of the ambulance in a stretcher, and he was rushed to the back of the emergency room and placed on a brown hospital gurney that had white tissue paper halfway falling off of it.

As Devon sat on the gurney, the blood from the gauze slowly oozed down the side of his face and just as he took his right hand to wipe his face two doctors approached him. Instantaneously Devon screamed,

"I'm scared! I'm scared! Mommy, help me!!! Mommy, help me!!!"

"There, there, little fella we're not going to hurt you! Under the circumstances how are you ma'am? I'm Dr. Luke and this is Dr. Maxfield."

"Well I'll be better once I know how serious this is."

"Well let's take a look here," said Dr. Maxfield.

"What's your name son? I'm Dr. Maxfield but most of the kids call me Dr. Mac!" Dr. Maxfield had dark wavy hair with a clean cut goatee, and he reminded Devon of his father Chippy.

"Dr. Luke and I are going to fix you up ok buddy?"

Dr. Luke who was a female doctor with short brownish blond hair placed her cold hands over Devon's cheek.

"It's ok sweetie, we're here to help you ok? It looks like he's going to need stitches ma'am."

"Stitches, I figured that, how many?"

"Well we won't be able to determine that until after we're done, but it doesn't look too bad. He'll definitely be scarred for life though."

"Oh lord his Dad won't be happy about this," worried Marsha.

"Ma'am how did this happen," asked Dr. Maxfield.

"Someone was chasing him and he wasn't looking and ran into a fence."

"He ran into a fence? Devon, is this what happened?"

"What you mean Devon is this what happened? Ain't that what I just told you?"

"Ma'am please remain calm, these are precautionary measures that we must take."

"Wait, I know you ain't trying to say that I abused my son?! Don't come at me with that bullshit! Lord, please forgive me for using the Devil's tongue!!!"

"Ma'am please, do not take this the wrong way," said Dr. Luke.

"How am I supposed to take it? You're painting a picture like I'm a bad parent or something. Stitch my son up so we can get up out of here!"

Dr. Luke stood behind Devon as he peered up to see an upside down face. Devon noticed how pretty she was but that still didn't stop him from squirming because he wanted her hands off of him. He sensed how upset the doctors made his mom and he grabbed Dr. Luke's hand and threw it off his face.

"Devon," yelled Marsha. "Stop it boy!"

"That's ok, he's just scared," said Dr. Luke. Dr. Maxfield grab a needle from the tray and said, "Ok lil man this won't hurt a tough guy like you too much!"

As the doctor started placing the needle towards Devon's eye, Devon's tiny lungs expanded as he inhaled a deep breath of air. Marsha was holding his left arm with her left hand and tears began to flow down her cheek. As she wiped her tears with her other hand she noticed a brave but menacing look on Devon's face that she never had seen before. It was the look of bravery but yet she noticed his eyes had rage! Marsha eased the tension of her grip around Devon's arm and stepped away as she watched her son take on the stitches like a little warrior. It was at that moment that the image of Darryl chasing him went through Devon's mind. All he could think about was getting revenge. It was as if he didn't even notice the needle going in and out of his eye. The anger that Devon felt seemed to possess him to the point where nothing would disrupt his vengeful thinking. It was at that precise moment that the seed of the beast within Devon impregnated itself within his tiny heart. Devon stared up into the white hospital ceiling and at that point he felt pain no more.

Damaged Father's Plea

I'm supposed to Honor my Father and Mother, isn't this true?
If I've never been taught then what should I do?
With your guidance I'm trying to teach my son how to be a man,
But if I've never been taught then tell me how I can.
I pray dear Lord that you show me a sign.
Help me make my son's life way better than mine.

David V.M. Kennedy

After Devon received his stitches he was congratulated by the doctors. Dr. Luke raised her hand and gave Devon a high five and said, "You were a big boy today Devon!"

"Thank you," Devon replied.

"I have a lollipop, do you want one?"

As Devon nodded his head yes Marsha said, "boy, talk with your mouth and not with your head!"

"Yes, Please, I want one."

"Ok, here ya go sweetie, you are so cute!!!"

"Thank You," said Devon and Marsha simultaneously as they prepared to leave the hospital.

The young mom and her well-mannered intellect walked out of the hospital to an awaiting car. Inside of the car was Devon's Aunt Sarah who was Chippy's older sister. Sarah was tall for a woman and she stood about 5'9. Sarah was the type of woman who commanded attention no matter where she went or what the circumstances were. Although she had African American features she and Chippy had the same mother and father, and her Italian bloodline was very noticeable. Sarah had long jet black curly hair that went down to the middle of her back, and her skin was very light, and it was smooth as cream cheese. She was a very beautiful woman who loved Devon as if he were her own.

"Hey! Is my baby ok? Come here and give Aunt Sarah a kissy kiss!" Devon smiled and blushed so hard that his light brown cheeks turned red.

"Hi Aunt Sarah, See my head?"

"I see, I see, I heard you tried to head butt the fence," Sarah said sarcastically. "I liked that fence. So what did you go and get it all bloodied up for?"

"Aunt Sarah! I didn't try to head butt the fence! Darryl was chasing me."

"Darryl? From up the street, ain't his mom on LSD," she asked Marsha.

"Now that bitch ain't never took care of her kids! He knows he is too big to be picking on Devon. Marsha you need to go handle her ass! I'll do it! You want me to smack dat ass?"

"No Sarah, and quit talking like that around Devon please."

"Hell, ain't nothin' he ain't heard already from my raggedy mouth brother Chippy anyway!"

Even though Sarah meant no harm, conversations like this were the norm around Devon. He was such a "mama's boy" that he rarely went outside to play with the other kids in the neighborhood. Like a Joey attached to a mother kangaroo Devon never wanted to leave his mother's presence. If one were to engage in conversation with Devon they might question, is it genetics that made this young adolescent so intelligent, or is it the simple fact that he was constantly exposed to adult situations? Although Devon rarely understood what was going on around him, the thing that he did well was pay attention. Whenever he listened a constant question that would storm his brain was "why?" Devon always tried to figure things out so that he could understand. He asked question after question until it registered into his brain. The old saying goes "Children are like sponges" but what many fail to realize is that the wetter the sponge is then the more it will soak. When kids are exposed to constant adult situations then their minds will mold based off of their experiences. "Curiosity may have killed the cat, but this combination of curiosity mixed with a constant exposure to ignorance served as a daily diet for the beast within.

Sarah continued driving, and as she approached Marsha and Devon's home, she reached up towards the rear view mirror with her hand as the bracelets that covered her forearm slid down to her elbow. After she adjusted the mirror she noticed Devon had somber whimpers as if he was a new born puppy begging for attention. Just listening to Sarah talk about Darryl caused the beast inside Devon to stir. He replayed the chase over and over through his head and he could do nothing but cry. Devon did not cry because he was afraid or in pain. He cried because the beast within wanted to seriously hurt Darryl but he couldn't. Devon wanted paybacks and he felt helpless because he was too small.

"Are you ok baby? What's wrong? Did Aunt Sarah make you cry?"

"No Aunt Sarah."

"Well Devon what's wrong does your head hurt," asked Marsha. "Are you ok?"

"Yes mommy," Devon said as he inhaled every tear and sign of mucous while trying to portray toughness.

"So why were you running sweetie?"

Devon raised his tiny first grade voice and said, "It was that big kid ma, the 12 yr. old, he said he was going to beat me up! I swear when I get bigger I'm going smash his face with a brick!" Marsha was shocked by Devon's outburst and she replied,

"Devon, now you know better than that, violence begat more violence." With a bewildered look on his face Devon inquired,

"What does that mean?"

Marsha was about to retract her statement, but then she remembered this is Devon the same kid who at the tender age of three had already been reading small children's books.

"Simple my son, if you ask for trouble than you're going to get it." Without hesitation Devon replied,

"Well he asked the wrong person!"

Sarah pulled her 1971dodge challenger in front of Marsha and Devon's house as her shiny tires splashed a pothole that was filled by water from the neighborhood kids playing with a water hose. Marsha pulled up the long chrome lock and as the young mother opened the heavy cherry red door, she noticed that Devon's father was waiting at the front door of the house with a visible look of disgust on his face. Marsha lifted the black leather seat forward to let Devon out, and as she grabbed his hand his left foot got caught on the seatbelt while his other foot touched the ground. "Oops! I got you Hun!"

As Devon regained his balance he caught eye contact with his father. Chippy opened the screen door and walked down the four stepped stoop and said,

"What in the hell happened to my son?!"

"Your son, don't you mean our son," asked Marsha.

Sarah walked around the front of the car and as she placed her big red bug eyed looking sun glasses on her face she said,"Chippy, shut yer ass up! You see the damn boy's been traumatized now stop all of that got damn yelling!"

"This ain't got shit to do with you Sarah so stay outta this shit!"

"Chippy, go sit down," Marsha demanded.

"Don't you tell me what to fucking do! If you were watching him this shit wouldn't have happened!"

"Get out of my face Chippy I don't have time for you right now!"

"Look I'm outta here," said Sarah. "Marsha don't pay his stupid ass no mind." Sarah held out her outstretched arms toward Devon and said,

"Come here baby and give Aunt Sarah a kiss MWAH!!!" Sarah walked pass Chippy and as she headed by she playfully yet forcefully shoved Chippy's head in a manner that dared him to retaliate. "Bye stupid. And quit being a stranger!"

"Whatever sis, I ain't thinking about you!" Chippy took a look at his son's head and stormed up the steps back into the house. Marsha and Devon followed hand in hand, and as Marsha closed the door Devon let go of her hand and sprinted up the stairs so that he could watch his favorite Stud Racer cartoon. Marsha placed her car keys onto a glass table that was encased by oak. As she stood upright Chippy came out of nowhere and jumped in her face.

"What da fuck is your problem Marsha?!"

"What are you talking about Chippy? Get out of my face!"

"You know what the hell I'm talking about! How you gonna embarrass me in front of my sister like that?"

"What? Embarrass you, what da heck are you talking about? Our son is upstairs with stitches in his head, and you said I embarrassed you?"

"Yeah, you stupid bitch, that shit was embarrassing!!!"

"Who you calling a bitch? You ain't gonna sit here and disrespect me like that, where are my keys? I'll be back when you calm down!"

"Your ass ain't going nowhere!"

As the young couple argued Devon ran to his bedroom door, and he slowly closed it. He was confused about why his parents were disputing. He immediately began to think that they were arguing because of him. He slowly walked to his blue car shaped bed and reached for his stuffed animal cat that his mother won for him at the county fair. As he embraced the black and white cat he stared into the stuffed animal's eyes as if he was hoping that it would see his eyes filling with tears so that it would ask him what is wrong. Devon cried as if that screw from his accident was lodged into his eye.

The couples' argument intensified, and Devon screamed for his parents to stop.

"Mommy, Daddy, please stop, please stop!"

The commotion was deafening, and his tiny voice went unheard. Devon lay in his bed helpless and baffled while continuing to think that this was his fault. He turned off his bedroom light and lay across his bed. He turned on his nightlight that was in the form of a green bookworm that had a green pajama hat. The bookworm had a white face where the bulb lit up, and it had an expression that looked as if it was smiling and saying to Devon that everything would be okay. He turned off his T.V. and lay on his back. His eyes were heavy from the long day as well as crying for what seemed an eternity. The sun had just set and as he stared at the ceiling he noticed red and blue flashing lights appear. They came from his window and the projection from outside appeared to hypnotize him as he cried himself to sleep.

The following morning Devon woke up to find one of his mother's best friends Valerie in the living room watching T.V.

"Good morning Devon," she said with a smile.

"Good morning Aunt Valerie, where's my mom at?"

Even though Valerie wasn't Marsha or Chippy's sister Devon still referred to her as his Aunt. She was like a sister to Marsha and she helped her raise him since he was a baby. Valerie worked as a nurse during the third shift and she came to Devon's house after her shift. Devon sat at the kitchen table and he noticed a plate with scrambled eggs and buttered toast on it.

"What's that? These eggs are brown!"

"What do you mean, what's that? They're scrambled eggs! Aren't you hungry?"

"My mom's eggs are yellow and fluffy. These ain't yellow. Where is she anyway?"

"Boy, if you don't eat that food! You got people out here starving to death and you're complaining about eggs being fluffy!"

"Well they don't look right. And what's that black stuff? Where's my mom?"

Before answering Devon Valerie took a deep breath and sighed. She was confused about how she was to tell Devon about what happened the previous night, and when she started to speak Chippy walked through the door. At that moment Valerie exhaled a deep breath and looked to the ceiling and whispered, "Thank you Jesus!" because she was now off the hook and didn't have to explain what had happened.

As Chippy headed towards Devon, he noticed that his father was wearing the same clothes from the day before, and he had a long scratch on his face.

"Hey Valerie, thanks for watching Devon," said Chippy with an embarrassed look on his face.

"Look, I don't even know what to say to you. Out of respect for my friend's child I'll just get my things and leave!"

Valerie rolled her eyes as she finished cleaning up Devon's plate that had only the scrambled eggs left scattered over it. She scraped the food into the trash and put the plate into the sink. As she walked out of the kitchen into the living room towards the front door she calmly stated, "You really need help." Chippy could do nothing but sigh as he put his head down in shame. He knows that he was wrong for what had happened but the damage had already been done. Now he had yet another burden which was dealing with Devon.

"Where have you been Dad? Why do you have the same clothes on? What happened to your face?"

"Go brush your teeth; we're getting ready to leave," demanded Chippy.

"Make sure you wash your face too!"

Without hesitation Devon obeyed his father and walked upstairs to the bathroom. Even though Chippy never answered where he had been, Devon still needed to know so when he came back downstairs he asked again.

"Where were you at Dad?"

Chippy ignored his son's inquiry because he didn't know how to explain where he had been the night before. Although Chippy spent the night in jail for fighting with Marsha, his son's interrogating questions made him feel much worse than the night before.

"Devon just eat this sandwich and get your shoes on!!!"

"I already ate and you don't have to yell."

"What did you say to me boy?"

"Nothing," Devon said respectfully.

"That's what I thought you said. Now get your shoes on and let's go!"

"Where are we going?"

"To see your Mom, now hurry up!"

"Where is she? Why didn't she tell me that she was leaving?"

Chippy could do nothing but ignore his son as they walked to the car, because he was too embarrassed to tell him the truth. He and Devon drove back to the same hospital where Devon received his stitches. Devon was curious as to why they were going there and why his mother wasn't home to fix him his favorite pancakes for breakfast.

"Why are we here Daddy and where is mommy at?" asked Devon. Chippy sighed and stated,

"Mommy and Daddy got into a little fight son so mommy is seeing the doctor, but she's going to be ok."

"A fight, Is that why you were yelling last night?"

"Huh? You heard me yelling?"

"Yeah, I yelled for you guys to stop but you didn't hear me. Were you fighting because I ran into the fence? I'm sorry Dad."

Chippy began to tear up as he looked his son into his eyes. It was as if he was staring at a miniature version of himself. He placed his hands on Devon's narrow shoulders and he said,

"Son, I am so sorry! Listen to me Devon, none of this is your fault! I don't want to you ever think that your mother and I argue because of you. Do you hear me?"

"But Dad you got mad when we came home and you started yelling at mom, so if it wasn't my fault then why were you mad?"

"It's complicated son, I don't know how to explain."

After being released from jail, Chippy had gone to the hospital to see Marsha before he went home to pick Devon up from the house. He had already expressed his regrets to Marsha and surprisingly she forgave him. Maybe it was her spiritual background that allowed such prompt forgiveness. Despite what had transpired Marsha loved Chippy and in spite of popular belief he loved Marsha more than life itself.

Even though Chippy was wrong for putting his hands on Marsha one must understand that Chippy was raised by a man who lost his wife during Chippy's toddler years, therefore he never had the chance to experience the comforting love and support of a woman until he met Marsha. Chippy's foster father came from an era where it was still believed that women were a bit inferior to men. This type of ignorance was instilled in Chippy so it really came natural for him to strike Marsha when he felt the need. The beast within Devon had a blueprint long before he or Chippy ever came into this world. Regardless if Chippy was right or wrong Marsha loved him and forgave him, but she specifically declared, "Do not bring Devon to the hospital!"

In spite of heeding Marsha's warning Chippy's conscious ate at him, and he felt that he had to take Devon to see his mother. As they walked down the hallway to Marsha's room Devon noticed that some of the other doors to the rooms were open, and he couldn't help but look inside some of them. His heart started to race as he noticed a little girl his age in one of the rooms with a cast on her arm and bruises on her face as if she had been punched repeatedly. The little girl's lip was swollen and Devon noticed the same black stitches that he had in his eye were similar to the ones in the girls lip except for the fact that she had a lot more. The sight of the little girl made Devon daydream of how his father beat up his mother. He began to grind his teeth, and he clenched his fist as he pushed the door to Marsha's room open. As they entered Marsha's room, Devon shouted, "Mommy are you alright?!"

With tears streaming down her face Marsha let out a slow painful breath as she tried to re-position herself in the bed. She wore a light blue hospital gown that tied around her neck and the bow hung loose and looked as weak as a spider web swaying in the wind. As she propped herself up on the pillows, her blanket and sheet slid down toward her knees. Devon noticed a large patch of blood surrounded by tubes that were hanging from his mother's side. As she came to a somewhat comfortable position she replied, "Yes baby I'm ok."

"Mom, what happened? What happened to your face?! Did Dad do this? Did he?"

Devon couldn't believe the sight of his mother's face. If he didn't know any better he wouldn't have recognized who she was. The entire left side of her face was swollen and her eye turned black and shut as the other looked perfectly normal. Dried up blood corroded around her lip and slobber fell to her chest due the fact that she could not completely close her mouth. Devon slowly and gently laid his head on his mother's stomach afraid that even the slightest touch would cause his mother to hurt. Tears poured down his face and he cried so hard the he struggled to catch his breath

"How could you?! How could you do this to my mom?! She didn't do anything to you! How could you?"

"Son, I'm so…

As Chippy became choked up with tears, he wiped his dripping nose with his swollen hairy knuckles that had small abrasions on his middle finger. The sound of Chippy's voice sent a piercing sensation down Devon's spine. As Devon wiped away his drenched cheeks he hardheartedly gazed into his father's eyes and said, "I hate you!"

"Get away from us! I hate you so bad!"

"Get away!" he screamed "You monster! You're an evil monster!"

"Devon, No," said Marsha faintly. "No, please don't say that son; please he's your father."

Chippy saw a rage on his son's face that reminded him of how he felt the night before when he and Marsha got into their altercation as he punched and slammed her to the ground. Each blow that he delivered was replayed in his mind as if it was a movie being played right before his eyes. As he stared off into space with tears streaming down his bearded cheek, he relived the fight through his mind, and he could feel the cracking of Marsha's ribs; he could also hear the loud impact of his fist pounding her face.

As Chippy stood dazed and shocked at Devon's reaction all he could do was cry. His tears flowed like the Niagara Falls. He stood at the foot of Marsha's bed sobbing with a pathetic look on his face as his arms dangled like a toddler wishing someone would pick him up and carry him away. Devon stood with his tiny fist clenched as if he was ready to engage in a heavyweight championship fight with his Dad. He stood in front of his father with a strong stance as he breathed deeply through his nose while he exhaled from his mouth. It was as if he had just finished a short sprint, and as he gritted his teeth he stared menacingly at Chippy. One can only imagine the thoughts that went through this 6yr old mind. It was as if Devon could feel every ounce of blood flow through his entire body. Countless emotions went through Devon's head and at that precise moment the beast within Devon's tiny little heart had been disturbed.

Women's Curse

Since we've eaten the apple we've experienced nothing but pain.
Am I wrong to question the meaning of life? I ask you; what is there to gain?
When I lost my virginity, the experience made me hurt.
To give life is a miracle, but excruciating pain is what
I felt at the time I gave birth.
You see pain is the essence of this woman's worth.
Why have you forsaken me? That is my question.
Your answer is simply prayer, therefore when I use it you
quickly denounce my depression.
Lord, I do apologize for questioning you each day and every night.
My promise is to polish your heavenly armor, and I promise that I will
continue to fight.

David V.M. Kennedy

Devon briefly visited with his mother due to the fact that she could not bear the heartache of having to look at her son through two distended eye sockets. Her facial impurities were as if Satan himself had erased her angelic splendor. Her beauty temporarily disappeared as easy as a child wiping soft crayon away from a whiteboard. Even though her injuries that were sustained weren't life threatening, and the battery looked far worse than it was, Devon showed very little sympathy for Chippy as he watched his father cry as they left the room.

"Why did you do that daddy?" Devon said in a demanding tone.

Dim wittedly Chippy replied,

"I don't know son, daddy and mommy got into an argument, and I got angry and did something that I shouldn't have done. I am sorry."

Chippy was truly remorseful, and at this moment he experienced anguish far greater than the physical pain that he imposed on Marsha. Chippy wanted more than anything to have Devon's forgiveness. He begged for his son to forgive him, and like his mother Devon eventually accepted his father's apology. Meanwhile in the hospital, Marsha lay in her bed gazing somberly at the cracks in the ceiling. Caught in her daydream of despair, she didn't even realize that her nurse had entered into the room.

"Honey, are you ok?" said the nurse in a non-distressing voice.

"Oh yeah, I'm sorry, I didn't even hear you come in," said Marsha.

"That's ok, sweetie you just get some rest. My name is Nurse Jacqueline Fable, and I'll be taking care of you."

Jacqueline Fable was a 28 yr. old Caucasian woman who was a single mother raising a son who was 1 yr. older than Devon. Jacqueline was about 5ft 2in tall and had long stringy hair that went down to the middle of her back. She had not by any means a hefty build but a body that would be described as pleasantly plump. Her white skin was as pure and smooth as soft vanilla ice cream, and her face was as if innocence was a birthmark embedded upon her cheeks.

"Hi, Jacqueline It's nice to meet you. So what's the damage?"

"Well, that all depends on which body part."

"Don't beat around the bush ma'am. Please be blunt with me."

"Ok, First Marsha let me check your vitals? Can you move your arm?"

"Ouch! Yes, a little bit but not too far my side really hurts."

"Well that's probably because you have a few cracked ribs."

"Oh, No, How many are a few?"

"Three to be exact, was that your husband and son?"

"Well my boyfriend and son actually."

"Your son's a cutie pie; let me guess he's about 5 yrs. old?" Jacqueline admired. With a smile of gratitude Marsha replied, "Well six actually, do you have any kids?"

"I sure do. I have a 7yr old myself, they're so sweet and naive at that age!" laughed Jacqueline...

Instantaneously, Marsha's face had dropped like the atom bomb that hit Hiroshima. It was at that subtle moment, that she realized some of the tainted thoughts that could be going through her baby's head.

"Did I say something wrong?" Jacqueline asked apologetically.

"No, No, I'm sorry I just drifted, must be the pain pills!" Marsha said sarcastically.

"Your boyfriend did this to you didn't he?" Jacqueline hesitantly asked.

The uncomfortable silence in the room could have awakened the dead, and the look on Marsha's Face told the whole story. It was a story that Jacqueline knew all too well. Jacqueline's assessment of Marsha could have qualified her as a psychic traveling from the future predicting the young couples' brawl as it happened in full detail. Like Marsha she had endured an abusive relationship from her deranged husband for years, and therefore she recognized the signs.

She expressed to Marsha, "Sweetie you are too young and beautiful to put yourself through this, no man has the right to beat a woman, regardless of what has happened!"

"With all due respect Nurse, please don't judge me," proclaimed Marsha.

"No my dear you misunderstand, I've been in this predicament before, so trust me when I say this, get out now while you can!" cautioned Jacqueline.

"You went through this? If you don't mind me asking what happened?"

"Well, my ex-husband used to have a drinking problem. Every night he would come home and force me to have sex with him."

"Oh, no I'm so sorry. Chippy is not like that at all. He doesn't drink anything but beer and he never drinks enough to get drunk. We just got into a little argument and I said some things. That's all. I love him."

"Well I kept telling myself that I loved my husband and I tried to fool myself that he loved me!"

"So what did you do? It's obvious that you are no longer with him," said Marsha curiously.

"Oh that's easy! I took a bottle to his head!"

"Ouch! It hurts to laugh! So you hit him with a bottle? You didn't kill him did you?"

"No of course not but I did take out a little more frustration then I should have! It's just fortunate that I'm a nurse! After a few days I healed that sucker right up!"

"Weren't you afraid that he would retaliate?"

"I would have been if he wasn't tied up!"

"Jacqueline, stop! It hurts to laugh!"

"Oh, he thinks that I'm the craziest bitch to ever walk the earth, and if he sees me walking down the street he'll cross over to the other side!"

"One can only imagine what you did to him Jacqueline!"

"Yep, and those images would end right up in a horror flick!"

As the two ladies bonded Jacqueline finished her duties, and she noticed a melancholy look upon Marsha that resembled a wet dog left outside on a cold dark winter evening. She embraced Marsha with a heartwarming reassuring hug, and as Marsha cried, each tear dropped as if they whispered thank you as they hit the floor.

"Listen here sweetie you take my number and call me after we get you all fixed up. Maybe we can get the boys together for a play date or something!"

"That sounds good Jacqueline; it was so nice to meet you. Thank you so much!"

"Anytime Marsha, Anytime!"

Jacqueline's shift had come to an end, and as she walked through the York Hospital parking garage she couldn't stop thinking about Marsha. She opened the door to her 1969 dodge dart and she began her drive to her father's house to pick up her son Daniel Fable. Jacqueline reminisced about the brutal beatings that she suffered from her ex-husband. Her recollection of the events were so vivid, that she immediately pulled the car to the side of the road while she gasped for air as sweat streamed from her pores.

Jacqueline's thoughts were so realistic that she had to peek into the vanity mirror just to reassure the purity in her face was unscathed! "My God!" she screamed.

"Please dear lord, have mercy on that poor child's soul! She is just a baby herself dear lord, please protect her with your merciful arms!" she prayed.

Out of the Darkness Came the Light

Out of the Darkness came the Light.
Out of the Blackness came the White.
When cast asleep throughout the Night,
One awakens with the Sun bright.
In the daytime Shadows overcome the Light.
Perceived inferior Shadows are consumed by Bright.
As the Sun ascends high Majestic and White,
Dusk makes the Sun inferior to the Night.
Out of the Darkness came the Light.
Out of the Darkness came the Light.
Dawn awakens cold and wet with green grass as Sun rises high and bright.
Darkness consumes the Sun while hot rays cool reminding us that out of the Darkness came the Light.

David V.M. Kennedy

Her strong faith in her Catholic upbringing helped to rehabilitate the physical and mental abuse that she sustained during her marriage. After the departure of her husband, she took on the responsibility of single parenting like an overprotective lioness fending off ravenous hyenas. Even though Jacqueline could relate to Marsha's spousal abuse, she had yet another obstacle and that was being a single Caucasian mother who had to raise her son in a predominantly black community.

Jacqueline had a son who was about the same age as Devon and his name was Daniel Fable. Daniel Fable was Jacqueline's sole purpose for living, and it was his childhood wholesomeness that eradicated any suicidal thoughts that ever entered her mind after the domestic violence that she experienced. Even though Jacqueline witnessed many traumatic situations as a nurse she simply could not get over Marsha due to the fact that once upon a time she was the same victim who lay in a hospital bed.

In spite of her abusive experiences Jacqueline was able to escape from her relationship, and she was also able to fight off depression while she continued to raise her son. Jacqueline lived with her father after the passing of her mother in order to care for him. The home where they resided was in a neighborhood that was once dominated by Caucasian middle class citizens. As time moved on the presence of the African American culture took its precedence in the once dominant white community.

Even though York, Pa had a diverse culture there was still some racial tension that spilled over from the race riots in the city after a woman was targeted and shot because she was driving a car that was similar to the one driven by a young African American boy who was targeted by a local Caucasian gang. Jacqueline entered her father's house and her son Daniel Fable (or D.F. as his family called him) rushed to the door. D.F. was a 7yr old boy who had a short pudgy build. He had the same ivory skin complexion like his mother, and his face had and appearance as if his daily ritual was to bathe with soap made from the tusk of elephants in the African wilderness. His rosy cheeks were complimented by the fruit punch mustache spread across his lip. He wore a blue and black flannel jacket with a matching blue baseball cap that had the inscription of the letter D.

As Jacqueline approached her son, D.F. ran and jumped into his mother's arms like it was the first time he had seen her in years.

"Hey precious, you're trembling, what's wrong?" asked Jacqueline.

"It's those men mommy! Those big black men mommy, they're going to get me!" D.F. proclaimed.

"What are you talking about D.F.? No one is going to get you."

"Well Grandpa said that they're taking over, and if we don't move soon than we're in trouble! He also said that they stink, and they smell like chicken!"

"Daniel Marcus Fable! Don't you ever let me hear you talk like that again!" Your Grandpa is just down right ignorant! Don't you dare think different about people just because of the color of their skin!"

Jacqueline had previously had the challenge of convincing her son that Black people were not a threat to him. One night while D.F. was asleep an African American man had broken into their home. D.F. had awakened from his sleep to find the thief staring at him face to face. Since this experience, he developed a phobia and every time D.F. would notice a black man passing by as he played or stared outside his window; he would scurry upstairs to his room and hide under his bed.

"Listen baby, not all black men are going to get you ok?" consoled Jacqueline.

"I understand what happened to you was very scary and he was wrong for breaking in, but just because he was black, does not mean that all black men are bad, do you understand?"

"Yes mom but why does Grandpa always say bad things about them? He scares me when he says things."

"Your Grandpa is just ignorant and that means that he doesn't know any better. That's what he was taught to believe as a child, and sweetie I am not raising you that way do you understand?"

D.F. responded with a satisfactory nod as his mother smiled with assurance, unconscious to the fact that she had just given her son words of wisdom that would change his life forever.

Two months had gone by and Jacqueline was at home opening the curtains of D.F.'s bedroom window as she would do every morning just to reassure her son that he had nothing to be afraid of. Although D.F. seemed to have suppressed the traumatic memory of the home invasion, Jacqueline did this as a constant reminder to let him know that the actions of one person shouldn't cause the mindset of another to prejudge an entire race.

Jacqueline had experienced the racial riots in the city of York, Pa during the 60s, and she made sure to raise her child based on intelligence rather than ignorance. Jacqueline prepared her son's breakfast while he dressed himself for the day. After feeding her son, Jacqueline drove to the hospital for work as she hummed her favorite Bee Gees tune. As she went through a stop sign she had to slam on the breaks! "Hey, you moron!" she yelled out of her window. Another driver ran the stop sign at a four way intersection, and he narrowly missed hitting her car. Without hesitation the stranger not yet known to Jacqueline was Chippy, and he sped down the street in his 1969 Dodge Charger.

Although Jacqueline had no idea who was the culprit that almost demolished her car, she prayed to God for forgiveness and asked him to watch over the distraught driver. Chippy was driving, and he ran through the stop sign and the reason that he wasn't paying attention was because he was trying to eject his eight track tape from the deck. He had no clue that he almost sideswiped Jacqueline's car, and he calmly went about his business as if nothing happened.

As Chippy inserted his eight tracks tape he began to sing, "Oh Mercy, Mercy, me, Oh things ain't what they used to be!" As Chippy continued his Marvin Gaye ballad he noticed the back gate was left open to his house, and he had a feeling that Marsha wasn't home. They were always conscious of having the gate closed while they were home, because the squeaky noise that it made when it opened was equivalent to having an alarm while they were there. Chippy thought to himself…

"Ain't this a bitch? Now where is this chick at? I work my ass off, and there ain't no food made! I swear, these bitches nowadays."

Marsha was at her friend Valerie's house getting her hair done while Devon played across the street at King Memorial Park. Even though the play area was considered a park to the locals, most would consider it to be simply a playground. Memorial Park sat across the street from the west end projects, and it was also adjacent to an old factory mill. The mill and the park were separated by a brown murky watered creek that was named Codorus. Broken glass covered the basketball area that had two full sized courts with just one of the rims having a net hanging from it. Just across the street from the projects was a swing set that had three solid steal swings that were in the form of space rockets. Marsha sat on a kitchen chair with her feet propped on a set of metal crossbars as Valerie stood behind her as she braided her hair.

"So girl what you been up to?"

"Oh nothing Valerie, I'm just trying to make it that's all."

"Well you need to try to make it without that psycho boyfriend of yours!"

"Come on Valerie give Chippy a break. He doesn't know any better and he's a good father."

"Yeah, I give you that but he has some real anger issues Marsha. I'm telling you the boy ain't got it all."

"Look, what happened is over with and we've moved on. He promised that he wouldn't do it again. Besides he doesn't know any better. Look at his upbringing."

"Girl, don't use his upbringing as an excuse! You were adopted too!"

"Yeah but it's not the same."

"Well what's the difference? I bet Seth would never put his hands on you girl! Well he would, but not like that, and damn that boy looks good!"

"Well then why don't you go out with him Valerie? And to answer your question, the difference is the fact that the Promises' raised Sicily and I together. Not only that I know my real mom. Chippy never knew his father or mother other than his baby years, and you can't count that. His adoptive mother passed while he was a baby and to top it off he was raised by a single Old Italian guy."

"Well, I kinda get your point Marsha but that's still no excuse. By the way what's up with your biological Father? You never say much about him."

"Well that's probably because I don't know him."

"You mean you don't even know his name?"

"I don't have a clue Valerie. Let's face it; my biological mom was a slut!" I don't even think she knows. She said me and Sicily has the same Dad but I don't look anything like his people."

"Yeah, you can tell you and Sicily are sisters but she definitely has other distinctive features."

"Exactly, I have two other sisters, and one is almost 6ft tall and the other has green eyes! Heck if "Papa was a rolling stone" my momma was a runaway truck filled with boulders!!!"

"Marsha you are so crazy… Wait who's knocking on the door?"

One of the neighborhood girls was banging on the screen door as she screamed, "Ms. Marsha, Ms. Marsha!" She was wearing a dark blue pair of jeans with a hole on the right pant leg, and her knee was visible with a quarter sized brush burn or strawberry on it. Her shirt was pink, but it had a large grape juice stain on her right side just under her chest. Her hair was done in a style that had Afro Puffs, and the part down the middle was crisp and straight as if someone used a ruler to draw it down the middle of her head making her look like she came straight from the beauty salon. Marsha jumped up with half of her hair braided into corn rolls while the other half laid combed over the left side of her face. As she hopped up from her seat a large black comb that Valerie had still in her hair fell to the floor simultaneously while she kicked over a jar of green hair grease.

"What is it," she asked.

"It's Devon! Hurry," yelled the little girl.

Marsha sprinted across the street, and while she ran it was as if her feet barely touched the ground. One could easily envision why she was so highly regarded as the best sprinter in the state of Pennsylvania. As Marsha approached Devon she noticed blood coming from his mouth.

"Oh God, No!" yelled Marsha. "What happened?"

"I was swinging and Devon walked behind me," said one of the neighborhood boys.

"Devon, you gotta be more careful sweetie. Mommy's here," she said as she kneeled down to put her arms around him.

"Valerie go get me some ice!"

"Ok and I already called Chippy! He's on his way!"

"Valerie, no, please, tell me that you did not call him!"

"Sorry, I thought that he should know," said Valerie with no real remorse.

"Darn it! Come on Devon, let me get some ice on that, are you ok?"

"Yes mommy, it doesn't hurt that bad but my lip does feels funny."

"That's because it's getting swollen, son, come on."

As Marsha started to walk Devon towards Valerie's house she saw Chippy speeding down the street towards them. As Chippy arrived at the park he noticed Marsha across the street holding Devon with an ice pack on his mouth. He got out of his car and slammed the door with all of his might.

"What is wrong with you woman?" yelled Chippy. Marsha simply ignored Chippy's irate behavior as she comforted her son.

"I can't even come home from work to relax because you can't care for my son!"

"Look Chippy, don't you see our son is in pain? I ain't trying to argue with you right now," Marsha said calmly.

"It's bad enough that you didn't have my fucking food cooked, and now you got my boy sitting here with a bloody lip!"

"Watch your mouth Chippy don't you see these kids out here?"

"Man, fuck that shit; don't tell me what to fucking do!"

As little Devon sat clutching his mother like a joey does a kangaroo, he began to cry but his tears were not from the pain of the rocket swing but from the soreness of his heart. Once again, Devon couldn't help but feel dejected, because all of his parent's arguing appeared to be his fault. He couldn't understand why his father was so upset when it was just an accident. He did not mean to get hurt. The hunger of the beast within was stirring. Conflict and

Hostility are two main ingredients for a recipe designed to allow the beast within to nourish. Inside Devon's 6yr old brain was a conscious that began to mold. Questions raced through his head faster than the speed light. As the Anger around him intensified he could do nothing but hold on to Marsha for dear life as he gazed with a remorseful look on his face into the sky. Although Devon was physically only six years old, mentally the beast within had grown and begun to mature.

UNLEASH

So young and so pure you're still my baby boy,
It hurts so bad to see others try to steal your joy.
On the outside, a coward is what many think that they see,
But your bottled emotions will set the beast free.
I've overprotected you. I've done all that I can.
The time is now baby boy. Unleash the beast and follow God's plan.

David V.M. Kennedy

Although Devon's run in with the rocket swing didn't seem to be anything but a busted lip, Marsha was concerned about his face. She couldn't quite put her finger on it but something just didn't look right with Devon's appearance. Marsha scheduled an appointment with the dentist about Devon's teeth in order to be on the safe side.

"Devon, get your shoes on I have to take you to the dentist for your check up!"

"Ok mom, do you know where my Stud Racer shirt is?"

"No, ask your Dad he washed clothes last."

"Dad, do you know where my Stud Racer shirt is? I'm getting ready to go to the dentist."

"I just saw that shirt; go check your bottom drawer. And close your damn mouth," chuckled Chippy.

"What do you mean? My mouth is closed."

"Well it's a good thing that you're going to the dentist. Maybe he can fix those two loading docks hanging from your mouth! Shit we're moving today so you might as well stay here and help me. I can use those big ass teeth to load the appliances on the truck!"

Even though Chippy was joking with Devon he noticed that his son wasn't laughing and that he had a sad look on his face.

"Come here! Let me see those hands!"

At that moment Devon's face lit up like a Christmas tree! This was his time to shine in front of his Dad. Since Devon could remember there wasn't a day that would pass without his father showing him how to fight. Boxing was Chippy's passion, and he always wanted Devon to get into boxing. Devon loved to perform in order to make his father proud of what he had learned. The two watched countless hours of boxing matches and Devon's favorite boxers were Sugar Ray Leonard and Muhammed Ali.

"So what you got? Stick and move! Stick and move! Keep your hands up! Tuck that chin!"

"Ouch, Dad that hurt!"

"Well, keep ya hands up! Now stop being a little chump and hit me back! You ain't gonna hurt me, hit me!"

"No, I'm tired and Mom is waiting for me."

"Boy you better stop being a little punk! Take this!"

With his hands open Chippy through a jab at Devon's chest flicking him with the tip of his fingers. The impact left a stinging sensation right under Devon's esophagus. Devon bent over and clutched his throat while tears began to stream down his face.

"What is going on," asked Marsha

"Get up boy and stop being a little Sissy," yelled Chippy.

"Chippy, knock it off! You see he's crying!"

"I know he better get up and swallow those damn tears!"

"Chippy we gotta go. Come on Devon."

"He ain't going anywhere until he fights like a man!"

"Quit pulling his arm Chippy you're hurting him!"

"He ain't hurt. Now let's go! Get them hands up!"

Devon hopped to his feet and took his stance with his hands up and his chin tucked just like his father taught him. The intensity in his face was never witnessed before by Chippy. It looked as if Devon was possessed with anger! His eyes literally looked like they had fire in them! Chippy stood 5ft 9 but he squatted down so that he was Devon's height, and he gave Devon and open handed hook towards Devon's head.

"That's it Devon! Way to slip that! So what you gonna do, huh? Now what? What? Wh…Ouch!"

Devon gave Chippy two left jabs to his right cheek and as Chippy leaned left to roll with the punches Devon clocked him in the mouth with a thunderous right hook! Instantaneously, Devon dropped his hands to his side and noticed his father's lip.

"Dad you're bleeding I'm sorry!"

"That's what you get," exclaimed Marsha

"Don't be sorry son! That's what I'm talking about! I'm ok, a little blood ain't gonna hurt me. Give me some skin!"

Devon's face lit up with joy as he stared at his Dad's lip. Although Chippy was simply being the typical young York, Pa bred father, he had no clue what he had done for his son. Chippy unleashed the beast within, and to Devon it felt good to see his father in pain. The six year old could do nothing but laugh inside as his father wiped the blood from his lip.

"Um, you might wanna get some ice on that," said Marsha.

"Hush woman, a little blood ain't gonna hurt anybody."

"Yeah but me not willing to kiss that puffy lip of yours will! Come on Devon let's go."

Chippy rushed to the bathroom to the surprise of a swollen upper lip. He could do nothing but laugh as he gently touched it while staring into the mirror. While Chippy stood gazing in the mirror, Devon and Marsha went to the dentist in order to have his teeth looked at.

Marsha and Devon walked to her car and Devon chuckled to himself as he opened the car door. The mere thought of Chippy touching his lip easily amused Devon. It was at this moment that he had developed a bit of confidence in his ability to fight. Chippy was also impressed, and as he stared into the mirror he stated, "My son can be the next Champ of the world in boxing. Yeah, I'll start training him now, and when he turns nine I'll get his amateur career going. As quick as his hands are now, ain't no tellin' how good he'll be! We'll move right up out of this ghetto!"

As Marsha buckled her seatbelt she said,

"Devon put your seatbelt on, you ok?"

"Yeah, I got Dad good huh?"

"You sure did! And you know what, he deserved it!"

"Why did you say it like that?"

"Like you really wanted him hurt, is it because he hit you?"

Marsha didn't know how to react to Devon's inquiry, so she briefly stared straight ahead as she was about to pull up to the dentist office. As bad as she wanted to answer yes to Devon's question, she knew that for the well-being of her son that she couldn't express her true feelings. As the car came to a complete stop Marsha shifted the gear to neutral and as she pulled up the emergency break she briskly turned to Devon and said, "No I said he deserved it, because I felt like he was playing too rough with you. So by you bustin' that mouth open he won't play as rough again! Now let's go get those teeth checked!"

Life Is Short

Life is short, L-I-F-E.
Look closely it's smaller than S-H-O-R-T.
When people take life for granite
G-R-A-N-I-T-E
It stretches the imagination into
Greed Rage Anger Neglect Ignorance Tumultuous Envy.
So think about life. L-I-F-E
Love Is Forever Expressing

L-O-V-E

David V.M. Kennedy

Devon smiled as he got out of the car and proceeded to the dentist office. When the assistant escorted Devon into the dental office she sat Devon in a brown chair, and she then placed a white X-ray machine on Devon's cheek. The machine was cold and it gave Devon Goosebumps when it touched his face. After what seemed like an eternity the X- rays came back, and the dentist had disturbing news.

"Hi ma'am I'm Dr. Calhoun."

"Hi Dr. Calhoun, I'm Marsha and this is Devon."

"Well let me cut to the chase. Did something happen? Your son's jaw is slightly realigned. It's nothing major but this is why his teeth protrude the way that they do. He already has a natural overbite due to his mouth being too small for his teeth but with this slight realignment will make his teeth stick out a little more than normal. For now it will be pretty noticeable but in the future he will grow into them so to speak."

"Well he did have an accident with a swing that was in the form of a rock-et, but it didn't seem serious enough to take him to the emergency room."

"Well that would have done no good anyway ma'am. It would have just been a waste of time and money so it's a good thing that you brought him to me."

"So I take it that there is no surgery needed?"

"No ma'am, not at all. Like I said he has a natural overbite anyway it's the slight realignment just makes his teeth stick out more. Trust me he'll definitely grow into them. He'll be okay!"

"Well that's reassuring, so does he need braces?"

"As of now I'm going to say no because like I said his jaw is the issue. Let's give it some time before we make a decision on braces. For now his mouth may look a little awkward but he'll be fine. You're gonna be on handsome little fella!" he said as he patted Devon on the back.

"Well you're the doctor," said Marsha.

After Devon's appointment he and his mother drove home and as they entered the home they found Chippy on his knees on the floor bent over with his face in his hands. The telephone had a long cord that stretched from the kitchen and the hand piece was just dangling off the edge of the couch and a faint voice could be heard over the phone line.

"Hello? Hello? Chippy," said the voice.

"Chippy, what's wrong? Hello? This is Marsha who is this? What's going on?"

"Hi this is Anna Piccolo, Augustus Piccolo's sister, we met once. My brother just passed."

"Passed, how? He didn't have any major health issues."

"Well he was found lying in front of the Princess Street center. There is an investigation going but for now they are saying that he fell and hit his head."

"Oh no, I am so sorry Anna. Is there anything that I can do?"

"Just take care of Chippy. My brother was all that he had."

As Chippy laid in the living room grieving, memories began to flow through his mind about this kind Italian man that took him in as a son amidst the racial tension and divide in the community that happened during his childhood. Augustus Piccolo was from the "old school" and he would often tell Chippy,

"In my house, you're my son and I love you, but to the rest of the world you're just a dumb Nigger! Until this world loses its ignorant way of thinking you're always going to be viewed in a certain way. I am going to prepare you for the realities of life. You gotta be tough Chippy, you gotta be tough!"

Augustus Piccolo would often tell Chippy stories about his biological father Arthur Soriano and how the reputation of the Soriano name came to be. He would tell him, "You're Dad walked the beat of his own drum! He didn't take no shit! One day a police officer pulled his sister over and began harassing her so she went and got him, and without hesitation he confronted the cop. He walked right up to the cop and slapped him with an open hand and dared the cop to call for back up!"

Even though Arthur Soriano had this toughness it wasn't because he was an overwhelmingly physical person. Soriano had a way with his words and he had a persona that was second to none. Arthur Soriano was a martyr and he had a way of making his family believe that they were prominent during a time period where racial divide was prevalent. He was also a very intelligent and charming man who had the ability to uplift his people. Although his death was kept hush Augustus Piccolo would often say to Chippy, "Them Italians killed him! I know they did. Your mom's people killed my best friend!"

Chippy took Mr. Piccolo's death very hard, and he and Marsha became closer after Mr. Piccolo's death, but as time went on they still had one more physical encounter. This time Marsha had simply had enough, and their previous altercation was a defining moment. Lying in the hospital bed was an experience that Marsha never wanted to experience again. She vowed that she would never allow a man to put his hands on her again, and if it did happen then she would make him suffer the dire consequences! During an argument, Chippy had smacked Marsha with an open hand across the face, and without hesitation like a raging bull charging towards a Matador, Marsha grabbed a hammer from the kitchen counter and she wacked Chippy across the head.

Chippy was knocked out as quickly as lighted match trying to keep a flame in a hurricane! Other than a minor concussion Chippy was ok from the blow. His pride was more hurt than his head. After reflecting on what happened Chippy thought to himself, "Damn, What the fuck has gotten into me? I know better. Why can't I control my anger? I love Marsha so much, but sometimes she just makes me so upset! I don't understand these broads nowadays. Damn, I wish I had my Mother to talk to. Why me Lord? What did I do to deserve this? Why did you take my Father before I even got to know him? Why did you take the only Father that I ever knew?! Please, tell me, I'm asking why did my Mother abandon me?! All that I ever wanted was to be loved! Why is it that my own Mother doesn't love me?!"

Subtle Inquiries

I have an inquiring mind; therefore it's something that I need to know.
Why hath thou forsaken me? Am I a mere villain in your sadistic show?
Am I a man in this world, or am I my inner child?
Like the animals you created can you set me free and let me run wild?
I feel like you've created a Beast and my prey is
Answers that I hunt through the night.
Even though I appear to be vicious, I easily
startle and I can't contain my fright.
I have an inquiring mind, so God I need to know why,
Do you hate me too? Am I really a bad guy?

David V.M. Kennedy

After their last fight, Chippy never physically harmed Marsha again. He took possession of the house that was left to him after Augustus Piccolo's passing, but later he had to sell it due to the city wanting to expand the parking lot for a company that sold dental supplies. Chippy's back yard faced College Avenue and the company across the street needed space for their employees so they bought out the residents on one side of Hope Ave.

Even though the house was sold it wasn't worth much; therefore Chippy and Marsha had to use most of the money for funeral expenses as well as some of the debt left behind by Augustus. Chippy also gave most of the money to his Aunt Anna, because she was eventually diagnosed with a terminal illness and the money helped her offset her medical expenses. Due to having to tie up loose ends Chippy ended up missing more work than he usually did. He felt that he owed Augustus his life; therefore he did everything imaginable to make sure Augustus' sister was comfortable.

Eventually, Chippy and Marsha had to move and the realities were that they were a young couple in their early twenties with no real education; therefore they had to move into the projects on the north side of town. Marsha was able apply for government assistance where she would only have to pay $90 for rent each month, but in order to qualify she would have to manipulate the system by stating that she did not know who the father of her child was on the application. She also had to state that she had no financial assistance from him. As Marsha sat at the government assistance office she pondered about what she was about to do. Morally she felt that making a false statement on the application was against all that she was ever taught growing up. The Promises simply didn't raise her to deceive. Marsha contemplated signing the paperwork, and she bit her lip while tapping her fingers with her left hand as she held a black pen with an artificial purple flower attached to the top of it.

Marsha knew that what she was doing was wrong by popular belief; however she also knew that she had no other means of living. She could always move back into her parent's home but then that would leave Chippy homeless. Besides knowing that Chippy wouldn't have a place to live, Marsha also didn't want to deal with the stressors of living with her parents. As she hesitated to fill out the application she noticed a Caucasian lady crying as she stood in line. The lady looked no older than twenty years old and she was visibly upset as she held a baby while two little boys who appeared slightly younger than Devon chased a toddler girl around the seating area. The toddler's nose was running profusely, and she was wearing a white stained T-shirt as well as a saggy diaper. The little girl's feet were bare and as she fell to the floor her diaper made a mushy sound while her black bottomed feet slightly kicked into the air as she rolled on her back.

As Marsha considered whether she really wanted to fill out the paperwork she overheard the young woman getting irate at the agency counter.

"I need this place, you gotta help me," exclaimed the disgruntle lady.

"I'm sorry Ma'am but there is nothing that I can do, rules are rules," stated a woman behind a glass window.

"This is bullshit! Where are me and my kids supposed to live? What am I supposed to do?"

"Ma'am, you stated on your application that the number of adults living in your home were two therefore that disqualifies you, I'm sorry."

"Yeah, but my boyfriend's unemployed we have no income!"

"Again Ma'am, I'm sorry, but the rules are the rules. Try our employment assistance program."

Even though Marsha was brought up in a religious household and taught that it was not right to tell a lie, her survival instincts kicked in, and after over hearing the young woman's conversation she had no qualms about what she had to do. Marsha prayed out loud, "Lord please forgive me, and bless that family." Marsha thought to herself, "There is no way that I can mention Chippy on here! If they denied a white family then I guarantee that I won't get assistance!" Without any further hesitation Marsha completed the application and when her number was called she took a deep breath and she gingerly walked to the woman behind the glass window.

Ignorant

I-G-N-O-R-A-N-T...What does this word mean to you?
I know what it says to me.
I...Similar to this word in the beginning it starts with I, or better yet me;
therefore your actions are critical to whatever the outcome could be.
G...Oh I see, this is the role that you're striving to be. So you're a G? Well
Gee! That's great, but are you a G when there's death served on your plate?
So, now you say you're a G and you think you are tough? Actually you're
neither, NOR do I think that you truly understand this stuff?
I-G-N-O-R...Did I forget the E or did I simply IGNORE? No, I didn't because
like your life there was purpose, so now you just need to explore! You should
explore like an ANT. Although small it carries weight on its
back that others simply can't.
So think about that tiny bug...Don't IGNOR the ANT...It doesn't
matter what you do, just don't be IGNORANT.

David V.M. Kennedy

As a result of Marsha falsifying the application her approval for an apartment was granted. Chippy tied up his loose ends with his father's property, and the young couple moved to the Parkway housing projects or "P-Way" as the youngsters referred to it. Although "P-way" was project housing, it did not have the stereotypical appearance of being drug infested or tacky looking by any means. Even though the average income was moderate or slim to none, the standard tenant was ambitious and hardworking, and it was very common for someone to lend a helping hand to any neighbor in need. Devon and his parents moved to 192 Parkway Blvd. Their apartment was the beginning home of a set of row houses that had a humongous acorn tree in front that sat directly on the corner of an alley and Parkway Blvd. Just west of Devon's apartment was a neighborhood of homes on N. Pershing Ave. that were older colonial style houses, but they were all very well maintained. The neighborhood wasn't considered upscale, but to Devon it was the richest area that he's ever seen. In comparison this particular area was to Devon as if Hope Alley was like a third world country.

After Devon's family settled into their new home he went to his mother to see if it was ok to go outside.

"Mom, Can I go out and play?"

"Devon, we just got here sweetie, you need to unpack your things and get your room together."

"Mom, please? I saw some other kids outside can I please go play?"

"Ok, I'll tell you what, go unpack all of your toys and help your dad put your bed together and if he says it's ok then you can go outside. Is that a deal?"

"Yes Ma'am," Devon replied as ran through the living room from the kitchen towards a set of wooden steps that led upstairs. As Devon was about to turn to take a step up the first two steps that winded into the full set of stairs, Marsha called out,

"Devon, tell your Dad that I'm walking down to Sister Jane's corner store! I'll be right back!"

"Ok, Mom, I will, can you tie my shoe first?"

"No, I gotta go! Tell your Dad, you need to learn how to tie your shoes! I'll be back I love you!"

"Love you too!"

Devon sprinted up the stairway and as his shoelaces tapped the wooden stairs he acted listened to the rhythm of the sound as he sang "conjunction, junction, what's your function?" As Devon entered his room he saw Chippy on his knees putting his bed together.

"Hey, Slick! Hand me that Phillips screwdriver."

"Yes sir and I know that it's the one that looks funny too!"

"Ah, So I see that you've been paying attention! Good job son. Now come here and let me show you how to screw this bed together. Ok, grab firm here and put that bad boy Phillips in here, and remember righty tighty leftie loos-ey!"

"Huh, what the heck is that supposed to mean?"

"It helps you to remember that whenever you screw or twist something you tighten to the right and loosen to the left; and quit cussing!"

"I didn't cuss."

"You said heck didn't you?"

"Dad, heck ain't a bad word," Devon said with a laugh. "You use bad words!"

"Ok, you just asked me 'what the heck does that mean' so what is the difference between me saying, what the hell does that mean? Exactly, there is none; it's all about how you say it! And I don't want to hear you saying ain't any more either. That's bad English. You need to always speak in a way that is professional when you are in a professional environment. You have to be like a switch. When you're around your boys you can use slang but around me I want professionalism unless I say otherwise. Just remember son, being a black man in this society means that you have to be three times better than the next man!"

"Why is that Dad?"

"Simple son, in this world there are always going to be certain people that don't like you for the color of your skin; therefore you need to always be three times better than the next man. I don't care if it's school, sports, or work. Always be three times better and don't settle for less."

"So, when you say people do you mean white people?"

"Look at me boy! I said certain people. I did not say white people. It's true that a lot of white people don't like us for whatever reason, but that is just being ignorant. They don't know any better. Trust me there are plenty of black people who would treat you worse than a white person would! Shit, even during slavery them dumb ass Africans sold their own people! I don't give a fuck what color the person is; if he's ignorant then he's ignorant!"

"Dad," Devon said with excitement.

"Stop cussing!"

"Shut up boy," said Chippy with a smile.

"Dad, why do you cuss so much? Mom says you need Jesus. Oh, and she went to Sister Jane's."

"Ok, I hope she brings me some Midland Chips! To answer your question I cuss because I like it!"

"Can I cuss Dad? You sound cool when you cuss except for when you're mad."

"No, kids can't cuss."

"Well, my friends in Hope Alley did!"

"You said there's no difference, so what's the difference between me saying shoot and the S word?"

"Boy I swear, the more that I teach you the dumber I get," laughed Chippy. "I tell you what, you can cuss around me but you better not let your Mother hear you! You hear me?"

Excited Devon replied, "Yes sir!"

"Ok, give it a try."

"Dad, when the fuck are you gonna get my bed done," asked Devon with a big smile on his face!

"When you give me the God damn rest of the screws," laughed Chippy!

Marsha's latest episodes with Chippy would have forced the average woman to leave the relationship, but she felt something special for him. Both of their childhoods were unique and the dysfunctional upbringings that they had formed a bond that was hard for her to sever. Marsha always contemplated on whether or not she should leave Chippy, but when she thought about leaving the relationship she would think of her son and end up giving Chippy another chance.

Contrary to belief, Chippy did love Marsha but he only treated his woman the way that he did because that was all he knew. If one is taught to abuse with no repercussion then one will continue to abuse. Marsha had a way of calming the beast within Chippy but, the young couple still had arguments and Marsha decided that enough was enough. Chippy moved out and Marsha had to face the harsh reality of raising her son without his father in the home. Marsha also had to figure how to explain to her son that his father would no longer be living with him.

FIGHT

F-I-G-H-T
I've been in so many, so now here is my plea.
F... Take this letter and while you're at it, add you!
I don't want to do it anymore; I mean it I'm through.
IG... Attach the F to these letters, and it's the abbreviation for figure.
My cognitive thought becomes weary as my obstacles get bigger.
H...Not much to say right now; therefore I'm done with IT.
On the other hand this letter's important,
because it means that I can take a HIT!
T... Let's take this letter and make it stand for true.
F-I-G-H-T
Will you fight for me?
Regardless of what I said, I will FIGHT for you!!!

David V.M. Kennedy

Devon had already begun elementary school at Jacob L. Devers which was about a one mile walk from his home. Although he wasn't the most extroverted kid, he was similar to a chameleon, and he had the ability to easily adapt. Even though Devon had no problems to adjusting to any social situation, the one problem that he could not deal with was being ridiculed. For some strange reason the mentality of the "typical Yorker" was like the old "crab in the barrel" cliché. In this community it seemed that whenever a person was doing well in life there would be a mass ordeal of negative opposition. They say that "misery loves company" and if that's the case then the people of York, Pennsylvania would make "misery" evict them from her home due to it becoming overcrowded. Devon came home from school and as he walked into the door he sang "My mama and your mama were hangin' the clothes. My mama socked your mama right dead in the nose! What color was the blood?"

As Devon opened the screen door to go inside the main door was already open, and he walked into the living room and tossed his black and yellow hat on the couch next to his mother who was sitting while she talked on the phone.

"Hey Valerie, what's up girl," asked Marsha

"Hey girl, how you doin'," asked Valerie on the other end of the phone line.

"Marsha, Guess what I heard?"

"What you hear Valerie?"

"Girl, you remember Sheri?"

"Sheri? No, who's that?"

"Girl you remember Sheri the one who that they say is a lesbian now!"

"Oh! Yeah I know who you're talking about. Ain't her man locked up for 5 years?"

"Yeah, Marsha, and that's why she's a lesbian now! Talking bout she gonna keep it tight until her man get out," laughed Valerie.

"I know right? So what's up with her?"

"Girl, she was up in the newspaper talking bout she trying to put together some Parkway Day."

"Parkway Day, what's that supposed be?"

"Girl it's probably some stupid way for her to make money to send to that fool in jail! Talking bout she tryin' to bring the community together! Girl please, she needs to go on with her ugly ass! That bitch so ugly she gotta trick or treat over the phone!"

"Valerie! You are so crazy! Now that's pretty ugly!"

As Marsha continued her conversation with Valerie she noticed Devon peeking into the refrigerator and she said,

"Devon, did you wash your hands?"

"Oops, no Mom I didn't, where's Dad? I gotta show him something. Dad! Where are you? Mom, I thought Dad was off today."

While Devon continued to yell for Chippy Marsha quickly rushed Valerie off of the phone.

"Valerie let me call you later I have to talk to Devon."

"Ok, Marsha, wait what are you gonna tell him?"

"Bye Valerie!"

As soon as Marsha hung up the phone Devon came from upstairs and he said,

"Mom, where's Dad? Isn't he off work today?"

"He is Devon but he's not here."

"Aw man, I wanna show him this flyer that I got from school! Look, it's for boxing lessons! When is he coming home?"

"He's not Devon."

"Huh? What do you mean he's not?"

"Just what I said, he's not. Listen your Dad and I have decided that we were not going to be together anymore. He's not going to live with us okay?"

"Why, is it because yous guys are always fighting?"

"Exactly, let me see that. Humph, well you know you ain't boxing right?"

"Huh. Why not?!"

"Because I said so that's why."

"Are you serious? Come on man!"

"Who do you think you're talking to? Don't you come on man me!"

"But Dad said that he wanted to put me in boxing lessons soon! That's not fair!"

"Life's not fair now go to your room!"

Although Marsha knew Devon had a passion for boxing she had her reasons for not letting her 6yr old son take up the sport. As Devon slammed his bedroom door Marsha stared into space and wept as she heard her son crying from his room upstairs. With Chippy gone she had no financial support and without a job she felt like the weight of planet earth itself was now upon her shoulders. Marsha's last resort was for full governmental assistance but after numerous attempts of applying for work she had no choice. No one seemed to want to hire a young black woman with only a high school education. Marsha applied to several fast food restaurants and not one offer was given to her.

As Devon's cries turned to soft whimpers Marsha's face turned to stone. She had the look of a rhinoceros ready to charge the first person that she saw. Rather than crying and feeling sorry she wiped her face and she swallowed her pride as she grabbed the phone book. She sighed as she dialed the number for governmental assistance, and her thoughts were of all of the obstacles that surely were to come.

The next morning Devon awoke and prepared for school. As he went into the bathroom to wash and brush his teeth he snatched the boxing flyer off of his dresser and he crumbled it as hard as he could. He was so angry that he threw the paper with all of his might into the garbage can that was between the toilet and the sink.

"Ouch! Stupid sink! I almost broke my stupid hand," pouted Devon.

"I can't do anything. Stupid Dad! Stupid Mom! Everybody else can box, so why not me?"

"Devon," yelled Marsha from her room.

"Yes?"

"What are you doing boy?"

"Nothing!"

"Well what was that noise?"

"What noise? I missed and cut my hand and I'm getting a band aid."

"How did you cut your hand? Come here and let me see."

"I don't know, I'm okay, I can take care of it!"

"Whatever, hurry up and come eat or you'll be late for school!"

"Okay!"

In spite of living in the projects, Devon would like to refer to his home as the "nicer" part of the projects. Indeed Parkway was not by any mean luxurious, but residents had a special type of pride that they had in themselves. It seemed that every tenant had the mentality of "I'm not poor, I'm just broke." Parkway residents had a plethora of ambitious people. They were "go getters." The neighborhood kids liked to think that their side was the best side, and they always competed with each other whether it was in sports or so called "representing" during the typical childhood fights. The "other side" was to Devon and his friends anywhere past Front St which intersected south of Parkway Blvd. Most of the projects toughest kids lived on the "other side" and a good quantity of them had to pass by Devon's home as they journeyed to and from school. Two of the toughest kids on the "block" were kids named "Flave" who was three years older than Devon, and "Spoon" who was around Devon's age.

One day Devon had an altercation at school that would change his life forever. It seemed that the daily ritual for the neighborhood kids was to pick on Devon by calling him "Bucky beaver" because of his teeth or chastise him because his clothes were better looking than the average "poor" child. Devon was a very bright and articulate child and he had been labeled "gifted" by the test that he took in school. Although he did not dress "nerdy" the other kids knew how smart he was and they teased him constantly. Even though Chippy was no longer in Devon's life full time, he did spend an ample amount of time with him before he moved out. Chippy was an avid boxing fan, and he and Devon would never miss a fight on T.V. Devon would always emulate Muhammed Ali, and just like his mother's feet his hands were noticeably quick, therefore he should not have been afraid of the kid who went by the name "Spoon".

Despite the fact that Devon had thorough training from Chippy, the one thing he lacked was a "killer instinct." When it came to confrontation Devon was afraid of his own shadow! It seemed like every day Marsha either had to get a call from the school about someone picking on Devon, or he would run home because he was being chased by the neighborhood kids. Although the residents of Parkway had a lot of unity they still seemed to find a way to chastise those who the average resident felt was better than them. The thought of a person achieving more than them seemed to get under their skin; therefore they would demean or degrade that person anyway that they felt fit. This "crab in the barrel" mentality by the adults in the community easily trickled down to the youth and Devon was a prime suspect of ridicule.

"Mommy, Mommy, Help, Mommy," screamed Devon as he came sprinting home from school.

"Boy, what is your problem?" questioned Marsha. Devon panted heavily and he spoke as if he had a Latin tongue and he said,

"This guy is chasing me, he pulled my scarf and choked me, and I didn't do anything to him! They keep pushing me and hitting me upside the head!"

Marsha was already stressed from the daily routine of struggling to put food on the table, and whenever she became angered to where she couldn't take it anymore, her sweet and beautiful glow turned into the ferocity of a raging bull! Marsha was already aware of the challenges of being a single parent. She knew that she was about to endure more obstacles than the runners at the steeplechase events during her recent track meets. Marsha made it clear to her son that enough was enough. She grabbed Devon by the arm and literally threw him outside the door off of the three step porch where Spoon stood unafraid of the fact that an adult was alongside confronting him. As she threw Devon out the door she screamed at the top of her lungs,

"Boy, I am tired of you running in here crying every day and telling me that someone is chasing you! If you don't stand up for yourself they're gonna always pick on you! Either you get your ass out there and fight him, or you fight me!"

Devon knew that his mother was serious, because the only time she would even think of using curse words was if she was beyond upset! Marsha realized that this wasn't the right thing to do but she felt that it had to be done or else Devon would run for the rest of his life. Spoon's reputation was he was the best fighter pound for pound in the projects, and one of the reasons was his brother was an amateur boxer who taught him how to fight; therefore he had the skill set needed to box and it seemed that no one could beat him.

Mother's Command

Each day you grow, but I'll still see you as my baby boy.
It hurts so bad to see others try to steal your joy.
On the outside a coward is what many think that they see,
But your bottled emotions will set the beast free.
I've overprotected you. I've done all that I can.
The time is now baby boy. Unleash the beast and follow God's plan.

David V.M. Kennedy

Even though Marsha tossed her son into the belly of the beast, and that this wasn't the customary thing to do, she felt that it had to be done or else Devon continue to be afraid of not only bullies but adversity in life itself. Although Spoon had a reputation for being a seasoned fighter at a tender young age, Devon now had no choice but to stand up for himself. Spoon swung at Devon as soon as his feet came off of the steps, and instantaneously Devon's instincts took over. Devon and Spoon squared each other up while both stood in a traditional boxing stance for right handed boxers. Devon's smooth style and lighting quickness beguiled the neighborhood crowd as he ducked and dodged Spoon's flailing punches. As Devon slipped one of Spoon's left handed jabs, he dropped his right hand while he moved to the left of Spoon. Spoon countered quickly with a left handed cross that caught Devon flush on the jaw! He then hit Devon so hard that Devon's neck made a crunching sound as his chin was knocked into his left clavicle!

Marsha's motherly instincts were about to take over as she stepped towards the two mini featherweights. She was ready to separate them until she saw the look that was in her baby's eyes. Marsha prayed to herself,

"Lord Jesus, please forgive me, why am I letting this go?"

After witnessing the look on Devon's face Marsha knew that she had to let the fight continue. If she ended this miniature brawl then Devon would never hear the end of it, and he would be scorned for the rest of his life! As

Marsha retracted her steps she caught Devon's eye, and he glanced at her with a frightening look. Devon's face was so intimidating that Satan himself could have looked at him, and he would have run away crying with fear! It was in this miniscule moment that the sight of his mother's face triggered a flash of painful memories. The image of his father punching and kicking his mother sent chills down his spine; and as Spoon came with a right roundhouse punch the next thing that was heard was uproar from the neighborhood crowd!

"Ohh!"

Even Flave who was there to pretty much looking out for Spoon had to cringe. As Devon ducked the right roundhouse punch, he gave Spoon a vicious left uppercut that connected flush over Spoon's mouth and nose! As Spoon's head jerked upward and back, Devon came with a thunderous right cross that landed dead smack in the middle of Spoon's jaw! In spite of Marsha going against her morals by letting the boys fight, she was not only shocked but pleased to an extent as well. She immediately halted the fight,

"Ok, now stop! Devon you get in the house, and Spoon you come with me."

"Get your hands off of my cousin," yelled Flave.

"Flave you better shut your mouth and show some respect before grab my belt and whoop your behind and then go tell your mama," demanded Marsha.

"I'm sorry Ms. Marsha, please don't, please don't tell my mom."

"Apology accepted now the two of you let's go!"

Marsha took Spoon home and explained to his parents what had transpired and as Devon sat at home he was in disbelief that the kids actually were cheering for him to win. Marsha returned from Spoon's house and as she came through the door she said,

"Now honey I don't want you to think that fighting is the answer, but sometimes you just have to defend yourself. Although what we did was wrong, I'm sure that kid won't mess with you again!"

Devon concurred with a smile of confidence and he acknowledged that his days of running from his fears were over. The next day Devon walked to school with a new attitude. He strutted with a swagger because he knew that today he didn't have to run home from school. While basking in his glory, Devon wasn't paying attention and…Screech! A green station wagon slammed on the breaks causing Devon to scurry across the street. "Sorry!" he yelled as he dashed down the street towards his school.

Utopia

Dear Father you created us in your image, and you've given us free will.
This little light of mine will shine as darkness
tries to shade me from what's real.
It seems that since Genesis we've been on a never ending Exodus,
Yet through blasphemy and tyranny you've always been next to us.
Mankind has always been searching for that picture perfect place.
My road block is ignorance so help me detour, and save the human race.

David V.M. Kennedy

In the station wagon were Marsha's former nurse Jacqueline Fable and her son Daniel Fable who were on their way to drop D.F off at his school.

"Whew! That was close; do you have on your seatbelt D.F.?"

"Yeah mom, c'mon we need to hurry up!" said the seven year old D.F.

Even though the Fables lived on the south side of town, Jacqueline had an early errand to run that day on the northern part of town where she had almost hit Devon. As she continued to drive D.F. to his school, she thought to herself,

"Hmm, why does that kid look familiar?"

"You ok mom?" interrupted D.F.

"Oh, yes honey mommy was daydreaming; let's get you to school my little angel," gleefully exclaimed Jacqueline.

She pulled to the front of St. Patrick's elementary school which was a small school located in the central part of the city. As Daniel Fable got out of the car to head to the playground, Jacqueline's face beamed with joy as a host of D.F.'s friends came running towards him. To say that D.F. was popular amongst the neighborhood was an understatement. D.F. was the All-American boy that everyone simply wished that they could adopt after they met him. This kid was the epitome of charm and wit. Everyone around the neighborhood loved him, and in their eyes he could do no harm.

One day D.F. accidentally threw a baseball through one of the neighbor's windows; and before he could utter the words "I'm sorry," the young woman instantly at the sight of his puppy dog look melted like a Hershey's kiss left in the Sahara Desert, and gave him a dollar to go catch the ice cream truck! This kid truly was the "All-American boy." Although the notoriety of Daniel Fable was prominent, this particular day was going to temporarily demote his status.

Jacqueline, who was thirty six years old worked at the hospital for 15 years, and throughout her tenure she witnessed any and everything imaginable. She was immune to trauma like a polar bear is impervious to the cold during a winter storm in Alaska. She without a doubt had ice in her veins. This particular day those veins would erupt like hot lava, because as she walked down the hall she noticed her father being rushed to the emergency operating room. Jacqueline sprinted to the head nurse to request off in order to be by her father's side, but by the time she got to the room he was already pronounced dead.

As one could imagine, Jacqueline's tears flowed as if the Niagara Falls came splashing through the hospital walls. After trying to pull herself together, she left the hospital to go and pick D.F. up from school. Automatically D.F. sensed that something was wrong because his mother's bloodshot eyes looked as if they were sprayed with mace.

"What's wrong with you, Mom?"

"Huh, oh nothing baby, I'm ok."

"Then why are eyes so red?"

Jacqueline knew that there was no easy way to break the news to her son, therefore she looked D.F. into his eyes and said,

"Daniel, Your Grandfather just passed."

"Passed? What does that mean?"

"He's dead honey. He's gone to heaven to be with Jesus."

"No more Grandpa?"

"No sweetie, there's no more Grandpa."

The two of them wept as Jacqueline drove back to their home on the south side of York. As she headed east on Parkway Blvd toward N. George St, she heard a booming sound of something hitting her car.

"Good Lord what was that," screamed Jacqueline.

"Daniel, are you ok?"

"Yes Mommy, I'm fine.'

"Oh my God, Devon, get down," Jacqueline panicked.

While Jacqueline warned D.F. to get down a brick came hurling threw the air smashing the passenger side of her green station wagon. Jacqueline happened to be looking at Daniel when a group of African American teens threw a brick from where they were standing which was on the corner of Front St and Parkway Blvd. Jacqueline brought the car to a stop, the brick barely missed Daniel's head and it landed into her lap. Jacqueline looked up in pain and as she began to push the brick off of her lap, she saw the mob of teens coming toward her. One teen who stood about 6 feet tall wore a white T- shirt and black pants yelled,

"This is 112, you stupid white bitch!"

"Mommy," screamed Daniel.

"It's ok baby, don't be scared!"

"Give me your fucking money bitch!"

"No! Leave us alone," demanded Jacqueline.

The ignorant thug noticed Jacqueline's black leather purse lying on the floor near Daniel's feet. As he reached inside of the broken window, pieces of glass fell into Daniel's lap.

"Mommy, help!"

Without hesitation Jacqueline grabbed the brick from the floor and threw it right at the thug's face. The brick hit the thug in the nose and blood spattered all over Daniel. Jacqueline screamed,

"Get away from my fucking son you bastard!"

Jacqueline pressed the gas pedal as hard as she could, and as the car took off the thug was still hanging inside of the passenger door. The force of the car made the thug bang his head as he fell out of the window onto the ground. Daniel began to cry and he yelled,

"Mommy I'm scared! They did it again, Mommy the black men did it again! I hate black people!"

As Jacqueline drove to safety heart slowed down after it felt like it was going to jump out of her chest. She pulled into a fast food restaurant parking lot that set across the street from a post office and turned to her son and said,

"Daniel! What did I tell you son? You need to stop thinking this way! All black people are not bad people! Remember that time when I told you that someone stole my wallet and the police caught who did it?"

"Yes, I remember."

"Well guess what race that guy was?"

"I don't know, Black?"

"No Daniel, he was white. Also the guy who robbed your favorite corner store on Pershing Ave was white. And remember the kid who stole your skateboard? What color was he?"

"He was white," D.F. said slowly as the wisdom from Jacqueline began to make sense.

"Exactly Daniel, and just like the Spanish kid who stole your bike and the Asian man that broke into Mrs. Coleman's car, they all did bad things, and they all were from different backgrounds. I don't want you judging people by the color of their skin D.F. Good and bad people come in all forms. You need to judge a person's character, and that is what is inside here, your heart. I know that you're going to miss your Grandfather, but some of the things that he taught you were just downright evil. I can't blame him too much, because he was raised that way. This particular mentality is a beast that plagues our society, and when I say plague I mean it destroys the mindset of the world that we live in. So Daniel from this day forward I want you to open your mind and learn about as many different ethnic backgrounds as you can. What I mean by that is that you need to appreciate how people who are different from you live. If everyone could live their life this way then the world would be a better place. Do you understand?"

"Yes Mommy I do, I really do understand."

After the mourning of her father, Jacqueline continued to work at the hospital while maintaining a steady income. Unfortunately, the house that she inherited was too much for her lone income to bear. D.F. was outside playing with two boys who lived across the street.

"Daniel" called Jacqueline.

"Yes mom, what is it?" inquired D.F.

"Listen son, we are going to be moving next week because mommy can no longer afford to live in this house, ok?"

"Moving? I don't want to move! Do we have to? What about all of my friends?"

At that moment anxiety jumped inside of D.F.'s body as if he was possessed by a spirit named Fear! He was so well known and complacent with his current friends, that he didn't think he could possibly befriend another.

One week passed by but to D.F. the time felt like it was the very next day. The mother and son packed their belongings and headed to the northwestern part of York to live at a place called fireside on Atlantic Ave. As they moved into their new apartment Jacqueline could only encourage her son to go outside and try to mingle and meet new friends.

Even though D.F. possessed a lot of charisma, he lacked confidence in his social skills. He began to literally close himself off to the outside world. Every day that he came home from school, he would stay in his room until it was time for dinner where he would come out momentarily. Jacqueline took notice of this sign of depression and took the liberty of forcing D.F. to go outside to the park and play.

"Sweetie you can't make any friends if you don't go outside and play so take this brand new basketball and go to the park!" D.F.'s face lit up like the fireworks on the 4th of July!

"Oooo! Mom, thank you!"

"You're welcome honey, now go outside and play. Make some new friends.

D.F. had an immense desire for basketball, and he took his new ball to the park where he saw a group of kids at the basketball court.

"Check out the chubby kid!" one of the children stated.

"Yeah, looks like he took a bath in hot dog water!" another shouted as they all exploded in laughter.

D.F. ignored the comments and pulled up for a jump shot. Swish! The sound of his brand new ball splashed through the nets like an Olympic high diver earning a perfect ten entering into the swimming pool. He had a shot so pure that the kids in the old neighborhood nicknamed him "Saucy!" In spite of being slow as molasses, his overall talent was smooth like butter. Each kid challenged him to a game of one on one,

"Yo, Twinkie butt! Let's play one on one! You suck!"

"Ok, I'll play you but my name is D.F. why are you calling me names? We just met so why are you making fun of me?"

"All man, give me the ball," said a nine year old black kid that looked small for his age.

"Check the rock," demanded D.F.

The little boy who went by the name of "Boog" was known around his neighborhood as the best basketball player his age! Even though Boog was small in stature he was lightning fast and very strong for his age. Not only was

Boog notorious for his basketball skills but he had his way with the little girls around the block. A group of girls were playing off to the left of the basketball court called Lincoln Park and as Boog noticed them watching him and D.F. play. After every basket he made he would say to D.F.,

"Boom! In your face Twinkie butt, ladies love Boooog!"

D.F. and Boog were playing the first to eleven points wins and Boog went up 5 to 0. D.F. became very annoyed because he got tired of hearing,

"Boom! In your face Twinkie butt, ladies love Boooog!"

As the two kept playing, D.F. grew tired of the sneers from the crowd. Again the mentality of the "typical Yorker" always seemed to be one that needed to degrade people. What was it that made people think this way? Did the parents of this small inner city not realize that their children's behavior was simply the outcome of how they were being taught at home? All D.F. simply wanted to do was make friends. D.F. was a very good ball player but his confidence began to sink to an all-time low do to the fact that the negativity was overwhelming.

Even though Daniel's sureness in his abilities steadily began to decline, Boog shot and scored on another basket, and even though they were playing by ones, his shot from the three point line. Boog was bringing his best game and he was putting on a show for his peers! Boog was ahead in the game 6 to 0 and he said to Daniel,

"I'll give it to you, you got game but you keep letting them get to you. Now I'm gonna beat you 11 to zip!"

D.F. turned around and looked under the basket and a group a ten kids yelled,

"Twinkie butt, Twinkie butt, Boog's beatin' Twinkie butt!"

At that moment Boog dribbled to his right and D.F. took the proper angle while cutting him off. He reached in and stripped the ball right out of his hands and then he turned around and made a layup.

"7-1 you, and it's make it take it! You're done, I got this," stated D.F.

"That was luck, said Boog.

D.F. went on to defeat Boog 11-8, and three other kids waited patiently to play the winner. D.F. defeated and annihilated all challengers on the court, and he gained the respect of all but one of his peers. Even though he remained humble as he went victorious, a kid known as "Slick Nick" wasn't impressed. Slick Nick was a tall lanky dark skinned African-American boy who looked like he was ten years old. He lived on the "other side" of the projects. Slick Nick and his crew would frequent Lincoln Park, because they knew that there were more white kids there to cause trouble with. In spite of Slick Nick willing to cause trouble among white kids, he had an infatuation for white girls! Lincoln Park was at least 2 miles west of the Parkway Projects and one would wonder why this ten year old boy and his elementary school henchman were able to venture so far without adult supervision. These particular types of children had parents who really didn't care if their child would wonder off, because they were more concerned about themselves. Slick Nick was ten years old. His mother was twenty four. His Grandmother was thirty nine. He had no relationship with his Grandfather or his Father, because he did not know who they were!

"Give me that ball Twinkie butt!" demanded Slick Nick.

D.F. stood shocked and in disbelief as Slick Nick snatched his ball and stared at him daring him to take it back!

"Hey! What you do that for," asked D.F.

"Because I felt like it, now what are you gonna do about it you stupid Honky," replied Slick Nick.

"I ain't no Honky, and I don't even know what a Honky is!"

"A Honky is you! You little white punk! White boys can't play no basketball you stupid jerk! Why don't you go hang out with your little rich friends?"

"I don't have any rich friends."

"Yes you do, all white people are rich! My Mom said white folks got money, ya'll got it made!"

"Well your mom is wrong, because we ain't rich!"

"Don't be talkin' bout my Mom you stupid Honky!"

"Huh? I didn't say anything about your mom!"

"Oh, so you getting loud?"

"What are your talking about?"

"I'm talkin' bout this you stupid twinkie butt honky!"

Slick Nick shoved D.F. to the ground making him hit his head onto a pole that faced a small creek behind the basketball court. He then took D.F.'s ball and kicked it toward Roosevelt St which was west of the basketball court. Even though Boog didn't know D.F. he ran after his ball to retrieve it for him. As the ball went bouncing into the street a motorist passing by in a red Mazda turismo abruptly blew the horn at Boog as he tracked down the ball. The loud sound startled the group of kids, and they all scurried from the park leaving

D.F. standing alone covered in dirt staring at Boog and the ball from a distance. D.F. began to walk towards Boog as tears streamed down his face. He was not only embarrassed but totally confused about why Slick Nick did what he did to him.

Mother's Plea

On this joyous and beautiful day why is it so hard for me to enjoy?
My duty to you Lord is to comfort and nurture,
and it's not to harm my baby boy.
In the beginning you created Adam,
and afterwards you blessed him with Eve,
I know that it's your will for us to be together, and our
separation is also hard for me to believe.
Patience is a virtue and through Christ I know I'll go far.
Bear with me Lord my baby's wounds are deep, and with your hands I'll
easily heal his scar.

David V.M. Kennedy

Incidentally, inside of the car was Marsha on her way to pick Devon up from baseball practice. She saw the entire incident with D.F. transpire as she was getting closer to Boog. After blowing the horn and passing by, she looked through her rear view mirror and she saw D.F. gather his basketball. Marsha stated with concern,

"Aw! They shouldn't have done that to that poor kid!"

As Marsha pulled up to the field, Devon came sprinting to the car full of excitement!

"Mom, Guess what?"

"What is it baby," asked Marsha.

"The coach said that I can start pitching fast," Devon exclaimed.

"Isn't that what you're supposed to do," Marsha said sarcastically.

"Well, yeah, but I didn't know that we could. Everyone else pitched slowly, so I thought that's what we were supposed to do."

"Well I'm no expert at baseball, but I'm sure that you are supposed to try to strike them out the best way that you can."

Even though Marsha didn't like baseball she did understand a little about the game, and she made sure that she attended every game Devon had. Devon was a starting pitcher for his 7 to 8 year baseball team, and he told his coach that he was pitching slowly, because all of the other kids were pitching slowly too. He was so naïve that he thought that it was a rule to pitch the ball slowly, because they were only seven and eight year olds! Devon's coach exploded with laughter after discovering his young player's immature approach to the game. He explained to Devon that he was able to throw the ball as hard as he could as long as he threw strikes. When the Parkway kids would get their rival games together, Devon was always picked to play with the kids that were three years older than him. Due to the fact that he played with the older kids his athletic skill was enhanced.

Despite Marsha attending every game, she really hated going to watch because she felt that it was too boring. Although she disliked the game she knew that Devon had a passion for it, therefore she would always be one of the loudest people cheering in the crowd. Since Devon was no longer ignorant of the rules he became a dominant pitcher, and he also hit multiple home runs! Devon was so proud that he couldn't stop ranting about his success to his friends and family. Although Devon was proud of his achievements there was still was one void in the back of his mind nagging him like a bitter wife would do to her husband during a long unhappy marriage. Devon wished Chippy would come to his games but each time he scanned the crowd, his father wasn't there. One day Devon asked Marsha,

"Mom, have you seen my Dad?"

"No, Devon I haven't seen him since he moved out."

"Is he ever coming back?" Marsha took a deep breath and responded by saying,

"I don't know Devon. It's complicated."

"What do you mean that it's complicated?"

"I mean that it's hard to explain. Your Dad and I just aren't getting along so we feel that it's best for all of us to not be in a relationship together."

"I wish that he would come to my games Mom; here take a look at this"

"What's this?"

"It's a certificate saying that I was selected to the All-Star game this weekend coming up, and this is paperwork for club baseball. My coach said that I am too good to be playing at this level and that he wants me to play travel ball," said Devon modestly.

"Good job Devon! I'm so proud of you! Travel ball? Where do they travel?"

"I don't know, but they go all over Pennsylvania and they get real uniforms! They even get to stay in hotels just like the big leagues! Can I do it?"

"I'm sorry Devon, but with your father not here it's just me taking care of our home and right now I can't afford to put you into travel ball. Besides, that takes a commitment and there is a lot of time invested."

"Aw Man, Please!"

"Boy, what did I tell you about 'aw man' do I look like a man to you?"

"No Ma'am, but Mom the coach said that I was good! He said that he could see me playing on TV one day because he's never seen a kid my age with so much power and control! You have money; you have money to get your hair and nails done every week!"

"No! Now, don't ask me again, or I'm gonna beat your behind!"

"This ain't fair! I never get to do anything!"

"Boy, shut up and go to your room! You better be thankful that you're able to play baseball at all! You got kids in these projects that wished that they even owned a baseball bat and glove, and here you are complaining about travel ball! I ain't white, I ain't rich!"

"Well my friend K. Ritt ain't white and he gets to play! What's being white got to do with it?"

"That's not what I said boy, and I could care less about a K. Ritt! Go to your room!"

As Devon marched through the living room, he forcefully walked through a curtain of beads that separated the living room from the kitchen. He opened the beads so hard that one of the strands snapped, and a string of beads fell to the kitchen floor with some rolling under the refrigerator and oven. At that moment Devon knew that he was in serious trouble so he took off running out the front door!

"Boy, I'm gonna beat your behind! Where's my belt?!"

Marsha was unable to locate her leather belt before Devon got out of the door, so she grabbed one of her canvas sneakers that had a rubber sole out of the pantry where the washer machine was. Devon sprinted out the door and he ran to the right towards Front St. He had a thirty yard head start, and before he knew it Marsha was grabbing him by the arm! It was as if the gun went off for the 100 yard dash and Marsha shot out of the house like a greyhound chasing a rabbit!

"Boy, didn't I tell you to get your butt in your room," said Marsha as she pummeled Devon with her sneaker. Her voice was rhythmic with each blow to Devon's buttocks. It was as if she was beating him while performing a song!

"Mommy, No! I'm sorry! I'm sorry!"

"Now get your butt back up to that house and you go to your room! And you better dry that face up! Shut up!"

Even though Devon didn't actually do anything worth getting a beating for, he found himself in his room pouting and crying not fully understanding why he was punished. Marsha loved her son with all of her heart but whenever she had to punish Devon she would often tell him, "this will hurt me more than it hurts you." Devon never understood how she could possibly feel more pain than him, because he was the one with welts on his leg.

Marsha was cracking under the pressures of being a single mother, and although she wanted the best for her son there was simply nothing that she felt that she could do. Every child needs discipline. Every child does not need to be punished by force for every little mistake that they make. Sometimes a swat on the backside is needed to grab the attention of a disruptive child, but repetitive force is unnecessary. Marsha only disciplined Devon the way that she knew how, and yet again the beast within Marsha was passed down to her by her parents. This slave mentality of beating to reprimand dates back to the beginning of man.

Rather than using brute force, Marsha could have simply brought herself down to Devon's level by explaining why he was unable to play in a fashion that he could understand. In order to compromise, emotions have to be set to a moderate level. Devon could have possibly triggered a thought that would have given Marsha an idea on how to get Devon the funds to play. Instead of resolving their issue in a calm manner, Marsha now sat in her living room with guilt and remorse while Devon lay in his bed with the beast within grumbling and ready to unleash.

It came time for Devon's All-Star game and the night before he tossed and turned, because he was full of anxiety. The next morning he discovered that his mother had come down with the flu, and she explained to him that she wouldn't be able to make the game. With a repetitive cough Marsha stated,

"I'm sorry baby, but mommy won't be able to make it to your game today."

"That's ok mom, you just get better," consoled Devon.

"I'm going to send my friend Janine so she can tell me all the details, ok?"

"Ok, I like Ms. Janine, She's pretty!"

"Yes, she is now whatever you do, I want you to have fun and try your hardest ok? Make Mommy proud!"

"Ok, Mom, I will. I just wish that my Dad would come, have you talked to him yet?"

"No, Devon, listen he ain't worried about you! All he cares about is himself, and he could care less about you or me."

"So, are you saying that my Dad doesn't love me?"

"What, no Devon just get ready for your game, and don't worry about him I think that I hear Janine outside, hit a homerun for me!"

"Ok, Mom I will do that!"

After Devon raced out of the door to meet Janine, Marsha began to break down crying in tears. Her heart was torn and not because her sudden illness wouldn't allow her to be present at the game, but because she had to resort to one of her friends rather than her own child's father to be there. Marsha hated that she had to now play the "MAD" role, which is Mom and Dad. Regardless of how strong many single mothers are the burden of raising a child without the help of the father is a strain. Without the father the child is deprived of the daily nurturing, and the mother tends to be bitterer than the norm, because she is frustrated with the absence of the father. Some moms are just mad. They get to the point that they take out their anger on their children while unconscious to the fact that they are doing it in spite of the father who is no longer there.

Paper Daddy

What is it dear Lord, why am I off on this vicious caper?
Aw, who cares? I gotta get this money, I gotta get this paper.
In the beginning you blessed Adam with Eve, and that seemed to ruin his life.
Solomon was a King and he had more than one wife.
My life has been miserable, and it's been destroyed since day one.
My first born is a blessing, but now it's time for me to have fun.
Father God what did I do to deserve this?
It's not my fault that I can't express my love!
Teach me dear Lord, because me my son's life is in peril so please send us your blessings from above.

Although Chippy never watched his son play a baseball game, he still heard stories about how well Devon was doing and always responded in a proud fashion. Devon would occasionally bump into his father as he played throughout the neighborhoods, and every time they saw each other Chippy would express his affection by giving him money. One day Devon was going to Sister Jane's corner store and as he stopped at the intersection before he was ready to cross the street, he saw Chippy pulling up in his 1969 Dodge Charger. The color was a champagne looking color with a black top, and Devon was in awe of the sound that the engine made! As Chippy approached the stop sign he heard Devon yell,

"Dad, Dad, over here!"

"Hey Slick, what's happening? I heard you were kicking butt in baseball!"

"Yes sir! I have a wicked fast ball Dad! I made the All-Star team too! My coach said that I was the best that he's ever seen at my age, and that he wants me to play on his travel team!"

"That's good Slick, I'm proud of you! When's your first practice?"

"Well, I can't play, Mom said I can't," said Devon as he lowered his head.

"What the fuck do you mean you can't play?"

"She says she doesn't have the money and that she won't have time to take me where we travel."

"What? What the fuck does she mean that she doesn't have time? How much is it? I'll pay for it!"

"For real? I have the paper here in my pocket! It will cost $50 a month for dues."

"Aw hell, that ain't shit! Here, take this one hundred dollar bill and put in your pocket! Don't lose it! Where are you going anyway, to the store to get some chips?"

"Yeah, but not for potato chips though I don't have enough money for that. I'm just gonna buy some penny candy."

"Boy, what did I tell you about eating all of that candy? If you're gonna eat candy eat chocolate but not too much! Here take this $20."

"Thanks Dad!"

"You're welcome. So what's your Mom been up to? Ain't no hard legs coming around are they?"

"Hard legs, what are hard legs?"

"Dudes, Devon, sheesh the more that I teach you the dumber I get!"

"Oh, no not that I know of, I haven't seen anyone around, when are you coming back home?"

"Well, I'm glad that I ran into you, you're about to have a little brother! Get in I want you to meet someone."

"For real, I'm about to have a little brother? My mom said to come straight home after I go to the store can you take me home first?"

"Boy, get in this damn car, I ain't thinking about your mom! I'm your father, besides we're not going to be there that long anyway!"

"Ok, Dad cool, so when will my brother be here?"

"Any day now son, we're going to meet his mom now. Her name is Ms. Paula."

After Chippy's separation with Marsha he later took on a new relationship and moved down the street within the projects. Chippy moved on the "other side" with his new girlfriend who went by the name of Paula. Paula was eight years older than Chippy, but looked as if she was five years his predecessor. She stood about 5ft7 inches tall and she was a pretty lady with a very loud and distinctive laugh! Paula was a natural born comedienne and she always had a smile on her face as she often amused the kids in the projects. Paula had three children from her previous marriage, and one was a boy who was about five years older than Devon and two daughters which one was Devon's age. Paula allowed Chippy to move in with her with the notion that his relationship with Marsha was over. Devon was a little bashful when he met Paula, but she immediately lightened the mood when he and Chippy walked through the door.

"Hey, Paula," yelled Chippy as he and Devon walked inside the home.

"What? Can't you see me coming down the steps? You don't have to yell!"

"I want you to meet my son; Devon this is Ms. Paula, Paula Devon."

"Nice to meet you Devon, but you can just call me Paula. I ain't an old fart like your Daddy! Look at him wearing purple sweat pants! Dah! Looks like a purple boa constrictor wrapped itself around his legs, Dah! And is that a fanny pack around your waist? Dah! What do you got some purple ribbons for your hair in there?" Dah!

"You're funny Ms… I mean Paula!"

"Yeah, funny looking," said Chippy.

"Funny looking, Chippy you so ugly that your birth certificate is an apology letter from the condom factory, Dah! You so ugly that you scared the crap out of the toilet, Dah! No, you so ugly that when you joined an ugly contest the judges said sorry no professionals allowed, Dah!"

Devon cried tears as he laughed so hard at his Dad as Paula continued to make fun of Chippy. As Devon began to dry his face, Paula's oldest son and her youngest daughter walked through the back door from outside. The son looked to be in his early teen years and the daughter was a pretty little girl who was the same age as Devon. Her name was Shayla, and she had beautiful slanted eyes, with dimples in her cheeks and her hair was done into two long pony tails. Devon was captivated by how cute she was and he stared at her with his mouth agape. He did notice however that her skin was lighter than the rest of her face in the corner of her forehead. Devon thought that it was a birthmark and he said,

"I like your birthmark, that's pretty cool!"

"Birth mark? I know you ain't cuttin!"

"Cuttin? I ain't cutting."

"Yeah, you cuttin', your teeth big when you sneeze you stab yourself in the chest!"

"Now that's some big ass teeth," laughed Paula's teenage son.

"What, why are you talking about my teeth," asked Devon.

"You started it, lookin' like a bucked tooth beaver!"

"Shut up, you don't even know me, ugly! You look like you got a map on your forehead!"

"Boo! That was weak; your teeth are so yellow that when you smile traffic slows down!"

"Shut up, stop laughing at me," Devon yelled as he saw Chippy and Paula join in the laughter. Tears began to stream down his face as the "cuttin" continued. The beast within Devon began to get annoyed and as he began to cry his father said,

"Boy, you better toughen up and dry them tears! I know you ain't crying! Be a man!"

Devon looked at Paula and her children as they continued to laugh and as he stood up from the kitchen table he slammed one of the chairs that had a round cushion with a metal back support to the ground and in his pre-adolescent voice yelled,

"Fuck you! Fuck all of ya'll"

"That's what I'm talkin bout, Devon," applauded Chippy. "Now get over here and give me some," he said as he reached out to give Devon a high five.

At first Devon was shocked at his father's reaction. He thought that he was going to get into trouble for cussing until he remembered that Chippy said that it was okay to cuss around him. One has to question how a parent could allow their child to be on the same level as them by engaging in adult language. The bible says to "honor thy father and thy mother" therefore respect should be given and not only to ones parents but it should also be given to elders in general. Devon only did what he was taught and after receiving praise for his outburst he felt pretty good inside. Internally the beast was feasting on Devon's rage, and yet again Ignorance seemed to be the most satisfying "nutrient" for the beast within.

"Dad I gotta get back home before my Mom gets worried."

"You're right let's get out of here Slick, I'll take you home."

"Man, I love this car Dad! Can I have it when grow up?"

"So you like this classic, huh?"

"Hell yeah, what the fuck kind is it?"

"Look Devon, If you're gonna cuss then at least do it right? There was no reason to say 'what the fuck kind is it' that shit didn't even sound cool," Chippy said as he and Devon closed the car doors simultaneously.

"You gotta know when to cuss Devon. I only say that you can do it around me because I don't see a difference between saying shit and shoot! You have to be like a switch Slick. There is a time to speak proper and a time to speak slang. When you're handling your business than you speak professional, and when you're hanging with your friends then you can speak your slang. You got that?"

"Yes, sir I got it."

"Don't address me as sir either."

"Why? My mom says that I should respect my elders and say sir."

"She's right but I'm your father and to me sir reminds me of slavery too much, so I don't wanna be called sir. After saying sir if an adult tells you not to call them sir then respect that."

"I got you Dad, I get it. Well thanks for the ride home. When will I see you again?"

"You know where I'm at; I'll be living with Paula and your new brother. Don't forget to give your mom that money; do you still have it in your pocket?"

"Yeah I got it, thanks, later Dad!"

Even though Devon hadn't seen his father on an everyday basis, Chippy seemed as if he wanted to step up as the father that Devon always wanted and needed. Whenever Devon would see him in the neighborhood, Chippy would go out of his way to see that his son had money in his pocket. Marsha never asked Chippy for anything, and she never took him to court for child support, and the reason why she didn't was baffling to her girlfriends. As Devon approached the front door of his house, Marsha was in the living room sitting on a brown leather love seat talking on the telephone to Valerie. She heard Chippy's car engine rev as he screeched his tires while he sped down the street.

"Hold on Valerie, I know this ain't Devon being dropped off by Chippy!"

"Mom, guess what," yelled Devon as he stormed through the front door.

"Boy, where were you at? I was getting ready to yell for you! I know that wasn't your Dad was it?"

"Yeah, he picked me up from the store and he gave me money for baseball!"

"Valerie let me call you back. This fool done gave Devon a hundred dollar bill!"

"A hundred dollars," asked Valerie in shock.

"Yes girl, a hundred dollar bill! Who would give an eight year old child a hundred dollar bill? He's so stupid!"

"Girl, you to need to get domestics on him, especially if he has money like that!"

"Valerie what did I tell you? I can take care of Devon by myself. I don't need him."

"Ain't nobody said you couldn't, but think of all of the shoes you can buy! Girl, we could go shopping every week!"

"I don't want his money! I don't want anything to do with him! And what do you mean, we?"

"Girl like I said, get the money," Valerie reiterated.

"Bye Valerie, I'll talk to you later."

"Devon," yelled Marsh as she hung up the phone.

"Yes?"

"Get down here!"

"Yes, Mom what's up?"

"What's up is your behind if you pull that crap again!"

"What, I told my Dad that I had to go home, and he said that it would be ok!"

"What did I tell you?"

"You said to come straight home from the store."

"Exactly, now get your butt back upstairs and take your pants off! You gonna listen to me! Where's my belt?"

"Mom, No," Devon yelled as he ran upstairs to his room.

Marsha followed Devon upstairs, and as he pulled his pants down tears began to flow down his face. He stared directly into his mother's eyes with the look of despair. Confusion was the main course in the smorgasbord of the Ignorance Buffet. Devon wanted so bad to ask his mother why she was about to whip him, but he knew that if he was to murmur one inquiry then she would erupt with anger. Marsha took her thirty two inch leather belt that Chippy once wore and struck Devon ten times across his buttocks and hamstrings. As Devon lied across the bed, one tear dropped from his right which was the same eye that he had stitched from his prior traumatizing experience in Hope Alley. As he wiped the tear from his face he rubbed his right index finger over his scar. While Marsha struck him with the belt her rhythmic scolds went unheard, because the beast within had taken over Devon's mind.

Although the belt left welts on Devon's legs, he lied on the bed as if no one was even touching him. He took his whipping like a warrior. Inside the beast within questioned him,

"What did you do to deserve this? If you didn't go with your father than he would have been mad. It's already bad enough that he doesn't come to your games. You don't need any of them. I am here for you. You can't even feel this belt, because I am protecting you. You just do as I say and everything will be fine. Look how tough you are, she's done, she's breathing hard, and you're not even crying! Just do it my way Devon, I'll take care of you!"

The Beast's Plea

Day and night you confuse yourself, and often you tend to question why.
I have all of the answers for you, so I'm telling you to give me a try.
These people don't understand you,
and they wouldn't last one of the easiest days in your shoes.
The pressure would make them fold like a blanket,
and repetitively they'd sing the blues.
This is the beginning of your conclusion, in other words the start of your end.
I have erased all of your doubts. Our new journey is here; I am the Beast Within!

David V.M. Kennedy

Even though Chippy and Devon spent more time with each other, Devon's father and son excursions would soon come to an abrupt end. Chippy and Paula gave birth to a son, and a year later they had a daughter. It had been over a year since the last time that Devon saw his father, and on Devon's tenth birthday Chippy saw him playing on the playground at a school on the other side of the projects called Jefferson. Chippy was now driving a new white Dodge Duster and the engine had the sound of a race car! Devon was in awe of the car, and once he discovered that his father was driving, he did a back flip off of the monkey bars as he landed in a pile of wood and hay mixed.

"Dad," yelled Devon with excitement.

"Hey Slick, happy birthday, let me see them hands!"

"You don't want any of this Dad!"

"Boy, you're getting big!"

"Yeah, and I play football too! I'm the quarterback!"

"Ok, Slick, I see you! How did that baseball ever go?"

"Oh, it didn't. My mom didn't sign me up. She said that she didn't have time."

"What the fuck? What you mean she doesn't have time? You know what, fuck that, it's your birthday so let's go have some fun! You wanna go bowling and shoot some pool?"

"Heck yeah, I just went bowling with M… uh my mom!"

"What da hell you stuttering for, those are some big ass teeth in the way?"

"Ha, Ha that's funny dad, uh how's my little brother?"

As Chippy was about to explain, Devon took a sigh of relief, because he almost told his father about Marsha's new boyfriend Marcus Bond. Marcus was a former Marine vet who served in Vietnam and he was ten years older than Marsha. He had a short afro styled hairdo, and he had dark brown skin with dimples in his cheeks when he smiled. He stood about the same height as Chippy and he had green tattoos of three different women's names on his forearms and chest.

"Your brother is getting big," said Chippy.

"He's actually walking already. You also have a little sister now!"

"Sweet, now I have more brothers and sisters than my boy K Ritt!"

"Oh yeah, so K Ritt only has one? I thought he had a little sister too."

"He does and now I have three! Oops."

"What you mean oops? What da hell you mean three? What's going on Devon?"

"My mom showed me a picture of my new sister. She said it was an underground or something, I don't know."

"You mean an ultrasound, that bitch is pregnant," yelled Chippy.

"What the fuck, to who?"

"Some guy named Marcus," said Devon.

Although Chippy saw Devon here and there, he rarely saw Marsha and he didn't realize that she was pregnant. Matter of fact Marsha was pregnant a year ago but she lost the baby due to a miscarriage while frolicking with her niece one winter eve. Marsha slipped on a patch of ice, and the doctor's told her that she may never be able to have children again and this was mainly due to the internal injuries she suffered by the hands of Chippy.

"How many months is she?" inquired Chippy.

"I think eight," said Devon.

"Ain't that a bitch," exclaimed Chippy.

"So what's this guy like?"

"He's cool I guess, he comes to all of my football games! He took me to the Baltimore inner harbor last week, and we got to go to the aquarium too!"

"Hmm, Oh really, so I take it that he lives with you?"

"Yeah, Dad my mom got married. I thought you knew. I was the ring bearer. They went to the Poconos for the honeymoon."

"Honeymoon huh," asked Chippy with a concerned and determined look on his face.

"Dad, you ok?"

Devon was somewhat confused at his father's response, because Marsha had been married for some time now. After their afternoon of bowling and shooting pool, Chippy and Devon finished their food and Chippy took Devon home. He dropped him off in front of his house and as usual he would leave the scene before Devon could even walk through the door. He told Devon to come see him this weekend so that they could watch a fight together on T.V. As Chippy pulled off he noticed a green station wagon and a brand new Trans-Am parked in front of Devon's house. He thought to himself,

"I bet that's that broke ass nigga's beat up station wagon! He better hope that I don't see his ass. I'm the motherfucking Dad not him. If this mother fucker thinks he's gonna replace me then we got problems. If he wants beef, then I'll give him beef.

Contrary to Chippy believing Marcus drove a raggedy green station wagon, the car actually belonged to D.F.'s mom Jacqueline Fable. Jacqueline and Marsha took each other up on a play date that they previously planned for Daniel Fable and Devon. It was a winter evening when Chippy dropped Devon off and as he walked through the door he noticed his mom talking to the Nurse from the hospital that she was in after her and Chippy's altercation, and he saw D.F. sitting on the floor playing with his electric football game.

"Hey, Devon I have someone for you to meet," said Marsha.

"Aren't you the Nurse from the hospital, what's wrong with my mom? And why is my game out on the floor?"

"Devon," yelled Marsha.

"Don't be rude boy! This is Daniel."

"Hi, Devon, you can call me D.F." he said as he reached out his right hand.

"I'm Devon," he said reluctant to shake D.F.'s hand.

"So I hear that you're good in baseball, do you play basketball?"

"I'm ok, but I love football more."

"Cool, I play basketball, but I love football too! What position do you play? I play tackle!"

"I used to play tackle too, but I just finished my first season at quarterback. I like that way better."

"I have a football in the car Devon, do you wanna play catch?"

"I have a better idea D.F. I saw some friends outside! We can play pitch up!"

"Is that like smear da queer?"

"Smear da what?"

"Never mind, I think I know how to play, let's go!"

Devon was outside playing with D.F. and Jacqueline was finished conversing with Marsha and she was ready to leave.

"D.F. it's time to go," said Marsha.

"No, I'm not ready to leave!"

"Sweetie I have to run some errands, so can we please go?"

"Damn it mom, No!"

Devon's eyes grew big with amazement, because he never heard a kid that was only 10yrs old talk to their mother like that!

"Did you just cuss at your mom D.F.?"

"She gets on my damn nerves sometimes!"

"Where do you live? I can ask my mom to take you home."

"I live just up the street about ten minutes away. Mom Devon said that I can stay! Go home I'll be there in a little bit!"

"Let me check with Marsha."

"I heard him," said Marsha as she walked out of the front door.

"Now D.F. you need to apologize to your mother. Ain't no cussing in my house and that is very disrespectful to speak to your mother that way!"

"I keep telling him Marsha, but he won't listen to me! It's like the older he gets the worst his mouth becomes."

"D.F. tell you mom that you're sorry!"

"I'm sorry mom; I'm sorry Ms. Marsha can I please stay with Devon?"

"Please mom he only lives up the street; I can walk him half way!"

"If Jacqueline doesn't mind then yes, but it's getting cold out here there's supposed to be a blizzard tomorrow!"

Devon and D.F. convinced their mother's to let them hang out with each other and after playing for a while the two of them noticed that it was about to get dark. As the boys headed back inside Devon's home snow flurries began to fall.

"Mom, I'm gonna walk D.F. halfway home!"

"Ok, Devon you bring your behind right back, because it's getting dark soon and it looks like it's going to snow!"

"Ok, I'll run! Come on D.F. let's bounce!"

"Your mom is pretty tough, huh Devon?"

"Yeah, she thinks she is," laughed Devon.

"I saw a man go upstairs, was that your Dad?"

"No, that's my Stepdad Marcus. He's cool. Who's your dad?"

"I don't know."

"Oh, I'm sorry; you don't know him at all?"

"Nah, I mean I know of him. I just know that he used to beat the shit out of my mom!"

"Wow, I understand that one. My Dad beat my mom too!"

"You gotta know how to treat these women Devon! You gotta put them in check! My mom knows not to piss me off!"

As Devon and D.F. came to their halfway point they gave each other a high five and D.F. started to run towards his house and Devon began walking back towards his home. While Devon was walking home he remembered that he left his Walkman at Chippy's house and he wanted to run down the street to pick it up. Although his mother told him to come right back he thought to himself, "Sometimes you gotta let these women know!" At that moment Devon decided to go to his dad's house.

In spite of Marsha's warning Devon walked right past 192 Parkway Blvd. and headed down past Front St. Each step that he took seemed to make the snow fall harder and harder. What Devon didn't realize was that the blizzard that was predicted to come the next day was beginning to fall at that precise moment. The local news had issued a winter storm advisory, and Devon was clueless to the fact that the meteorologist called for over 3ft of snow that night. As Devon reached his father's house the winds became blistering and the snow pounded the ground as if God poured a gigantic bag of flour over the city of York. Devon knocked on his father's door as the snow covered his black and yellow winter hat.

"Hey Slick, what are you doing back here in this mess?"

"I was walking my friend home, and I remembered that I left my Walkman on the table. I've only been walking for 15 minutes and the snow just poured down out of nowhere! Can you take me home?"

"Paula has my car at her friend's house so when she gets back I'll take you home. Take those wet pants off and throw them on the radiator. I have some shorts that you can put on. Tell Shayla to make you some hot cocoa?"

"Ok, I need to call my mom can I use the phone."

"Paula's son is on the phone with his girlfriend, don't worry about it Slick you're with your pops!"

"Yeah, you're right I have no worries, huh?"

"What did I say? Your mom ain't too worried because if she was then her ass would have driven you to your friend's house! She's probably up under that punk ass dude of hers!"

It began to snow harder and the down pour lasted for hours. In spite of being safe at Chippy's house, Devon never told his mom that he was going to his father's place, and as time passed Devon and Shayla ended up playing outside in the backyard in the snow. As the two of them played, Paula's son joined in the fun and suggested that they build and igloo. Devon was having a blast playing in the snow until he realized that it was getting late.

"Dad I need to get home now, it's getting late," said Devon.

"Boy, its 3ft of snow outside, your with your dad you just stay right here," demanded Chippy.

Not thinking anything of it, Devon figured that he'd listen to his father and he continued to play. Even though Devon was safe, Marsha was at home eight months pregnant and she was worried sick that something had happened to her son. In spite of the snow being up to here waist, she decided to go out and look for Devon. Due to their constant arguing and bickering, Marsha never new exactly where Chippy stayed, therefore she had no clue if Devon was with him or not. After the storm had passed and the snow stopped falling, Chippy decided to have Paula's oldest son walk Devon home because Paula was stuck with the car buried underneath the snow at her friend's house. As the two arrived at Devon's home he knocked on the front door to be let in, and Marsha was furious when she opened the door.

"Boy where the Hell was you at," screamed Marsha.

"I was at my Dad's house," Devon said hesitantly.

Devon knew that his mother was not one to curse, but she was very irate and the sounds of her words were so piercing that it felt like a long hypodermic needle was jabbing at his eardrum. Marsha continued,

"You get your behind up in your room, and you stay there until I say that you can come out!"

"But Mom I…"

"Get your ass upstairs!"

Devon went to his room in tears confused more than ever because he truly didn't understand why he was being punished. He thought that if he didn't listen to his father than he would get into trouble. He knew that he shouldn't have gone to his father's house, but if his Walkman had gotten lost or broken then he'd be in trouble with his mother. The damage had already been done. Devon kept blaming "old man winter" for dumping the snow, because he would have made it home before dark if the storm didn't hit so hard. After this incident Marsha forbid Devon to see his father, and she made him stay in the house on punishment for one month straight! Devon cried as he lied in his bed until his head began to hurt. He bowed down on his knees as his white pajama pants with hot rod cars on them slid slightly down his waist. He folded his hands in front of his face as his thumbs touched the tip of his nose. Devon recited the Lord's Prayer, and he asked God to help him understand what was truly going on.

"Our Father, who art in Heaven, hallowed be thy name. Thy kingdom come, thy will be done, on earth as it is in heaven. Give us this day, our daily bread, and forgive us our trespasses as we forgive those who trespass against us. Lead us not into temptation, but deliver us from evil. For thine has the kingdom, the power and the glory, forever and ever. Amen. Why me Lord, what did I do to deserve this? Please help me!"

Even though Devon had a lot of time to think while he was on punishment, he still couldn't fathom why his sentence was so severe. Marsha later sat Devon down and said,

"Listen Devon, your dad doesn't care about you, he only cares about himself. He just wants to be in a relationship with me, and the reason he made you stay at his house was him trying to get back at me out of spite! When you get older you'll understand."

"So, my Dad doesn't love me?"

"No sweetie, don't think like that! He loves you but…"

"But what, there is no but! You just said that he doesn't care about me! You said that he only cares about himself and that he only cares about you! That's why he doesn't come to any of my games! He hates me! I hate him!!!"

"Devon," pleaded Marsha as he ran to his room slamming the door behind him.

Devon didn't need to be older to understand. He understood all too well that his whole existence has been a problem for his parents. It seemed that every argument that they had was geared towards being his fault. Devon's ego had been crushed as if a boulder dropped from the heavens and landed on his head. At a pre-adolescent age Devon began feeling miserable about life. The beast within began to mature as Devon became more and more depressed. After this brief state of depression, Devon's spirit would soon be uplifted. Marsha gave birth to a baby girl and she and her husband Marcus gave Devon the honor of naming his newborn sister. After the baby was delivered at the York Hospital Devon sat waiting patiently in his mother's hospital room. He reclined back in a brown recliner which had a slight tear in the leather underneath his left leg. As Devon fiddled with the tear, Nurse Jacqueline Fable came through the door with a small clear cart with Devon's sister in it.

"Hey, hey, hey, look who I brought to see you! Hi Devon, how are you doing?"

"Hi Nurse Fable, I'm doing fine! Is that my sister?"

"Yes it is would you like to hold her?"

"Of course you can," said Marcus as he patted Devon on the head.

"Wow, Marcus, she looks just like you."

"Devon, I want you to stop calling Marcus by his first name," demanded Marsha.

"What am I supposed to call him? He said don't call him Mr. Bond."

"I want you to call him Pop!"

"Pop," asked Devon.

"Look, Marsha he doesn't have to call me that. I'm okay with him calling me Marcus."

"No, it's disrespectful, and besides we are a family and I don't want people hearing him calling you by your first name. Do you hear what I'm saying to you Devon?"

"Yes Ma'am, She looks just like you Pop," Devon said with pride.

"Yeah, I guess you're right Devon, and look! She's opening her eyes!"

As Devon sat on the edge of the recliner with the back still reclined he carefully held his newborn sister while he looked into his sister's eyes and noticed that she had a distinct color about them. Her eyes looked as if they were as pure as platinum and Devon turned to his mother and said,

"She looks as if she has a Destiny mom. I want to name her Destiny."

Marcus and Marsha Bond looked at each other and smiled with amazement as they both said at the same time,

"Destiny, it is!"

Stability

Everyone has a story to tell, but my life is a mysterious fable.
Lord you have blessed me with so many gifts,
so explain to me why my existence is so unstable?
I'm like a motherless child who can't seem to love,
and although my heart is pure it seems to never be felt.
Lord, come into my heart and stabilize my mind, because only you can re-shuffle the cards that I've been dealt.
You've blessed me, and the world is like the weight of a trolley car, but I am strong and my existence is that stern cable.
With you as my conductor my life is no longer a mystery, and as my story unfolds, it simply tells that I am stable.

David V.M. Kennedy

Even though Devon had no objection to calling Marcus "Pop," at times it did make him feel uncomfortable. Every time he would say it the thought of his father hearing him call another man "Pop" would send chills down his spine. One day Chippy was on the south side of town in a barbershop that sat across the street from the city school William Penn Senior High School. As Chippy was in the chair getting his corn rolls undone, one of his neighbors from Hope Alley named "Green Eye" walked through the door. He stood the same height as Chippy but he was freakishly obese. He had a mouth full of rotted teeth, and he wore a long scruffy beard.

"Hey Chippy, what's up man?"

"What's up, Green Eye. How you doin' man?"

"Shit, I can't call it, you know me same shit different toilet!"

"I see you haven't changed much," laughed Chippy.

"Nope, only change I have is for this candy up in this machine right here!"

"Green Eye you need to leave that candy alone with your raggedy ass mouth, it looks like you ate a battery sandwich for lunch," Chippy's barber exclaimed.

"Fuck all ya'll, Yo' Mama ain't had no problems kissing this mouth. Oh, Chippy, guess what I heard?"

"What's that Green Eye?"

"I heard Marsha ain't letting you see your boy anymore, because her new husband is going to adopt Devon. What's up with that homeboy? Ain't no way I'm letting some cat adopt my son!"

"Yo, what the fuck are you talking about Green Eye? Who'd you here that bullshit from?"

"Uh, Um, I forgot who told me that. I heard it through the grapevine. Everyone is talking about it!"

"Sure they are Green Eye, just like everyone is talking about that fat ass stomach of yours," laughed Chippy.

"Fuck you Chippy!"

"Fuck me? You said that like you gotta problem. You got something you wanna get off of your chest?"

"Ya'll ain't gonna be fightin' in my mother fuckin' barbershop," exclaimed Chippy's raised his hands holding a set of clippers in his right one.

"It wouldn't be no mother fuckin fight anyway," said Green Eye.

"Yo, hurry up and finish my hair, keep talkin' shit Green Eye, I never liked your punk ass anyway!"

"I never liked yo' Puerto Rican lookin ass neither, fuck you and that bitch that won't let you see your kid!"

At that moment Chippy leaped out of the barber chair with a black cape and white strip tied around his neck. As he lunged out of the chair he used the foot rest to jump into the air as he gave a thunderous right hook to Green Eye's jaw.

"Who's a mother fuckin' bitch now you fat fuck? Get your fat rotten mouth ass outta this fuckin barbershop! I better not see you back here again!"

As Green Eye picked himself off of the ground, not once did he think about retaliating. He slowly walked out of the door with right hand under his mouth holding his jaw. As Green Eye walked up a flight of stairs, Chippy's barber said,

"Come on Chippy, you can't be doin' that to my customers man,"

"Shut the fuck up and cut my hair," snapped Chippy.

"Ok, we cool, we cool, I'm just saying. I'm trying to run a respectful business that's all."

"You're right man, my bad, I lost my cool, but that mother fucker had it coming!"

"Well I don't think his fat ass will be talking shit anytime soon, I think you broke his jaw!"

As Chippy's barber laughed and finished cutting his hair, Chippy stared into space with a look of dismay on his face. He knew that he wasn't really being the father that he could be for Devon, but yet his main focus was on the fact that another man was living with Marsha and taking over his fatherly responsibilities. Chippy began to plot on ways to make Marsha's life miserable, because he didn't want his son being raised by another man.

One spring evening Devon was in is room reading his favorite superhero comic book when he heard a loud sound of glass being shattered outside the front of his home.

"Chippy, stop it!" screamed Marsha.

"Where's that punk? Ain't nobody raising my son!" yelled Chippy.

Devon dashed to look out of his mother's bedroom window where he noticed Chippy standing with a baseball bat in front of his mother's car. He had smashed the mirror of her Mazda Turismo on the driver's side, and glass was scattered everywhere. All of the commotion drew the crowd of the neighbors out of their home as if Chippy was Paul Revere warning the town that the British were coming! The police were called and Chippy sped away in his white Dodge Duster leaving long black tread marks in perfect formation as he screeched down the road. Devon sat at the window stunned as if he was watching an action packed scary movie being produced right in front of his innocent little eyes. Devon's tears flowed at a snail's pace down his tiny cheeks as he attempted to scream, but became choked by his sadness as he could only whisper the word Daddy as Chippy zoomed down the street.

Shortly thereafter, Marcus came home from work to find his wife distraught from the event that occurred.

"Marsha! Honey what happened to your car? Marsha?"

"I'm up here," cried Marsha.

"Hey, baby, are you okay? What happened?"

"Chippy, came here, and he hit my car with a bat! He said that he heard that you were going to adopt Devon."

"Adopt Devon, where did he get that from?"

"I have no idea. He's just a fool!"

"Well he's not getting away with this Marsha, I know where he lives!"

"Marcus, no just leave it alone. He'll get his."

"No Marsha, I'm not leaving this alone! If I do then he'll think that he can just come here and do what he wants! That's gonna cost us a lot of money to get that car fixed! He hit the door too!"

"Marcus, please just let it go!"

"No, fuck that shit! He's gonna pay one way or the other!"

While Marcus and Marsha discussed what happened, Devon sat at the top step outside of his room hidden from his mother's room but close enough to hear the conversation. He now felt that he was in somewhat of a pickle, because he and Marcus began to bond. Devon really didn't know how to react to the fact that Marcus now wanted to harm his father. The next day unaware to Marsha Devon visited Chippy after school. He felt like he had an obligation to speak to his father, before Marcus went after him.

"Hey, Slick, what are you doing here? I thought your mom said that you couldn't come down here anymore!"

"She doesn't know that I'm here. I have to tell you something, but I don't know if I should."

"What is it son? You can tell me tell anything, you know that."

"Well, it's Marcus, Dad."

"What, don't tell me that mother fucker did something to you did he?!"

As Devon was about to explain to his father what was going on, Paula and Leann walked through the door with groceries. Paula was wearing a long wool looking overcoat with a red bandana tied around her head. She placed two brown paper bags on the kitchen table as Leann placed two plastic bags on the kitchen counter top by the sink.

"What's up Bucky beaver," said Leann.

"Shut up, Leann you ugly bitch!"

"Chippy, you better get your son," yelled Paula.

"Hey, hey, all of you just chill. Devon, keep the peace. Tell Leann that you're sorry."

"Sorry? She started it! I'm not telling her that I'm sorry!"

"Chippy are you gonna let him talk to my daughter like that," asked Paula.

"Forget this Dad, I'm outta here!"

"Devon, wait what did you have to tell me? Devon!"

Devon ran out of the front door and sprinted towards Parkway Blvd. He ran west back towards his home as fast as he could. Even though his father only lived a few hundred yards away, Devon felt like it was taking him forever to get home. He was hoping that no one saw him coming from his Dad's house so that they wouldn't tell his Mother where he had been. After feeling like he was in the clear, Devon slowed down and caught his breath before he got to his door. The beast within was so anxious to come out, and when Devon got inside he noticed that his Mom was in the kitchen cooking a big meal. This was peculiar to him, because Marsha rarely cooked big meals.

"What's going on Mom?"

"Hey baby, how you doin? I'm making your favorite; fried chicken, bake macaroni, and cabbage. I also made some rice and corn! Why don't you go upstairs; there is someone waiting to meet you!"

"And who is that Mom?"

"His name is Jeremy, he's Marcus's son. He's only three years older than you, and I know you've always wanted a big brother so now you have one!"

Jeremy Strong was an 8th grader at Edgar Fahs Smith Middle School. Even though Marcus claimed him as his son, he wasn't Marcus's biological child. Marcus was previously married to Jeremy's mother, and the parenting that he gave to Devon was the same way that he treated Jeremy. Marcus was a great man. He was a protector. He took care of his responsibilities, and he firmly believed that young men needed their fathers in their life. He also believed that in order for a young man to survive in society they needed the necessary tools to become a strong spiritual and responsible individual; therefore he had no qualms about treating Jeremy and Devon as if they were his own children.

Contrary to Marcus being a great father, he and Jeremy's mother did not see eye to eye, but she still allowed Jeremy to see him regularly because of the bond that they shared. Jeremy was the essence of happiness. Even at such a young age he exemplified what it truly meant to live life to the fullest. Jeremy had a medium brown skin tone with a proportionate but fairly large nose. He had a big chin that really became noticeable when he displayed his smile that would light up the darkest of rooms. Jeremy's greatest attribute was how respectful and well-mannered he was to his elders. In their eyes he could do no wrong. Marsha loved Jeremy and treated him with unconditional love and respect.

Although Devon received a lot of attention from his mother as a single child, he always wished that he had a big brother. Devon hated getting picked on by the neighborhood kids, and he always wished that he had someone to not only protect him but to talk to. In spite of Devon wanting a big brother, Jeremy's timing to meet him was impeccably off. Marsha grabbed two oven mitts out her kitchen drawer, and as she lowered the oven door to grab her glass dish of baked macaroni she said,

"Devon, run upstairs and go meet Jeremy. Tell him to wash his hands and get ready for supper."

"Aw man, do I have to? Can't you introduce him to me?"

"No, learn how to be a man and go introduce yourself, and what did I tell you about that "aw man"? I'm gonna knock you upside your head with this wooden spoon! Get up there and do what I told you to do!"

"Stupid, stinking, Mom," mumbled Devon as he walked upstairs.

"What did you say," yelled Marsha.

"Nothing!"

"Yeah, that's what I thought you said!"

As Devon got to the top of the stairs one of his toy cars that was about three inches in length slammed into his foot. Devon was very particular about his collection of toy cars, and kept them stored away in plastic container that was round and it had a picture of a big car tire. Devon walked into his room and saw Jeremy on the floor playing with his car collection and his wheel shaped storage bin was propped open with his cars scattered all over the room. Devon clinched his fist and said,

"What in the heck are you doing? Those are my cars!"

"Oh, hi I'm Jeremy, you must be Devon," said Jeremy as he extended his hand.

"Man, are you crazy," asked Devon.

"Why do you say that?"

"Those are my freakin' cars and you have them all over the place! No one touches my cars! Get out of my room!"

"Your mom said that I could play with them until you came back. I'm sorry, lil' bro!"

"Bro," asked Devon with a puzzled look on his face.

"Yeah, bro, we're brothers now! Here, take this car, it's yours! I used to collect cars, but I lost my collection in a fire and this one was the only one that didn't melt! Take it, it's yours!"

Devon stood in front Jeremy while staring at his hand. He couldn't believe what Jeremy was holding and about to give him. It was the mini die cast car of his favorite cartoon Stud Racer! It was the Mysterious 5! Kids loved Stud Racer but no kid could seem to get their hands on the Mysterious 5 car! Having this car would make Devon the talk of Devers Elementary school!

"Are you sure Jeremy? That's a rare car!"

"Here man, I'm getting too big for these anyway!"

"Thanks man and I'm sorry for yelling at you."

"No sweat, man call me big bro; I always wanted a little brother!"

It was at that precise moment that a simple gesture from Jeremy cleared Devon's mind from all of the conflict that he had going through his head. All of Devon's worries seemed to magically disappear as he slowly grabbed the white car from Jeremy's hand. All of the memories of the constant bickering and yelling from his parents left out his mind. All of the "put downs" and name calling from his peers were the furthest thoughts from his head. Instantaneously, Devon was at peace. For the first time in a long time Devon felt loved while the beast within grumbled with agony! Devon now had a stepfather who gave him his undivided attention, and he also had the big brother that he always dreamed of having. One key component to neutralizing the beast within is stability within the home. It is human nature for one to want to be loved. Everyone wants and needs to be a part of something that gives them the sense of family.

Although people need a sense of family to function normally in a society, in order for a person to be holistically healthy they must have five key elements in their everyday lifestyle. In order to have a strong sense of stability a person must be: Spiritually, Mentally, Physically, Socially, and financially healthy. One could argue that Devon already has all five components of holistic health, but to what magnitude is the question that remains. Devon has only been alive for ten years, and out of those ten years he is only cognizant of seven. 30% of Devon's young life was contributed to learning and the development of his personality. 70% of his pre-adolescent years were exposed to a barrage of conflict and turmoil. In order for the beast within to survive, it must nurture off of negativity! Jeremy Strong helped Devon neutralize the beast within with a simple gesture.

Imagine how life would be if everyone on earth were related to Jeremy Strong. The entire human race would prosper because of the simple fact that like Jeremy, they would be willing to give. Not only would they have the will to give, but like Devon they would recognize even the simplest act of kindness and appreciate what was done for them no matter how minuscule. Everyday people should go out of their way to do something as simple as Jeremy Strong. Envision being related to Jeremy Strong! How proud would it be to say that one is now the member of the Strong Family?

Ignorant Sleeve

In this fabric called life you're like an inexperienced tailor; therefore it's my garment that I'd like to retrieve.
I'd rather have my Righteous arms bare then to have them covered up with your tailor made Ignorant sleeve.
As my opinionated blood flows freely, Courage pulsates through my veins.
Therefore, I'll release the tightness of your Ignorant band around my neck, because it's like a collar of barbed wired chains.
As I undo my top button, I release your strangle hold and my vocal chords no longer hurt.
I'd rather dress myself with Knowledge so take your nasty cloth back, and I'll sport this Intellectual shirt.
As you laugh at my wardrobe, I realize some say it's out of style and visibly it seems so plain.
While you jest I'll cut up these sleeves of Ignorance, because God has hemmed my soul. Now I am empowered and I have so much more to gain.

David V. M. Kennedy

"Devon," yelled Marsha from the bottom of the step.

"Yes Mom," Devon replied

"You and Jeremy wash your hands and come eat!"

"Ok, we're coming!"

As Marsha headed back into the kitchen Marcus walked through the back door.

"He babe, how's it going?"

"Hey, what's up Marsha?"

"Are you ok Marcus?"

"Why do you ask that?"

"Well, you never say hey what's up Marsha. So what's wrong?"

"Look, you know what's wrong! I can't let this shit go!"

"Marcus, that happened yesterday, it's over with so don't sweat it. You're more of a man then Chippy will ever be!"

"Fuck that! He's gonna pay," yelled Marcus as he slammed his fist on the kitchen counter.

"What's all the hub bub, bub," asked Devon sarcastically as he and Jeremy came downstairs.

"Marsha I'm outta here. See that Jeremy gets home for me please!"

As Marcus walked out of the kitchen through the living room towards the front door, he looked Devon directly into his eyes with a look of disgust on his face. Even though he had no ill feelings towards Devon, the site of Devon's face reminded him of Chippy due to the fact that Devon resembled his father so much. Not once did Marcus stop to think how Devon would feel if something bad were to happen to his father. The only thing that was on Marcus's mind was revenge. As Devon and Marcus engaged in a brief stare down, Devon curled his lip and thought to himself,

"You better not do shit to my father!"

"Marcus, wait," pleaded Marsha as she chased him out the front door.

"What's going on lil bro," asked Jeremy.

"I don't know man; I think your Dad wants to fight my Dad."

"That's crazy! Do you know why?"

"Who knows, some stupid grown up stuff I guess. I do know that my Dad did something to my Mom's car but I don't really know why. Really I could care less. They've been fighting since I can remember. Did you like your food? This shit is good!"

"Yo, you better be careful! Your Mom is right outside, and she'll hear you cussing!"

"Bro, right now I don't give a damn. Besides my Dad lets me cuss. If she has something to say then I'll just go tell him. I don't even give a shit anymore! Let's get outta here anyway. Do you wanna go "nigga knockin"?

"Do you mean doorbell ditchin," asked Jeremy excitingly.

"Nigga knockin, doorbell ditchin, yeah it's all the same! Do you wanna do it?"

"Yeah, but man, we could get into some serious trouble if we get caught Devon!"

"Bro, we won't get caught! I'm fast and you're even faster than me so let's go!"

While Devon and Jeremy decided to go outside, Marcus emerged from his brother's house with his brother following behind wearing a dark sweatshirt with a black winter hat on his head. He strongly favored Marcus with the exception of being a shade lighter. The two men jumped into Marcus's silver Trans Am that had a big Firebird on the hood of the car. The two of them went on a search for Chippy like two Basset Hounds would do as if they were on a hunt for a rare silver fox. Marcus peeled his tires as he drove down Parkway Blvd. towards Atlantic ave. where D.F. lived. As D.F. sat in his room drawing pictures, he heard the rumble of Marcus's car engine as he passed by the Fable's home. D.F. ran to the window to watch the car zoom down the road and he thought to himself

"One day I'm going to have a car like that!"

"Turn off those lights D.F. we have to get up early so that I can take you to Steven's house," Jacqueline called from down the hall.

"Ok Mom, I just need to finish this picture!"

"D.F. get the door, I hear the doorbell ringing!"

"Alright, can I have some cookies?"

"Yeah, go ahead but see who that is first."

As D.F. walked down a narrow hallway from his room that led straight into a small kitchen, he stopped and turned around to face the doorway to his room as he heard tires screeching outside of his home. While thinking about the cookies that his mother had made, he decided to go answer the doorbell rather than go back and look outside of his bedroom window to see what the commotion was.

"D.F. what's up man, help us out," said Devon as he and Jeremy stood on a blue painted wooden front patio breathing heavily.

"Hey, Devon what's up? Who's your friend? What's going on?"

"D.F. this is Jeremy, Jeremy this is D.F. Jeremy is my Stepbrother."

"What's up D.F," said Jeremy with his right hand extended.

"What's up Jeremy, come on in? Did you guys hear those cars screeching their tires?"

"Yeah, we heard them, but I couldn't tell where they were coming from," said Devon.

"So why are you and Jeremy breathing so hard? Are you in trouble?"

"We just went Nigga Knockin' and some dude let his dog loose on us!"

"No offense D.F, but Devon don't say the N word in front of him," yelled Jeremy.

"What? D.F. is probably blacker than you Jeremy! Besides I'm saying Nigga, not Nigger. There's a difference."

"The N word is the N word Devon, there's no difference!"

"Whatever big bro, D.F. what do you think?"

"Well, I hear what you're saying Devon, but I'm not gonna say it!"

"Anyway, if it makes you feel better Jeremy we went doorbell ditching; there are you satisfied?"

As the trio started to head up the stairs that led into D.F.'s apartment they were startled by a loud crash, Boom!

"What da heck was that," asked Devon shockingly.

"Oh, shoot it looks like an accident up on the corner," yelled D.F.

"Let's go check it out," said Jeremy.

While the three adolescents sprinted about 50yds down Atlantic Ave towards Parkway Blvd, Devon led the way for the first 30yds until he witnessed what was going on before his eyes. His all-out sprint swiftly turned into a light jog until he suddenly came to a stop. Jeremy and D.F. who were not far behind caught up to Devon, and to their dismay they could not believe what was going on. As Devon stood in disbelief, he saw the car of his dreams smashed into a bent over street sign while Marcus and his brother held Chippy pinned against the Chippy's car.

"Take this you piece of shit," yelled Marcus as he punched Chippy in the left jaw with a thunderous right cross hook.

"Yeah you half breed mutt, you gonna learn not to fuck with my brother!"

"Fuck both of ya'll! You little bitches can't fight me one on one," said Chippy as he swung unsuccessfully at Marcus's face.

As the two brothers grabbed Chippy away from his car door, together they lifted him up over their shoulders and viciously slammed him to the ground head first! Chippy landed on his left shoulder but he was able to cling on the brothers enough to lessen the impact of the fall. His face still caught a small pothole in the street and his mouth bled profusely. As he tried to gather himself and rise to his feet, Marcus and his brother simultaneously kicked him in the rib section. Chippy let out a painful yelp as he heard a piercing scream,

"Dad, no stop it!"

"Huh, Devon, what is he doing here," thought Chippy.

"Devon, Take your ass home," yelled Marcus.

At that precise moment, Chippy caught an adrenaline rush from hell and he did a fireman's roll two times and quickly bounced to his feet as if he had never felt any pain.

"Who in the fuck you think you talkin' to? That's my mother fuckin' son you faggot ass bitch!"

As Chippy cursed at Marcus, Marcus's brother charged at him like a football linebacker was trying to sack a quarterback. Chippy quickly grounded himself and got lower than the brother and scooped him up off of his feet while body slamming him hard on the northeast curb of Atlantic Ave and Parkway Blvd. Marcus's brother banged his head on the concrete and instantly became knocked out cold. Chippy kicked him square across the face to make sure that he wouldn't get up. Chippy had a rage in his eyes that was worse than a stampede of angry bulls. Marcus saw his brother lying on the ground with blood spewing from his nose and mouth, and he ran the opposite direction towards his car. Chippy hawked him down from behind and gave him a vicious forearm to the back of his neck.

"Who's a fucking mutt now you little black monkey bitch! I should kill you mother fuckin' ass! You little bitches tried to jump me huh? I got something for you mother fuckers! Fuck with me again and you'll be fucking dead! You can have that bitch, and I ain't gonna fight over no fucking bitch, but you better not fuck with my son and I mean that shit or I will kill your ass! Do you fucking hear me mother fucker?"

"Ok, man, ok we're good, we're good. Please stop, I'm sorry, I won't do nothing your son. I'll treat him like my own. We're good."

"Yeah that's what the fuck you better say, and you can take this in case you change your mind!"

After repeatedly beating Marcus to a bloody oblivion, Chippy ended his barrage with a devastating kick to his face! As Marcus lay unconscious on the ground a few feet from his brother, Chippy turned towards Devon and his friends as he caught his breath and wiped the blood away from his nose. As Jeremy ran towards Marcus's side Devon stood still as he stared at Chippy from a short distance. The beast within grumbled as it thrived on the confusion that was in Devon's mind. Devon was scared and proud at the same time.

Even though he feared for his father's safety, contrarily he was proud that his father defended himself while stating that he would not let any harm come to his son. Devon ended the brief stare down and stood helplessly as Jeremy consoled Marcus. Devon didn't know what to say or do. D.F. put his arm around him and pulled him close as Devon's eyes filled with tears. Chippy got into his damaged car and drove off while the two brothers regained their consciousness.

"Come on Devon. My mom made cookies. Let's go get some and then I'll ask her to take you home."

"Why me D.F, why me, what did I do to deserve this?"

"It's ok, bro. let's get out of here. It looks like Jeremy is going home with his dad, so you can call your mom and let her know that we'll bring you home."

"Alright, thanks D.F." said Devon as he tried to hold back his tears.

Under Your Hat

You may question my judgment about this or about that,
But whatever you do just keep it under your hat.
I'm not a man of perfection, but I am true to my word.
Therefore, sometimes I must ask you not to repeat what you've just heard.
What I'm about to say to you is sure to cause a verbal spat,
But regardless of how you feel learn from my experience,
and keep it under your hat.

David V.M. Kennedy

Even though Marcus Bond and his brother wanted to retaliate, time passed on and Chippy and Marcus never had another altercation with each other. Marsha and Chippy eventually got on speaking terms with one another due to the fact that they had to raise Devon from separate households. Marcus landed a decent paying job at the local factory York Snacks and he and his family moved out of the projects to a two story townhouse in the suburbs north of the city called Cedar Village. Marsha had banned Devon from seeing Chippy for an extended period of time, but after a lot of prayer she eventually allowed Devon to visit his father again. Devon's visits to Paula's house to see Chippy turned into less quality time between father and son to what now seemed limited to Devon only stopping by to ask for money.

One day D.F. and Boog, who now became good friends with Devon, were shooting basketballs together on a basketball court at a place called Penn Park that was directly across the street from York High School.

"D.F. what time is Devon coming, I'm ready to bounce," said Boog.

"Isn't that him over there by the statue," asked D.F.

"Yeah, that looks like him, yo, Devon hurry up!"

"Hurry up for what Boog," yelled Devon.

"Man, just come on, I got something set up with these chicks!"

"What's up D.F. what's up Boog," said Devon as he approached and shook their hands.

"Devon, Boog claims that he has something set up, but I think he's full of shit!"

"I don't know D.F. I heard Boog kissed a girl already," laughed Devon.

"Kissed, I did more than kiss. I ain't no virgin like you too!"

"Virgin, I ain't no virgin! Devon's the only virgin around here!"

"Shut up you two, yous guys are both liars!"

"Whatever, Devon like I said I ain't no virgin, and I bet D.F. ain't either. If he is then that's about to change for both of you! Let's get up outta here!"

"Where are we going? Who are the girls?"

"Just come on Devon," demanded Boog.

"Yo, Devon ain't that your Dad in that white car coming down the street?"

"Yeah, I'm gonna see if I can get some money from him."

As Chippy drove closer to the trio, Devon noticed that his Dad had a new white car. He slowly drifted down Lafayette Street once he noticed that one of the boys was Devon, and he pulled over next to an all-white building that was the York City School District administration building. As Devon started to cross the street from the basketball court he slightly tripped over a raised piece of concrete just as Chippy revved the engine of his 1972 Dodge Challenger. The sound of the engine startled Devon as he regained his balance.

"Dad, whoa, when did you get this bad boy?"

"Hey Slick, so you like this huh? Wanna take a spin? Hop in and I'll let you drive it!"

"For real? But I'm only 14, I can't drive yet!"

"Boy, get in the damn car and let's go," laughed Chippy.

"I want to Dad but my friends want me to go somewhere with them."

"Well it's up to you Devon," said Chippy as he revved the engine. "Hold on Dad let me tell them that I'm not going. Can you give them a ride?"

"Sure son, hurry up though I just remembered that I have to run somewhere real quick so if they don't mind me making a pit stop I will."

"Ok, one sec…"

"Yo, D.F. Boog, my Dad wants me to roll with him, but he said that he would give you guys a ride."

"Whatever Devon, your ass is just scared of the Poo Nanny," laughed Boog.

"Fuck you Boog, I ain't scared of nothing!"

"Don't sweat Boog Devon, you know he's just messing with you," said D.F.

"Yeah Devon, calm your ass down, it's all good. We're straight, besides we gotta go meet Steven and Bluck before we go over there anyway."

"Which Steven, I hope you're not talking about Steven Buster! I can't stand that guy, he talks too much shit!"

"No weirdo, Steven Cartwright our boy, the one that you threw all of those touchdowns to last year? Duh!"

"Oh, well I haven't seen him and Bluck in a minute so shut up chump!"

"Yo, D.F. let's get outta here before this guy starts swinging on us," laughed Boog as he and D.F. gave Devon a handshake and a hug.

After exchanging pleasantries with D.F. and Boog, Devon headed back towards Chippy across the street. His head was down and his fist was clenched as he walked around the front of the car towards the passenger door.

"You alright Slick? If you wanna go with your friends then that's cool, I'll catch up with you later."

"No, I'm cool Dad; they just pissed me off a little bit. Let's go."

"Alright then let's go; put your seatbelt on Slick."

As Devon reached for his seatbelt he briskly pulled the straps over his lap and he locked the seatbelt into place. After locking the harness he placed his right elbow on the door as he rested his head in his right hand while Chippy drove away.

"Are you sure that you're ok Devon? Is there something that you wanna get off of your chest?"

"Huh, I'm cool Dad, It's just, I don't know…"

"What it is it son? Talk to me, now you know that you can talk to me about anything! I mean anything!"

"Well, the guys were just teasing me a little bit about being a virgin and they're going to meet some girls. They think that I'm scared to hook up with the girls, and they think that I bailed on them."

"Well are you afraid Devon?"

"No! I mean, I don't know Dad. I'm not afraid of girls but I don't know if I want to have sex. I mean I do but… I don't know, ugh!"

"Hey, hey, go easy on the dashboard Slick! I know that this is a used car and all, but it's a classic! Look son, it's ok to be a little nervous about having sex. Right now your body is going through changes and having certain feelings towards girls is natural. Wait, you do have certain feelings towards girls don't you?"

"Dad, what are you trying to say?!"

"Easy Slick, I'm just playing with you! Hey, you're my first born and the start of my legacy so I gotta make sure that you're straight. No pun intended," laughed Chippy as he pulled over to a post office across from a McDonald's on the corner of S. George and W. Princess Street.

"Wait here while I run in here and mail this, and lock your door."

"I'm 14 Dad, I think I can handle!"

"Whatever chump, we'll see how much you can handle when I get back how about that? I've been wanting to test those hands anyway!"

"You ain't ready old man!"

"Old man, if you think 31 is old than boy are you in for a rude awakening! You see these hands? Muhammed Ali wishes he had these speedy hands! Lock your door, I'll be right back."

Chippy headed up a flight of stairs into a post office that had the look of an old roman architecture with pillars. As Devon admired the coolness of his father's walk, he didn't notice Chippy's old nemesis Green Eye approaching the car.

"Hey little man, is that your Dad Chippy that went into that building," asked Green Eye as he approached and began to lean in order to talk to Devon face to face.

"Sorry bruh but I don't know you from a can of paint," exclaimed Devon as he locked his door and rolled up his window.

"I'm an old friend little man, I just couldn't tell if that was him or not! Was it?"

"Get the fuck away from me man, I don't know you!"

"Look here you little bastard, I know that was him! You tell him that he better watch his mother fucking back! You better watch yours too!"

As Green Eye yelled at Devon he slammed his fist on the hood of the car, and Devon jumped at the sound. Green Eye hastily walked towards McDonald's while he looked back as Devon opened the car door.

"Hey, what the fuck is your problem man?!"

"Shut the fuck up kid, you heard what I said," threatened Green Eye as he walked directly into a parking meter.

"That's what your fat ass gets," laughed Devon.

"You better respect your elders you little punk!"

"Fuck you, you fat nasty green eyed bitch! Ain't nobody scared of your nasty sweaty looking ass!"

"What did you say to me kid? I will fuck you up right now," said Green Eye as he approached Devon with his arms held out.

"What, am I supposed to run? Next time, give me a heads up and I'll pretend that I'm scared for you Funkmeister!"

"Keep it up kid and I'll slap the shit outta you!"

"Hey! What the fuck is going on," yelled Chippy as he trotted down the post office steps.

"Dad, this slobby dude told me to tell you that you and I had better watch our backs!"

Suddenly, Chippy became infuriated as he briskly jogged towards Green Eye! He had on a pair of suede steel toed boots with a pair of blue jeans and a white tank top undershirt on. His wavy hair was cut so clean, and his beard blended as if it were drawn on his face. Although Chippy had the look of a "pretty boy," the look on his face sent chills down Green Eye's spine! Green Eye began to quickly back pedal as Chippy got near.

"Are you threatening my son you fat fuck," yelled Chippy as he slapped Green Eye in the face with an open hand.

"No, chief I was just messing with the young buck, you know me!"

"Shut the fuck up," said Chippy as he slapped him again.

"Dad, chill, I think I see the cops down the street!"

"If I ever see your fat ass around any of my kids I'll kill your ass! Do you hear me bitch," threatened Chippy as he slapped him once again.

"Chippy we're cool man, we're cool."

"We ain't fucking cool! Get the fuck up outta here!"

Green Eye rubbed his left cheek as he turned and headed back towards McDonald's. His pants were hanging off and while the crack of his buttocks was exposed Chippy said to Devon,

"Now son, that is a disgusting nasty piece of a so called human being!"

"Dang Dad, you didn't have to slap him like a bitch did you," laughed Devon as he opened up the passenger door.

"Sometimes you just gotta let them know son," laughed Chippy as he entered his car.

The father and son laughed as they drove past McDonald's, because they saw Green Eye sitting inside next to a window rubbing his left cheek with his left hand while stuffing his mouth with a sandwich with his right one.

"Look at that piece of shit Devon! He ain't got anything better to do but to stuff his fat ass and start shit. Some people just have no purpose in life. Misery loves company Devon and that right there is a miserable person."

"What was that all about anyways Dad?"

"It was about nothing Devon. It was about not a damn thing! Green Eye is just a jealous person who tried to start a rumor about me and your mom and I nipped it in the butt. I really don't understand his type. Certain people just love controversy and need for others to feel misery in order to make themselves feel good. It's just sad that he'd rather see me fail when in actuality as fucked up as he is, I'd rather see him succeed in life. Those are the people that you disassociate yourself from Devon. Come on, get out I want you to meet someone, and then I'm gonna take you to an empty lot so that you can drive this baby!"

"Who are we going to meet?"

"Just get out and stop asking questions boy!

Devon and his father pulled in front of a set of row houses on Maple St and as they simultaneously closed their doors a woman who was a little shorter than Chippy walked out of the house and stood with her arms open as Chippy walked up the small stoop. It was a woman that Devon had never seen before, and she was as beautiful as a picture of a full moon taken on a clear summer night. Her skin was so smooth and her eyelashes were so long. Devon stared at her with his mouth agape as Chippy hugged and kissed her as if he forgot that he was standing there watching.

"Hey, son this is Mahogany. Mahogany this is my son Devon," introduced Chippy.

"Devon you didn't tell me that your son was this handsome! He looks just like you!"

Devon blushed and smiled; and not only because of the compliment but because of the fact that he couldn't remember the last time that he heard someone call Chippy by his name Devon. Even though the woman was drop dead gorgeous, Devon began to get a look on his face as if he looked at the wicked witch of the east! Inside Devon was boiling with anger, because this was supposed to be his time to spend with his dad and now it seemed that some strange lady was about to go along for the ride. Devon was not only disturbed that she was going with them but he was upset because his dad was treating her as if this was his new girlfriend.

"What about Paula? I was just at her house with my dad last week," he thought to himself.

Devon was so in awe of Mahogany's face that it took him a while to notice Mahogany's stomach. She was definitely pregnant and Devon was shocked to see Chippy rubbing her belly as he smiled from ear to ear. Chippy decided to take Devon and Mahogany to the bowling alley. As Mahogany invited the two inside of the house to while she grabbed her purse Devon whispered to Chippy,

"Dad, is that baby yours?"

Chippy smiled at Devon and concurred,

"Yeah son, you're going to have a new little brother."

Devon couldn't believe his ears. He now had two little sisters and one brother with one on the way. Chippy put his arm around Devon and said,

"Hey keep this under your hat."

"What about Paula Dad," whispered Devon?

"That's why I said keep this under your hat," demanded Chippy in a loud whisper.

Devon understood what Chippy was trying to say. He didn't want Devon to say anything to his mother or spill the beans to Paula either.

Although Devon was good at keeping his dad's secrets under wraps, he often wondered why his dad was dating two different women. Unknown to Devon, Chippy was just following in the footsteps of his father Arthur. To most people what Chippy was doing would be considered immoral, but Chippy did only what he was accustomed to doing. Even though he didn't know his biological father, he constantly heard stories about him, and he also witnessed the actions of his foster father Mr. Piccolo who was no saint either. Devon admired his father's every move, and watching him woo Mahogany erased all of his teenage doubts when it came to handling girls.

In spite of Devon realizing that Chippy's immoral behavior was unjustified, he still revered his father's every action. Chippy could do no wrong in Devon's eyes although one day while Devon was riding with his Dad in his new job's company van, this somewhat obsessive admiration of his father would now be tested.

"Hop in Slick, check out my new ride!"

"What happened to the Challenger Dad? Why would you get rid of that for this piece of junk?"

"I'm just kidding Devon; this is my new work van. I'm a courier and I deliver packages to people."

"Don't scare me like that Chippy; you know that I want that Challenger in two more years when I get my license!"

"You better watch your mouth boy, I got your Chippy!"

"Just kidding Dad, where are we going?"

"I have to make this drop and then I'm gonna take you to see a friend of mine."

"Does your friend have any daughters? I need a girl right about now," laughed Devon.

"Well, I'll have to say yes and no to that Devon."

"Yes and No? What do you mean yes and no?"

"Yes, she does have a daughter, but no she isn't your age."

As Chippy finished explaining himself, he pulled in front of Bantz Park on the western side of York. Devon's Grandparents the Promises lived near Bantz Park and Devon had quite a few friends in the neighborhood. Devon noticed two of his God brothers and a few of his friends playing football in the field by the basketball court.

"Yo Dad, there's John and Mark! I haven't seen them since we moved from Hope Alley! Can I catch up with you later?"

"Yeah Slick, but before you go I want you to meet someone. She's pulling up right now."

A grey van with the same company logo as Chippy's van pulled up behind the father and son as they sat waiting outside the back of a church that was across the street from Bantz Park. A Puerto Rican lady stepped out of the van and headed towards Devon and Chippy. At first glimpse Devon thought that the lady looked like Gloria Estefan from the Miami Sound Machine band. She wore a rainbow colored bandana that was rolled to fit like a headband, and her curly jet black hair complimented it to perfection. As she opened her arms to give Chippy a hug Devon's eyes grew big as he softly said to himself,

"Oh, my God, please tell me that she's not pregnant too!"

"Devon this is Gina, and Gina here is my son that I told you about Devon. Devon here is the daughter that I was referring to right inside of here!"

"Dad, you've got to be kidding right? That's not your child is it? Look Dad, I'm gonna go. This is too much for me. I'll catch up with you later. Yo, John and Mark, what's up…"

"Did I do something wrong Chippy? I didn't mean to scare your son off," said Gina.

"Huh, oh no he's fine. You know how it is when kids have to deal with someone other than their mother having a kid to their father. I'll talk to him later about it."

Chippy's escapades continued over the next few years. By the time Devon was sixteen Paula had given birth to one girl and four boys with two of the boys being twins. Mahogany also mothered three more boys leaving her with four. Gina had her girl and Chippy later had a daughter with a woman named Grace leaving Chippy with twelve children to five different women!

Even though Chippy's secrets eventually came to light, he would always tell Devon the infamous saying,

"Hey keep this under your hat!"

As Chippy's inhibitions came forth, he experienced unimaginable conflict with the mothers of his children. Paula and Mahogany didn't see eye to eye and Paula would often put Chippy out of her house which caused him to move in with Mahogany. Contrary to Chippy's hectic households was his mastery at doing what he called "keeping the peace." Chippy was notorious for saying his catch phrase "you gotta keep the peace!"

One day Devon was heading to Paula's house to ask his Dad for money to go to the movies and as he got to the door he heard Paula scream,

"Get the fuck out of my house! Forgive me Lord for using the Devil's tongue for you have saved me, but I can't have this wicked man living me in sin!"

"Paula, wait let's talk about this, you know I love you girl!"

"Love, Chippy you don't know the meaning of love! You are sick! I should have never taken you back! Hey Devon, forgive me for yelling but your Dad is a sick man! Did you know that you had another sister and 3 more brothers? I knew about the one brother but three? Your new sister is upstairs!"

"Come on Paula; don't bring my son into this. Keep the peace!"

"Keep the peace? I'm about to give you fucking piece, that's what I'm about to do! Lord give me strength! Look I'm not going to discuss this any further with those babies upstairs but you best believe that you will not be living here anymore! I am through!"

As Paula turned to walk to the kitchen, Devon headed up the stairs to the bedrooms where his brothers and sisters were and said,

"Dang Dad, you fucked up!"

"Don't you disrespect me boy! I'll cave your chest in!"

"No disrespect Dad, you don't have to yell! You might as well bring it all out!"

"What is he talking about Chippy," demanded Paula.

"Fuck it, I have another daughter! You happy? That's right, I have twelve fucking kids to five different women, and there are you satisfied? Don't judge me! You don't know shit about me! Nobody knows shit about me! All I have are my kids! Nobody loves me! Nobody ever loved me! Fuck!!! Devon look out for your sisters and brothers for me. I'll be back!"

Devon turned back as he got halfway up the staircase, and he sat on the steps and watched tears flow down his father's eyes. This 5ft9 half Italian half African-American man who was born under the stars of Leo had the heart of a lion but cried like a baby. Devon sat shocked and confused about what or if he should say anything as his Dad walked out and slammed the front door. The beast within had made its imprint on Chippy and Devon. Although Chippy had major issues, to Devon he was like Socrates the philosopher with all of his wisdom and philosophies that he had on life.

Even though Devon witnessed many arguments between his father and his "harem", he still viewed his father as a hero and continued to put him upon a pedestal. In spite of Chippy's promiscuity, Devon grew to understand things in life better, and he still could see his father doing no wrong. One of the reasons that Devon felt this way was because Chippy constantly drilled in his head that he should not to walk the same path as he did. Chippy sometimes contradicted himself, but he always cautioned Devon and demanded that he respect women to the fullest. Even though Chippy's way of thinking was hypocritical, he stressed to his son that he did not want him to grow up to act like him.

Scorn

Baby I love you, truly it's you I adorn, but now
The pulsation of my heart beats like a rhythmic scorn.
You've disintegrated my youthful exuberance, and now my heart turns old.
My memories of you are warm although you left me in the cold.
Baby I love you, truly it's you I adorn, but now
I realize that it's over; and you are just a heartless memory who has only known how to scorn.

Chippy was not by any means a saint, but regardless of his immoral behavior he did try to do his best at raising his children. Chippy made sure that he "kept the peace" with the mothers of his children in order for all of them to live in harmony as a family. D remained very close with all but one of his siblings, because Gina felt the need to take move with Devon's second oldest sister to Boston because she was ashamed that she had a child with Chippy. Marcus and Marsha eventually moved out of the projects into the suburbs in Emigsville, Pa. Devon enrolled into Central York High School where he was one of four black students that attended the entire school.

Although Devon was seldom picked on, he did have his share of squabbles due to the fact that he was an African-American. Devon maintained good study habits by staying on the honor roll, and in spite of a few verbal battles here and there his time at Central was very enjoyable. Marsha had landed a new job and Devon and Destiny seemed to get anything that they asked for. One day Devon came home from school and he discovered that his stepfather Marcus had stayed home from work.

"Pop, are you here, Pop," yelled Devon throughout the house as he set his backpack net to the stairs.

"Devon, I'm up here," said Marcus from upstairs in a faint voice.

"Ok, I'm gonna do my chores and the go to the playground to shoot some hoops!"

As Devon was doing his daily chores of washing the dishes he put on the headset to his Walkman as he listened to his Michael Jackson Thriller Album.

"I want to love you, PYT, pretty young thang," sang Devon when Ka-boom! Boom! Boom! Thump! Boom!

"Ouch! Devon, help me," groaned Marcus.

"Pop, are you okay, what happened," Devon called as he noticed Marcus had fallen down the steps.

"Ow, it hurts call your mom please!"

"Ok Pop, hold on, I'll get help!"

Even though Devon was a bright student, he had no clue of what was about to unfold. Marcus and Marsha had not been seeing eye to eye, and it was mainly because Marcus would not give up smoking Marijuana. Devon ran to the bottom of the stairs and saw Marcus still in his pajamas lying on the floor. Devon ran into the living room and picked up a white cordless phone and called Marsha.

"Mom, Pop fell down the steps," Devon said to Marsha on the phone.

"So, leave him there," Marsha calmly replied.

"Huh," Devon said with a puzzled look on his face.

"I said leave him there," Marsha repeated.

"But I think that he's hurt!"

"What did I say? Ain't nothing wrong with him! Leave him right there."

Marcus and Marsha had been having trouble in their relationship, and unlike Marsha's liaison with Chippy, she and Marcus never argued in front of their children so Devon had no clue that his mother was unhappy. Marcus was known to smoke marijuana and Marsha found out that not only was he smoking, but he would do it while Devon was with him. Although Marcus never literally smoked in front of Devon, he did partake in it while Devon would be in another room. Naïve to the whole situation, Devon did exactly what his mother told him, and he left Marcus lying at the bottom of the steps. Marcus eventually gathered himself and and after lying on the floor for thirty minutes he got up and went upstairs.

Marsha came home from work that evening and when she went up to her room she noticed Marcus was still in his pajamas and he was just sitting on the bed staring into space with the TV turned off. Marsha thought that Marcus's behavior was peculiar and his silence started to frighten her so she turned around and started to walk out of the bedroom.

"Where in the fuck have you been woman," yelled Marcus as he jumped up out of his sadistic daze.

"You know where I've been Marcus. I had to work."

"You've been off work for two hours damn it! Where the fuck was you?"

"Marcus you need to calm down and stop cussing at me," said Marsha calmly.

"Do you love me Marsha?"

"Marcus, please..."

"Do you love me?"

"Marcus..."

"Don't Marcus me, do you fucking love me?! How hard is that to answer? Do you love me?!"

"Look Marcus, let's talk about this later after you calm down, okay?"

As Marsha began to turn away to walk out of the couple's bedroom, Marcus delivered a crushing blow to the back side of her head between her ear and neck where her jaw bone connected. Marsha fell directly to her knees as she he her head on the corner of their mahogany wooden bed frame.

"Answer me! Answer my fucking question! Do you love me?"

"Marcus how could you," cried Marsha.

"I need to know! Do you love me?"

"You are crazy! Get away from me!"

"Come here woman! Get your ass up here, hmm, give me a kiss. Give me a kiss! You love me don't you?"

"Get your hands off of me! You're hurting me Marcus, you're hurting my face!"

"Ouch! You bitch, my fucking balls!"

Marsha sprinted down the stairs crying as her blue and white blouse draped over her right shoulder due to the top three buttons being ripped off. Devon was sitting in the couch listening to his Walkman on the highest volume as he drew up football plays in a notebook.

"Grab your things Devon, we're leaving!"

"Mom, what happened," asked Devon as he threw his headphones off of his head as they fell around his neck.

"Hurry Devon, let's go!"

"You motherfuckers ain't going anywhere!"

"Yo, Marcus chill," yelled Devon.

"Look Devon, you stay out of this! This is between me and you Mom!"

As Marsha went to grab her car keys, Marcus grabbed her by the hand and twisted her wrist as if he were a master at Aikido! "Marcus stop, you're hurting me, Devon help," screamed Marsha in pain.

Devon headed toward his mother and Marcus yelled,

"Get the fuck outside boy!"

In spite of being outweighed by twenty pounds, Devon was shocked and afraid but he briskly walked towards Marcus.

"Get your fucking hands off of my Mom!"

As soon as Devon came within arm's length of Marcus, he let go of Marsha's wrist and shoved Devon with all of his might! Devon violently hit the floor and the force of Marcus's shove made him hit the ground while rolling over backwards into the front door of their home. At that instant Marcus grabbed Marsha and threw her three feet in the air over the living room couch landing on the a large rectangular glass coffee table. As Devon gathered himself, he was a little dazed from banging his head on the door therefore he stumbled as he headed towards him Mom.

"Ouch, my back, my back," Marsha.

"Mom, are you okay, here I got you Mom, just hold still I got you!"

While Devon consoled him mother Marcus sprinted upstairs to the bedroom and grabbed one of three shotguns that hung over his bed. Devon gently sat his mother upright and asked,

"Can you stand up Mom? C'mon, we gotta get out of here?"

"I think I can Devon, but it hurts baby, it hurts," cried Marsha.

As Devon began to raise his mother to his feet the mother and son heard click, click!

"Oh shoot, Mom c'mon we gotta go! I got you mom, put your arm around my neck!"

Once Devon got Marsha to take a few steps toward the door Marcus met them 3ft away from the entrance with his shotgun drawn and pointed it directly at Devon's face and yelled,

"Motherfucker you ain't going nowhere! Sit your motherfucking ass down, you ain't going anywhere! If you don't step the fuck back I'll blow your motherfucking heads off."

"Marcus c'mon man, you don't wanna do this bruh, and c'mon man it's me Devon. Just relax and let's talk this out."

"Marcus please, I love you, yes I love you with all of my heart, please take the gun out of my baby's face! We can work this out! Please just drop the gun and take me upstairs and make love to me!"

"So you really do love me don't you?"

"Yes baby, I do, now lower the gun and let's go upstairs so that I can show you baby, I love you!"

As Marsha pleaded for Marcus to lower the 12 gauge shotgun, the sound of her words sent chills throughout Devon's body. The beast within was ready to unleash like never before, and Devon just stared at the tip of the barrel while looking directly into Marcus's eyes. Suddenly, Devon's fear turned into pure anger and his only thought was feeling disgusted and ashamed that he couldn't protect his mother. As Marcus began to lower the shotgun, without a second of hesitation Devon took a quick step to the right and Marsha fell to the floor as he pushed the barrel of the gun upward to the left away from his face. As the gun barrel pointed towards the ceiling a loud booming sound went off as the force of the shotgun caused Marcus to drop it to the floor.

Although Marcus dropped the gun, plaster from the ceiling dropped directly on top of Devon's head as he gave a thunderous right hook to Marcus's jaw! Marcus staggered back two steps and countered with a right haymaker punch. Devon ducked the haymaker and delivered a vicious uppercut that knocked Marcus out cold on his feet! As Marcus swayed forward, Devon gave him a right hook that landed flush across the left side of his chin! Marcus dropped to the floor and Devon retrieved the shotgun and stood over Marcus while he pointed it to his head!

"If you make one motherfucking move, then I'll blow your fucking head off! Mom, are you okay?"

"Yes baby, I'll be okay."

"Can you make it to the phone Mom? Call the cops!"

Devon's Plea

No matter how hard I try to be successful I just can't seem to better my life.
This beast within is consuming my existence, and it constantly causes people misery and strife?
What is it inside of me that is so detrimental
and keeps me from attaining my goal?
Dear God I need your help. I'm begging you; please release this curse placed upon my soul.
Your voice is the wind which speaks softly, and I'm like a
brittle leaf swaying on a tree.
Many may think that I've crumbled; but my true existence is the root and with your blessings I'm as happy as can be.

David V.M. Kennedy

Contrary to calling the police, Marsha phoned her older brother who gathered two of her younger brothers, and they rushed to her home. When the three brothers arrived Devon stood over Marcus with the shotgun pointed directly in his face as sweat poured down the side of his face. Marsha's oldest brother who stood 6'4 tall calmly placed his hand over the barrel of the gun and said,

"It's okay Nephew. I'm here. Give your Uncle the gun."

Even though Devon felt more secure that his Uncles were there for him and Marsha, he still had a fearful look on his face as he trembled when he took his eyes off of Marcus and looked into his Uncle's eyes.

"It's okay; here let me have the gun."

"Here Uncle, take it," Devon said as tears began to pour down his face. Devon released the gun to his Uncle and his other Uncle who stood 6'2 embraced him as he cried in his chest like a baby. Devon's oldest Uncle placed the safety switch on the gun and the sight of seeing Devon cry caused him to smash Marcus's face with the butt of the rifle! Devon's third Uncle who stood 5'11 kicked Marcus in the ribs and landed a fury of punches to his face. The two Uncles threatened Marcus by stating that if he ever tried to harm their sister and nephew again that they would kill him.

In spite of feeling like he lost his manhood, Marcus never even came close to having an altercation with Marsha again. Marsh knew that her daughter Destiny would eventually need to interact with her father so as time passed she allowed Marcus to have supervised visits. Marsha filed for divorce and Marcus obliged. After Marcus and Marsha's divorce, Marsha took Devon and his baby sister Destiny to live with her adoptive parents the Promises. Her parents welcomed them in with their open arms and they let Marsha know that she could take as much time as she needed to get on her feet. Her parents lived at 753 W. Locust St. which was located in the city on the west end of York.

Even though Marsha had no deadline, as time went on she felt pressured because of the fact that her father began treating her as if she were that little girl who once grew up in his house. "I've really got to get my own place," Marsha would often say. Devon had to leave his friends at Central York High School and enroll into William Penn Senior High which was a city public school where most of the kids from Devon's old neighborhoods went. Devon was already popular amongst his peers so fitting in wouldn't be a problem for him.

Although Devon had intelligence to go with his popularity, he wasn't really handling the divorce and traumatic encounter with Marcus too well. Marsha was a young single mother who was trying not only to make ends meet, but she also was trying to find herself as a person. Marsha eventually began to date other men, and Devon fell by the waist side due to the lack of attention that he was so accustomed to from his mother at home. He started hanging with "the in crowd" and his grades began to slip considerably. Devon was still playing football, and at this particular moment football was all he seemed to care about. Devon had been playing quarterback since he was eight years old, and he just led his team to an undefeated season and they were about to play for the State Championship. Chippy had never seen Devon play football even though he constantly heard how good he was.

In spite of not being a fan of football Chippy decided to attend the State Championship.

"Dad, what are you doing here," asked Devon as he came out of the locker room to warm up before the big game.

"Hey Slick, I felt like I needed to be here for you, besides I never got to see my first born play! I brought all of your brothers and sisters with me too! It cost me and arm and a leg to pay for them so you better make it worth my while! There they are over there at the snack bar," laughed Chippy.

"I got you Dad! You do know what a touchdown is don't you," joked Devon.

"Ha-ha very funny, yeah and I also know how hard it is to start Varsity as a sophomore at William Penn, I'm proud of you son!"

"Thanks Dad, I love you, enjoy this clinic that I'm about to put on!"

Devon was so excited to be playing in front of his father and siblings for the first time. Putting on a clinic was an understatement! Even though William Penn was undefeated they were considered the underdogs, because Central Bucks West High School was going into the State Championship their 3 time undefeated State Championships! Devon dazzled the crowd as he completed 76% of his passes for 467 yards and 5 touchdowns! Devon was selected the game's Most Valuable Player and his team won their first ever State Championship!

The following day at school one of the students who saw Devon interviewed on the news didn't quite agree with his "fifteen minutes of fame" and he made it a point to let the rest of the student body know that he wasn't pleased. The kid was a former basketball star who quit the team his freshman year, because he didn't like the coach yelling at him. As Devon came from the cafeteria the former hoop star bumped into him with his shoulder and said,

"Watch where you're going, Mr. Lucky to win the game!"

"Luck, I'm sorry but I don't believe in luck!"

"Whatever Devon, the referees gave you that bogus penalty! You suck! You wish that you were as nice as me on the court!"

"Whatever bruh, you don't even play anymore!"

"I don't need to play; I'm too good for that weak ass team! If you didn't have those fast receivers you wouldn't have done anything with your sorry ass sneakers."

"What do my sneakers have to do with this?"

"You suck like your sneakers! Those are played out like your mama! I heard that you have to live with your grandparents because your broke ass mama got beat up!"

"Hey man, you better watch who the fuck you're talking about! Don't talk about my fucking mom!"

"What you gonna do punk? You ain't shit!"

Without hesitation, Devon attacked the kid like angry dog would a cat and he beat the kid as if it were Marcus Bond himself that day he threw his mom over the couch and threatened to blow their heads off. The kid was beaten so bad that he was rushed to the hospital for internal injuries, and Devon was suspended from school for the first time ever! Marsha received a phone call from the principal who let her know that Devon was suspended and that he would probably be expelled. Marsha was furious, and after work she sped home to talk to Devon!

In spite of the fact that Devon placed the young man in the hospital, there are always two sides to a story but unfortunately for Devon, Marsha was only trying to hear the principal's side.

"What on God's green earth did you do," asked Marsha in a very demanding tone.

"The kid started making fun of me for being in the paper and on the news by saying that I sucked at quarterback," said Devon.

"So you beat someone up for that," questioned Marsha emphatically.

"No, he then said that I had to live with my grandparents because we couldn't afford a house, and that I didn't have a father!" At that moment Marsha's anger toned down and she digressed from yelling more and she quickly turned into the mild mannered nurturing mother that she was.

"Look son, I know things have been difficult for you, but you can't let out your frustration by resorting to violence. Remember, violence begets more violence," Marsha reiterated.

Even though Marsha's philosophy sounded very logical, Devon who was this same kid at three years old reading small children's books concluded that his mother was being somewhat hypocritical. He thought to himself,"

This is the same woman about six years ago who made me go outside and fight a kid who chased me home from school. Now that I defend myself, I'm being reprimanded, she should be the one chastised not me!"

Although Devon had these feelings inside, he kept them to himself because his mother had instilled the biblical saying, "honor thy mother and thy father" in his head. Devon was not only respectful but he also didn't want to unleash the beast that was inside of his mother either! Marsha went easy on

Devon because she felt that the suspension was enough. After Devon returned to school his teachers noticed a drastic improvement in his studies. His transcripts came in from his former school, and that following year he was placed into the gifted program for accelerated students.

Although Devon got back on track with his studies, he couldn't seem to avoid physical confrontation. Devon had witnessed so much at a young age that subconsciously those preceding parental battles had taken its toll. One day he was having a visit with his father at Paula's house. Three of Paula's older kids gathered around the kitchen table as the family played a friendly game of monopoly. Devon who was a strong competitor had started to take control of the game, and at that precise moment Paula's oldest daughter children started to "cut on" or "play the dozens" with him.

"Yo, Devon's teeth are so big, when he smiles people stop staring at the sun cause they think it's a solar eclipse!"

"Yeah, he looks like Bugs Bunny with a swollen mouth," said Devon's youngest brother named Edgar.

Even though the youngsters were doing this in fun, Devon didn't take to kindly to the wisecracks. This type of action took place every time he visited his father's dwelling. Devon would sometimes "crack" back, but each time he "cut" back it seemed that the entire household would gang up on him. Devon would get tired of the game real fast. It didn't help that Chippy would occasionally talk bad about Devon's mother in front of everyone either. Not only was it annoying, but it was also painful when his dad would call him a bum, or laugh at him because he didn't do "manly things" and knew how to cook and clean the kitchen.

Although Chippy wasn't purposely trying to offend Devon, he did. Rather than getting too emotional about it Devon would just get up and leave as he did on this particular day. Devon went home and picked up the phone to call D.F.

"Yo, what up," asked Devon.

"Nothing just chillin," said D.F.

"Yo, you wanna go hoop," asked Devon.

"Cool, I'll call the fellas," said D.F.

D.F. called Bluck, K-Ritt, Boog and Steven Cartwright and let them know that he and Devon would meet them at the park known as West Minister Park. Frequently the five amigos met another posse to play basketball for bragging rights. D.F. met with Devon at a place called Kiwanis Lake and he noticed that Devon didn't look like his usual self.

"Yo, what's up Devon? Why are you so quiet?"

"Huh, oh nothing man, I just have a few things on my mind."

"Yo, I meant to tell you! You should've come with me and Boog that day! We met some fine ass chicks!"'

"For real, dang it I knew that I should've gone with yous guys! Shit I was chasing after my damn Dad again. I'm sick of always having to hunt him down just to see him. The shit gets old. Besides every time I go over there Paula's kids always talk shit. Especially my youngest brother Edgar, he gets on my damn nerves! Sometimes I just wanna choke his little ass!"

"Well at least you have a father Devon, I don't even know mine."

"Well that's just it D.F. I think that I might be better off if I didn't know mine. So what happened with the girls?"

"Yo, this one girl had a fat ass! Her titties were fucking perfect! I played with them bad boys all night!"

"Was she me or you," asked Devon in their code language.

"She was you! You know that I love some black pussy! No offense but I need ass and thighs in my life!"

"D.F. you're a fucking nut! So did you get your dick wet? Did you hit?"

"Let's just say that she'll have a different lean to her walk! Devon you should have come with us! Paris was there!"

"What? Get the fuck outta here! Paris ain't even like that!"

"Ha-ha, I knew that you liked her! Yo, I think she's feelin' you too! You're right bruh she just chilled why we went upstairs with the other honeys. I know she was hoping that you were there!"

"Do you think that she likes me? I don't know man; she seems to like them thug type dudes."

"Nah man, Paris is too sophisticated for that! You need to get with that! I guarantee you that she'll let you hit!"

As the guys approached the basketball court on their bikes, Devon noticed that D.F. was listening to his Walkman and not paying attention to what was in front of him as he looked back to talk to him. "Yo, D.F. watch out," shouted Devon. D.F. turned to see what Devon was talking about and Wham! The tires on his green bicycle which the guys called a "bus", slid in a pile of rocks where

D.F. hit the ground hard stomach first. All of the guys at the park roared with laughter as he looked up at them with his face as red as a stop sign!

Everyone on the court was laughing except for one of the guys from the other basketball rival crew. D.F. had accidentally knocked over his "boom box" which the guys used as a timer by playing a 90 minute cassette tape which they broke down to 45 minutes for each half of basketball.

"Yo that wasn't funny fat boy that was my box," said the biggest guy on the court.

"My fault yo, I didn't mean it," said D.F. apologetically.

"You stupid idiot, I just bought that," said the kid as he pushed D.F.

In spite of D.F. showing his regrets or not, the big kid wasn't happy with the outcome of the bike accident. As D.F.'s shoulders were being shoved he tripped over one of the basketball and fell near the free throw line of the basketball court. As soon as D.F. hit the ground, Devon appeared like a magician returning from a disappearing act with a crushing blow to the kid's face! The sound of his fist hitting the kid seemed like a cinder block was attached to his wrist. The rest of the crew was astonished by how quick Devon attacked, and they couldn't believe the fury that was in his eyes! Devon continued to punish the kid with bone crushing blows while demanding him to apologize to D.F.

"Say you're sorry" said Devon repeatedly. After the scuffle the kid who was already remorseful said,

"Look man I just wanna play ball, you got me, I don't wanna fight you!"

Devon looked to D.F. and said,

"You ok bro?"

D.F. was shocked by how Devon reacted to the kid who threatened him. D.F. was by no means a fighter, but he wasn't afraid to stand his ground if need be. Watching Devon pummel the kid left D.F. amazed and concerned, and as he nodded yes to confirm that he was okay he thought to himself,

"Something's eating at my boy. This is so out of character for him."

Beautiful Butterfly

A true man's feelings for his woman should never inflict pain, although his everlasting love should continue to intensify.
He should uphold her in the highest of regards while making her feel as beautiful as the flight of a butterfly.
Unlike warm swift winds that alters the path of a butterfly while blowing it across the meadows,
Unconditional is what a man's love should be, while he remains stern like the stem of a rose with a touch as soft as its petals.
When a man embraces true love, then his heart should always swell with pride.
True love is the essence of God's intentions, and it feels good to have millions of butterflies inside.

Eventually Devon and the kid shook hands, and the two crews went ahead and played a friendly game of basketball.

As time passed, Devon, his mother, and his sister, moved out of his grandparent's house to an apartment on Hoke St in West York. Marsha had no furniture for the home except for Devon's bedroom suit plus a bed and dresser for her room where she and her daughter Destiny slept. Marsha started to date and was going through a phase where she began soul searching. Devon understood that his mother needed companionship, but he still felt a little uncomfortable about her dating. One day Marsha and Devon were driving home from church and Marsha had decided to stop by to visit her good friend Janine. On the way to Janine's house Marsha stopped by a corner store on Pershing Ave across the street from Penn Park. Devon noticed that his mother was talking to a strange man that he's never seen before.

Devon was unaware that this strange man had been dating Marsha for a substantial amount of time. As Devon sat in his mother's car, he stared at the strange man as if he knew him. After exchanging pleasantries Marsha got back into the car and she handed Devon a bag of potato chips he said,

"Who was that funny looking dude mom?"

"Huh, oh that was a friend that I went to high school with."

"Oh, well he sure did stare at your butt as you came back to the car! He's a weird looking dude."

"Hush Devon and quit talking about people," scolded Marsha.

"Why are you getting upset? You act like that's your man or something!"

"Shut your mouth Devon! Mind your manners, and I don't wanna hear another word!"

"What did I do wrong?"

"Not another word boy!"

Marsha drove away from the corner store, and the two of them left to go visit Janine. After their brief visit, the two got into the car to leave and as Janine and Marsha were exchanging their goodbyes, Devon noticed that the same strange man was about to get into a car that was parked a few houses down the street! As the man drove by Marsha and Janine, he slowed up and said something to Marsha before he drove away.

"Mom, is that weird guy following us? I know that I've seen him somewhere before!"

Marsha and Janine erupted with laughter, because they knew who the gentleman really was and it humored them that Devon had no clue. The man's name was Ben Able, and as Devon stared at the man as he talked to his mother he thought to himself,

"I know I've seen this guy before. Where do I know him from?"

Ben Able was to what most women would refer to as "Sexual Chocolate". He stood 6'3in tall and had the physique of an Adonis! Ben wore his hair cut low with a super clean hairline and a fade that blended as if his barber spent an entire day cutting his hair. Ben was a former All-State running back from William Penn Senior High who later graduated from Penn State University with a degree in Sociology. As Ben drove by Marsha's car where Devon was waiting the two caught eye contact and Ben smiled and nodded his head as if he was saying "what's up?" At that moment Devon said out loud,

"I know who that guy is! That's that chump who kicked us out of the gym!"

One day Devon and his crew were supposed to play basketball against the local recreational center called the Crispus Attucks or C. A. center. Devon, D.F. Boog, Cart, Bluck, and K. Ritt formed special bonds, and they became what the locals referred to as a "posse". Even though in many ghettos "posse" is a term known for being notorious or gang related, this crew was far from that! Devon, Cart and Bluck were by far the nerdiest looking of the bunch due to the fact that Devon and Cart had distinguishable mouth structures and Devon and Bluck wore glasses. K. Ritt had noticeable height which was why the promising high school basketball star had just about every major college offering him a scholarship. Contrary to D.F. being the "All-American white boy" Boog was the epitome of the "All-African American" child. To say that this "posse" had character was an understatement.

Devon and his "posse" would frequently walk the city of York as they searched for good basketball competition to play against. One day Cart learned about a basketball league that was about to begin at the C.A. where Ben worked, and the boys were required to have a coach if they wanted to play in the league. Cart was told by a friend that he would help the boys out and on their first scheduled game the crew showed up to the C.A. without a coach. Unknown to Devon and his crew, Ben Able had already had communication with the director of the facility that boys were representing that if they didn't show up with a coach, then they would not be able to play.

In result of the miscommunication, the boys showed up to play without a coach expecting to play. As Devon turned to watch Ben drive away in his 1985 BMW, he reminisced about that day at the C. A.

"Yo Cart, thanks for the hook up with this league bruh!"

"Yeah, I can't wait cause we're about to run through these cats," said Cart.

"Yo K. Ritt, I bet you don't dunk on nobody," Boog exclaimed.

"C'mon Boog, now you know that we're playing the C.A. and how much trash these dudes talk! When I dunk and hang on the rim I'll say in my Scarface voice, say hello to my little nuts! Yo, we're about to run these bums out the gym!"

"My boy Devon got that mean set shot," said D.F.

"Yeah, you can call him set shot willy," laughed Bluck.

"Go ahead Bluck, with your straight line brick laying shot," Devon retaliated.

"What can I do for you boys," asked Ben Able.

"Hi sir we're here to play are first game," said Cart.

"What time is your game?"

"We play at 3pm said sir," said Devon.

"3pm, 3pm, oh yeah I spoke with your director. Where's your coach?"

"Coach, what coach? We're just from the rec center. We don't have a coach," stated Devon.

"Well no coach, no game, bye!"

"What do you mean no coach, no game? We don't need a coach. We've been playing together for a long time! Besides Cart and K Ritt play high school ball," exclaimed Devon.

"No coach, no game! Game is cancelled! Bye," said Ben Able as he slammed the doors to the gym.

It all came back to Devon. Ben was that guy who refused to let them play without a coach. Devon remembered how the guys were furious as they left the gym, because they believed in their minds that Ben just didn't want his team to lose after he saw K.Ritt and Cart were playing knowing that they were State Champions at York Catholic High School. Even though Devon recalled who Ben was, he had no clue that Marsha and Ben had already made plans for Ben to move into Marsha's apartment. One day Devon came home from school and when he walked into the house he saw boxes and clothes piled in the living room.

"What the fuck," Devon said to himself as he looked at the array of stuff.

"Hey baby, how was school today," asked Marsha.

"Hey Mom, school was school. What's going on?"

"What do you mean school was school? I asked you how was school? Don't get smart!"

"I ain't getting smart. Whose stuff is this?"

"Oh, that's Ben's stuff."

"Ben, who is Ben?"

"You'll meet him in a few. He's on his way back home."

"What do you mean he's on his way home? What's that supposed to mean?"

"Just what I said, he is my boyfriend and he'll be staying with us?"

"What?! What boyfriend? What do you mean he's living here?! What about me and Destiny?"

"Boy, I don't have to explain nothing to you! I'm grown! I am the mother and you are the child! Open the door I just saw his car pull up."

"So when were you going to tell me all of this?"

"Tell you all of what… Hey Ben," said Marsha as she hugged and kissed Ben as he walked through the door.

"Ben this is Devon, and Devon this is Ben."

"Hey, what's up Devon, it's nice to meet you!"

"I'm outta here," said Devon as he walked into his room and slammed the door.

"I guess he didn't take the news so well huh Marsha?"

"I ain't thinking about that boy, I'm about to knock him upside his head for being disrespectful!"

"No Marsha, don't do that. It's cool. It's a lot for a teenager to take in. Especially with all that you told me that he's been through. I wish we could have told him sooner but with loss of my job and my eviction and all, I didn't even see this coming."

Although Devon didn't mean to disrespect his mother, he couldn't help himself and he lost his cool, because he was fed up with stepfathers after the Marcus Bond fiasco. When Ben moved in Devon was miserable and he started to go into a state of depression. Devon began to conjure up ways that he could make Ben's stay the worst that he could possibly could. Devon wanted Ben gone so bad that he started acting weird as if he was having mental problems hoping that Ben would just freak out and go away. Devon's tactics were to no avail; and after Devon figured out that Ben really loved his mother and was not going anywhere, he decided that for her he would try to accept Ben. Contrary to accepting Ben, Devon made it painfully clear to himself that he was not going to recognize Ben as a stepfather but only as a friend.

As time moved on Devon and Ben found a common ground in football. Devon also realized that Ben was actually the perfect man for his mother because he treated her like he's never seen a man treat a woman before. Devon fought hard to suppress the beast within, and even though the ignorance tried to take over Devon's mind, didn't give in to the temptation and he gave Ben a chance. Ben was a passionate football fan, and since the two had this in common they would often engage conversations about the game.

"Devon that was a good game that you had, but I don't know what the heck your coach was thinking!"

"What do you mean? We won 22-0."

"I'm talking about that offense! With the speed that you guys have and the ability that you have to throw the ball puzzles me as to why they are running the wishbone offense! Spread them out and let them boys go to work! Yeah you guys will probably win the county again, but this year will be tough to win State again!"

"Yeah, Coach keeps saying that he should change the offense, but he doesn't think that the guys will be able to pick it up."

"Well, ya'll better do something, because J.P. McCaskey looks strong this year!"

Ben panned out to be a great guy, but Devon still did not like the fact that he came into his family's life so quick without notice. Devon was very sensitive when it came to his mother, and he often felt that he was losing his mother's love because it seemed like she was never around anymore. Marsha was always a go getter and she always had a task to do. Whenever Marsha did spend an ample amount of time at home it seemed to Devon that her full divided attention was being given to Ben. Even though he had no choice, Devon accepted his mother's relationship but it was not without caution. He never made it aware to Ben although he did put in the back of his mind that, "If this man puts his hands on my mom, I will kill him!"

Together We Can

My feelings for you are so clear but I need to ask you why?
Why do I get shut down before I even try?
I am here for your every need,
But your selfishness symbolizes greed.
I get criticized for every move that I make.
Even the questions that I ask are a big mistake!
So tell me why?
Am I not your fantasy guy?
Don't look away; I want to stare into each eye,
To see if the love that I project is truly inside.
If it is than you sure can't deny,
That my passionate endurance gives you the ultimate high!
Come on let's go; we both need a ride,
But understand that this trip will boost each of our pride.
When the drive is over and we can go no more,
I'll hike to you mind with the sense of valor.
As a couple it's healthy to mentally compete,
But neither shall be victorious nor experience defeat.
We must open our minds to maximize and feel elated,
And we will always love each other and never feel hated.
So the next time don't question when I ask you why.
Together we can make, so let's give love a try.

David V.M. Kennedy

Ben and Marsha had developed a strong relationship, and they eventually decided to move into a bigger apartment. The family moved to 664 Linden ave. which was on the west end of town on a corner lot that intersected Belvedere St. Even though Devon was happy that Ben and Marsha developed what was the precursor to an everlasting bond, he wasn't feeling comfortable in his own household. Ben and Marsha eventually got married, and shortly after the wedding Ben asked Marsha if he could adopt Destiny. Marsha thought hard and long about Ben's request. Destiny who was only 3yrs old had no say in the matter, but Marsha's concern was about what Destiny's father Marcus Bond would say.

"Marsha, I really love you, you do know that right?"

"Well Ben I should hope so, I mean we did just get married," laughed Marsha.

"No, baby listen, I truly love you and I want to make this family complete."

Once Ben disclosed his heartfelt statement, Marsha took a deep breath, and her face slowly turned into a blank stare. After ten seconds of silence Marsha who had begun to insinuate looked Ben in the eyes and said,

"Ben, I love you with all of my heart, but I told you what the doctors told me after my miscarriage before Destiny was born. I'm sorry baby, but I can't have any more kids. The risk is too high. As a matter of fact they are requesting that I get a hysterectomy. We talked about this extensively Ben, I don't understand."

"Oh baby, no, no, no, that is not what I mean. Woman I love you unconditionally, and I will replace your womb with my heart! What I mean is that I want Destiny to bear my name. I want to adopt her."

"Oh Ben, Are you serious? What about Marcus? I mean he doesn't come around anymore, because he's strung out on that new drug crack cocaine, but it would only be fair to let him know; Don't you agree?"

"Yes, I thought a lot about that, and I put myself in his shoes and if he is against it then all that I can do is simply respect his wishes."

"Ok, well I know where he lives so I'll stop by to invite him over so that we can talk. What about Devon?"

Ben was sitting on the edge of his black leather love seat as he faced Marsha who was sitting on the sofa, and when she asked about Devon he slowly sunk into the back rest and said,

"Whew, you know Marsha I have to be a man and admit that I really never gave it a thought. I mean he's almost sixteen so I didn't think anything of it."

"Well that's kind of good, because trust me, Chippy wouldn't go for that anyway!"

Devon was now maturing into a young man, and in conjunction with his body going through changes, he often had questions but didn't feel comfortable talking to his mother about them. Devon already felt that she was constantly treating him like a baby. Marsha wasn't overbearing but she was a little overprotective. Devon would occasionally visit Chippy, but he didn't feel comfortable discussing girls because remarkably Chippy would always encourage Devon to have kids!

Although Devon knew that he was too young to have a child, he was constantly being pressured by his peers to have sex with a girl. Devon also had to deal with the pressures of being the starting Quarterback at William Penn Sr. High especially because of the demand to win. William Penn which was more known as York High developed a reputation for having the toughest teams in the State of Pennsylvania. With Devon having early success at York High this led to many confrontations due to the jealousy of his peers. One day Devon was coming from class and he ran into one of his best friends Bluck,

"Yo, Bluck hold up!"

"Yo, what up D," said Bluck in a slow monotone voice.

"Yo, Coach said that if we practice hard that he'll let us out of practice early! He said we should destroy Red Lion High for homecoming! What you wanna get into?"

"I don't know it's up to you. Uh oh, here comes your girl! Man every time I talk to you in the halls a fine girl walks up on us! My boy got babe magnets in his chest," joked Bluck.

"Whatever man, that's just Paris. I didn't even really meet her like that yet! Besides it's those dimples of yours! I swear when I grow up that I wanna be just like my boy Bluck!"

"Here she comes; here she comes, let me get my paper outta my book bag so that I can take notes!"

"Whatever Bl…"

"Hi, Devon how are you," asked Paris.

"Huh, oh, hi how are you? Your name is Paris right?"

"That's right, so you've been talking about me huh?"

"No, who that said that?"

"Uh, no one, how'd you know my name then?"

"Uh, you have it hanging on your necklace."

"Oh, so what are your eyes doing down here," said Paris as she pointed to her cleavage.

Paris was only a freshman, but she had a very mature and developed body. Devon was now standing 6'2 and Paris stood at 5'5 and she was star basketball player who was going to start Varsity as a freshman according to her coach. Unlike the other girls on the team who had a tomboy look, Paris was as feminine as a young woman could be. She had long natural brown hair that would easily curl if wet by water. Paris had the perfect proportion for what Devon liked. She had very firm full breast and her butt curved at the perfect angle as it connect to her thick muscular legs. Devon was in awe every time that he'd see her, but he never had the courage to approach her.

"Well first of all, I was looking at how beautiful your eyes were, and those pretty things told me in an instant that if you like these then you need to look further down south!"

"Oh really, did they now?"

"They sure did, and they also told me that they want me to look even closer at them and to make sure that I get your number so that we can meet some time after school!"

"I see you think you're somebody special, don't you Devon?"

"Baby you know what; to think that I'm special means that I'm unsure, but I know that I'll be special if I was with you!"

As Devon wooed Paris with his Chippy like playboy charm, Bluck smiled and shook his head as he walked to class.

"Yo, Devon hit me up at the crib later!"

"Ok Bluck, I'll get with you!"

Devon and Paris began to date, and they began to spend a lot of time together once the football season ended. Even though Paris was only fourteen years of age, she had already had multiple sexual encounters. Although she didn't have the reputation that she got around, word did get to Devon's crew that she liked him and that she would love to take his virginity. One day Ben and Marsha decided to drive to Baltimore, Md in order to spend the weekend at the inner harbor. Devon was two months shy of his sixteenth birthday, and he was sick of being ridiculed by his friends for still being a virgin.

Devon spent the night at Bluck's house and the two stayed up all night putting together a 90 minute music tape of slow jams.

"So, your mom and Ben went to B-More?"

"Yes sir! Yo, hurry up with that tape! Paris is coming through!"

"I knew my boy was about to get it in! I wanna be just like you when I grow up!"

"Whatever Bluck, as the whole posse knows Bluck got all da babes!"

Devon was the same age his mother was when she gave birth to him which was the tender age of fifteen. Paris was fourteen and about to turn fifteen in five months. On a crisp chilly fall evening in York, Pa, Devon and his teenage girlfriend was about to embark on a life changing moment.

"Hey Devon, I didn't think that you were gonna call, are you still at Bluck's house?"

"Yeah but I'm heading out are you ready?"

"Yeah, how long will it take you to get here?"

"Well I'm on my bike so no more than ten minutes. Do you have your bike?"

"Yeah, but I'm not riding it at night because my mom will kill me!"

"Ok, well I'll leave my bike here and walk. Where did you tell your mom that you're going? Is she home?"

"No, she's at work and I told her that I was staying at my friend Megan's house. Megan has my back! Oh and Devon, bring the Jim Hats!"

As Paris ended the phone call Devon slowly pulled the phone away from his ear as he stood mouth agape while Bluck played his Super Nintendo.

"Yo, she just said don't forget the Jimmies!"

"Get da fuck outta here, Paris said that? I heard she let one of the bruhs hit, but I didn't think she got down like that! Ya'll just met! I told you that she was feelin' you!"

"It's Jimmy, it's Jimmy," sang Devon.

"So are you gonna wear won Devon?"

"Hell yeah, why'd you ask that?"

"Because it's your first piece of the pie, how are you gonna get a real taste with a condom on? For my first I put mine on after I got the feel for a few strokes and then I stopped for a little and put it on. That way she didn't get pregnant and I felt good!"

"Damn Bluck, I never thought of it that way. You're a fucking genius my brutha!"

Little did Devon know was the fact that Bluck was giving horrible advice for having sex. What Bluck didn't reveal was that nothing bad went wrong on his first experience, but this was his older brother's advice who used this tactic, and he experienced numerous sexually transmitted diseases. Bluck's older brother was constantly making a visit to the Planned Parenthood Clinic to get help for an array of STDs. Devon left Bluck's house with two condoms in his pocket, and he walked west down King St past his fried Cart's house where he met up with Paris on the corner of King and George St.

"Hey Devon, I missed you!"

"I missed you too. When I walked by that guy over there he asked if I knew who you were and I told him yeah Beauty is her name! Damn girl you are gorgeous!"

"You look pretty handsome yourself Devon. So are you sure that your parents won't be back until Monday?"

"Actually, they'll be home Monday night so we have the rest of tonight and all of tomorrow! What about you, won't your mom wonder where you are?"

"Please, the only thing my mom cares about is that bottle of liquor that I just gave her money for! I just told her that I was staying at my girlfriend's house."

"Well let's do this then," Devon said as he kissed Paris on the lips.

The couple walked about 25 minutes to Devon's house on Linden Ave, and when they arrived he noticed that his Aunt Sarah was coming down a set of wooden steps on the side of the house that creaked loudly as she walked.

"Aunt Sarah, what are you doing here," asked Devon with a surprised scared look on his face.

"No, what are you doing here? I'm here to get some clothes for your sister Destiny. She's staying with me now instead of your Aunt Valerie. Who's this pretty little thang?"

"Oh, forgive me Aunt Sarah, this is Paris. Paris this is my Dad's sister Aunt Sarah."

"It's nice to meet you ma'am."

"You too sweetie, so I take it that you're about to go in here and knock my Nephew's socks off huh?"

"Excuse me," said Paris shockingly.

"Ya'll act like I ain't never been young! Devon's Mom and Ben are gone and here you two come at 9 O'clock at night strolling to the crib! Don't act like you're going to pop some popcorn and watch a VCR movie!"

"Well that's what Devon said we were going to do."

"Well he lied! Marsha doesn't even have a VCR up in that house! That's why I ain't staying here to babysit! Shit baby girl, this is my brother's child, ya'll don't have to lie to kick it!"

"Come on Aunt Sarah," said Devon with an embarrassed look on his face.

"Look ya'll be safe, and you better strap that Jim Hat on cause this fine lil thang looks like she's about to put that whip appeal on you!"

"Aunt Sarah you will never cease to amaze me!"

"I keeps it real Nephew, you know that!"

Sarah drove off in her new Chrysler convertible as Devon and Paris walked up the noisy wooden steps. When they got inside the house Sarah went to the restroom to freshen up, and Devon went into the kitchen to look for something to eat. Devon then reached in his pocket and threw in the cassette tape that Bluck made for him into the cassette player. Ben had a brand new sound system that had clarity and speakers with bass that would rock the entire neighborhood! As soon as Devon pressed play, a slow soothing bass track played as the sound of R&B artist Keith Sweat blared out "You may be young but you're ready, (ready to learn). You're not a little girl, you're a woman (take my hand)."

As the music blasted throughout the house, the young teenage Paris came into the living room and locked eyes with Devon as he extended his hand gesturing for her to slow dance with him. As Paris placed her head with her long silky brown hair on Devon's chest, he inhaled a deep breath as the aroma from her perfume mesmerized him. Devon's heart raced like never before and he felt like he was floating in mid-air. As the music continued to play, the lyrics marinated into both of their ears and the young couple truly believed that even though they were young that they were definitely ready.

A month and a half passed and Devon was running late for school. He started sprinting because he knew that if he was late another time than he would be issued Saturday detention at York High. As he got closer to the school he saw Paris 30ft ahead of him.

"Paris, wait up," he said as he tried to catch his breath.

"Devon, I'm late," said Paris with a worried look on her face.

"No, we still have 8 minutes. We have time to go to the cafeteria real quick. Do you want some fruit or something?"

"No Devon, I'm late," exclaimed Paris as tears began to flow down her face.

"You're late, late?"

"Yes Devon, and I am so scared! I don't know what to do!"

"Come here, come here, calm down, I got you, calm down."

"I can't believe this Devon! I'm pregnant! What am I going to do?"

"Are you sure? Maybe it's just stress or something. I learned in health class that sometimes that causes late periods."

"It's been almost two months! I just came from the clinic and the test was positive!"

"Oh shit," said Devon as his bear hug became an immediate release.

"What do you mean oh shit? What are we going to do?"

"I don't know Paris, I guess I gotta get a job and take care of it! I don't know! We gotta tell our parents!"

"My mom will kill me Devon, I can't do that!"

"Well, I love you Paris so maybe in two years we'll get married and raise our child."

"Devon, don't talk stupid!"

"Huh, what do you mean by that? What, are you saying that you don't love me?"

"Yeah but…"

"What the fuck do you mean yeah but? Ain't no yeah but!"

"Calm down Devon, please calm down!"

"Fuck that! This is some bullshit! My God why me? What did I do to deserve this? Why in the fuck did this have to happen to me?!"

The young couple knew that they had to tell their parents about their mistake, but they were not prepared for the emotional distress which lied ahead. The adolescent couple believed with all of their heart that they had mutual love for one another, but they really didn't know what love was according to most of the comments that their parents made during their courtship. This was Devon's first sexual experience so his feelings for the young girl were more elevated than hers were towards him. Devon's life had come to a sudden halt and time was not on his side. He felt in his heart that he could "man up" and except the responsibility of parenthood, but the question that still loomed in the juvenile couple's mind was "What are we going to do?"

Devon would stress daily as he went to school each day as he contemplated telling his mother while trying to deal with everyday life as a teenager. One of the common things that the students in his high school were notorious for was "cutting" or simply making jokes at the expense of others misery. Even though this was very common in York, Pa, and Devon had experienced this kind of behavior his entire life, it still remained his biggest pet peeve because kids took it too far. Although no one knew about his current teenage pregnancy situation, Devon carried this burden on his shoulders every day; therefore he was very sensitive and self-conscious about any and everything. The slightest comment about anyone's adversity would cause him to explode like a volcano.

"Ok, class put your notes away and take out your number two pencils," said Devon's English teacher who was a short middle aged Caucasian woman with a blonde short cut hairstyle.

"Today's test will be a test about expression. There is no way to fail this test unless you decide not to express yourself at all."

"Well 'Teach' I choose to express myself by not expressing myself on this test that you handed out," belted out one of Devon's classmates a chubby Hispanic teen boy that already had noticeable facial hair.

"Nice try, but if you don't express anything on that paper then you will get an F," said the teacher as she smiled from ear to ear.

"His big behind needs to express himself by buying a razor to shave that wool off of his face," said a heavy set African-American student that was known to constantly "cut" on people.

"Aw, so you cuttin' huh? I'll blow you, with your pimple face, go ahead Bumplestilskin," snapped back the Hispanic boy.

"Boo, that was weak. Yo' mama so fat that I took a picture of her last Christmas and it's still printing," said the heavy set African-American boy.

"Hey! That's enough, both of you shut your mouths or else that's gonna be Saturday detention for the two of you," scolded the Teacher.

"Thank you, some of us are trying to graduate you know," said sneeringly by one of Devon's female neighborhood friends nicknamed Moosh.

"Shut up Moosh with yo nappy head," said the heavy set African-American kid.

"No, why don't you shut up; you heard what the teacher said," demanded Devon as he stood up because he saw that Moosh was upset and about to "go off".

"I said enough! All of you, Devon sit down! And as for you go to the office," yelled the teacher as she pointed to the door demanding the heavy set African-American to leave.

"What about him, he tried to get in my face!"

"Go! And not another word!"

As the heavy set African-American kid slowly walked out of the door, he subtly pointed at Devon and said only what a lip reader could read which was "I'm gonna fuck you up after school!" Devon calmly shrugged his shoulders, and he held out his hands while he tilted his head to the left and raised his eyebrows and said to himself, "I dare you!" After class Moosh approached Devon and asked,

"Hey, are you ok?"

"Huh, oh I ain't sweatin' that guy. He ain't tryin' to do nothing," said Devon.

"Well I'm not talking about that Devon; you've been to yourself lately and that was out character for you to stand up and yell like that."

"Nah, Moosh I'm good. I just didn't like how he tried to talk to you that's all."

"Alright, If you so Devon, you know your girl's got your back!"

"I know Moosh, I'm good," Devon said with a halfhearted smile.

Ordinarily, Devon would speak what was on his mind, or if deemed necessary he would take it to another level by getting into a physical confrontation. Now Devon held it all in. Inside he desperately wanted to open up to Moosh, but the constant thought of what people would say and how they would look at him began to loom in his head. His whole well-being was in disarray, and the beast within had stood its ground. Devon felt like he had no one to turn to because he thought that if he talked to one of his friends than they would view him differently, and he couldn't go to his mother whom he was so close to because he felt like she was literally being taken out of his life. Chippy had his own problems with his womanizing and besides that he had too many kids to deal with.

Besides the fact that he felt Chippy didn't have time for him, Devon's main reason was the fact that he didn't want to hear his father continuously encourage him to have kids. Chippy would always stress that if he was able to have kids young then so could Devon. Chippy was not bashful when it came to letting Devon and his siblings know that he wanted to be a Grandfather. Even though Devon was Chippy's first born, he wasn't feeling that his status had much clout. Eventually he tried to discuss his problem with his dad but Chippy's whole philosophy seemed to be, "go on and make me some grandchildren!" Regardless of whether this type of parenting goes against the norm, this was the way it was and the way it has always been for Devon. One may opinionate that Chippy was an ignorant father, but Devon just took what he said and let it go in one ear and out the other when it came to him pushing for grandchildren. Devon really needed someone to turn to because the stress was becoming too much to bear, and he completely felt lost. He felt like he was out of touch with his mother, and his father simply just didn't make sense to him when it came to the topic of having kids.

In spite of feeling a sense of loneliness Devon's only way of coping was to consult D.F. and his mother Jacqueline. Jacqueline often shared wisdom as D.F. enlightened the quandary with his impeccable humor. The two would often combine like peanut butter and jelly as they uplifted Devon's spirit, but Devon didn't see them every day therefore their brief counseling just wasn't enough.

Although Devon was able to keep his sanity with the help of his friends, time was passing by and his girlfriend was ending her first trimester of pregnancy. He had decided that he wanted to have the baby, but regardless of what he thought this was not his final decision.

"Paris I have a job at McDonald's! We'll be ok, I'll take care of my responsibility."

"Devon are you serious? You're smarter than that; I know you believe that you will be able to take care of a baby working at McDonald's. What about college Devon? We are too young for this!"

"So what are you saying Paris? Do you want to get rid of it?"

"Devon I don't know what I want. I'm going to tell my mom. I think that she suspects something because she keeps asking how am I getting so fat."

"Well at first I thought that we should get the abortion, but now I want to have the baby. I want to be a father!"

"I don't know Devon. I'll let you know what I decide."

"You mean what we decide right?"

"It's my decision Devon, and you need to respect that."

Ultimately it was the young ladies decision, but Devon didn't want to agree with Paris and her logic. Devon finally decided to tell his mother since Paris was going to break the news to her mom. He knew that Marsha would go ballistic, but he had no other route to go. One day Devon met with his girlfriend at the park bench outside of his high school.

"Hey, how's it going," asked Devon.

"Fine I guess," said Paris as she brushed away dry bird poop before she sat on a green wooden bench.

"Did you tell your mom yet Paris? I think that we should keep the baby, I can work at McDonald's, and I still plan on going to college.

"Yes, I told my mom and she was not happy at all."

"Yeah I told my mom and she was beyond pissed."

"I know, her and my mom already talked!"

"What, when did this happen?"

"Just the other day, your mom came to my house."

"Well I told her that I wanted to keep the baby. Did she tell you that?"

"Devon I already got rid of them," Paris said as tears gushed from her eyes.

"How could you Paris? Why didn't you talk to me first! We could have made this work!"

"My mom forced me to! She said either get the abortion or get out of her house!"

Devon was stunned by the news that he heard from Paris and as he watched her cry he stopped and thought about what he just heard.

"Wait a minute, did you say them? What do you mean them?"

"Yes, Devon we had twins," Paris said loudly as tears and mucous poured out of her eyes and nose.

"You've got to be fucking kidding me, we had twins and you killed them?"

"Honest Devon I didn't want to, but my mother made me! How could you put it so harsh?! Before you said that you didn't think that we were ready and now you're acting like you really wanted to be a man? You then have the audacity to say that I killed them? What kind of monster are you Devon?"

At that precise moment Devon could nothing. His body went numb as he sat and stared into space while replaying his whole situation over and over in his head. He turned to Paris and as tears poured out of his eyes he said,

"I am so sorry, please forgive me."

Recognizing the Beast

After all that we've been through, I bet you still don't know who I am.
I'm like a wolf in sheep's clothing, and you're my prey little lamb.
You've been on this journey for so long,
and you probably still don't know where to begin.
It's not rocket science figuring out how to escape the beast within.
I am a universal conscious that's like a black widow,
and you're a fly waiting to be caught.
I masterfully manipulate your environment to disrupt your thought.
Unless you're blinded by my shield of Ignorance I am not hard to see.
Like money I'm the root of your destruction, and only education defeats me.
So now that you recognize, if we fought each other would you win?
My Ignorance is power. Good luck escaping the beast within.

David V.M. Kennedy

Shortly after the young bewildered couple's predicament, Devon turned sixteen years old and even though the adolescent pair's parents were against them having a serious relationship, they knew that the two would continue to see each other; therefore Paris began to use contraceptives. The traumatic experience brought the young couple closer together and Devon felt that he was more in love than ever before. He would often boast that he and Paris would get married when Paris turned 18, and no one could tell him any different. Devon would become furious when his stepfather Ben would laugh and say,

"I guarantee you that you guys won't get married!"

Although these types of comments seemed harmless, and even though it didn't appear to affect Devon, they did infuriate him, and he would often bottle up his anger inside. Football season was about to begin again, and Devon had to take a physical exam before he could play. The season prior, Devon was the only sophomore in his class to be awarded a varsity letter as he helped lead his team to an undefeated championship. Even though Chippy never went to any of his games, he did support Devon's dream to play college football. One summer he actually financed a trip for Devon to go to an invitational only football camp. Marsha and Ben were unable to take off work to drive Devon to the camp so Chippy volunteered to take him. Regardless how much Chippy knew about football, Devon saw this as a perfect opportunity to spend quality time alone with his father.

"Devon bring your bags down and put them in the trunk. I'm gonna drop you off at Paula's to see your brothers and sister before we leave."

"Ok, but why are you dropping me off?"

"I gotta run somewhere real quick. Here take this money to get some snacks and meet me at Sister Jane's in thirty minutes."

"Ok, I guess I'll see you in a few."

Devon briefly visited his family, and did as he was told. Just as he was walking out of the store with a brown bag full of snacks, Chippy pulled up in his Challenger with Grace the mother of one of Devon's sisters in the passenger seat.

"What's going on Dad? We gotta hit the road. I have to check in and you know that it takes six hours to get there! Where do you have to take her?"

"I know that Slick, and that's why we're leaving now get in she's going with us."

"Are you serious? You're taking her? I thought that it was just gonna be you and me like the good ol' days!"

"Aw man, you're getting too big for that anyway, quit getting all sensitive and mushy on me and get in the got damn car!"

Chippy drove six hours to upstate New York while Devon sat cramped up in the back seat of the Dodge Challenger. Devon appreciated what his father was doing for him by paying for the trip because he knew that the trip was very expensive for his family and he actually couldn't believe that his father had done this for him. Chippy knew how much football had meant to Devon, but the one thing that he failed to realize was that Devon wanted his presence at the games even more!

In spite of never attending the games, Chippy collected every article that he could about Devon, and he even recorded one of the radio broadcasts of the championship game. Devon was going into the season projected to be one of the best quarterbacks in the history of the school and Chippy recognized that and decided to sacrifice a few things to get him to the camp. As they drove along the highway Devon said,

"Dad, can you pull over soon? I have to go to the bathroom."

"Ok Slick, Mahogany do you have to use the restroom?"

"No Chippy I'm ok."

"Devon you need to hold it man, I wanna make up some time."

"What do you mean? I need to go now!"

"I mean just what I said, you need to hold it!"

"Oh, so if she would have said that she had to go then I guess we'd stop huh?"

"You better mind your tone boy!"

"Man, I don't wanna hear that shit!"

"What did you say to me," yelled Chippy as his foot pressed harder on the gas pedal.

"I didn't say anything!"

"Yeah, that's what I thought you said. Don't get knocked out! I'll embarrass your little ass!"

Devon sat in the back seat and pouted to himself for the rest of the trip as he gave Grace the "evil eye" every chance that he got. After a long silent ride that seemed like an eternity to get to, Devon's anger turned into smiles once he arrived on Syracuse University's campus! He was so excited that he actually hugged Grace when she and his father dropped him off and said their goodbyes. Chippy told Devon that he would return at the end of the week and wished him good luck.

One week later Devon packed his bags for his return trip home and he was ecstatic that he one a trophy during a quarterback competition and he couldn't wait to share the news with his Dad. As he stood in front of building where the campers checked out, Chippy pulled up just in time. Chippy got out of the car and walked over to grab Devon's bags as Devon said,

"Dad, check this out! I won camp MVP baby!"

"Yeah that's nice hurry up and get in the car," Chippy said angrily.

Devon was about to ask what was wrong until he noticed that Paula was sitting in the front seat! Even though Grace drove up to New York, it was now going to be Paula who was riding back with them to York, Pa. Devon said to himself,

"Oh my fuckin' goodness! They're gonna argue the whole way home, I bet you!"

Although Devon was no prospective candidate for the psychic hotlines, he was like a prophet predicting how Paula and Chippy would carry on.

"Bitch, what the fuck is your problem Paula?"

"I ain't know bitch ya hairy greasy looking grizzly faced mother fucker! A bitch is who you drove up here with the first time! Didn't he Devon? Didn't he bring that little dark skinned bitch up here with him?!"

"Devon don't sweat her, and keep my fucking son outta this shit woman!"

"Fuck you Chippy!"

"Fuck you back Paula!"

The two argued the entire drive home, and Devon felt miserable for the entire trip. He couldn't stop thinking of the fact that this was supposed to be the perfect opportunity for him and his father to catch up on old times and hang out like they used to. After the long drive Chippy dropped Devon off at home and drove off without even mentioning Devon's experience the entire trip. He didn't even say goodbye as he handed Devon his bags. Devon slowly walked up the noisy wooden steps of his apartment house to an empty living room with no one at home. Ben and Marsha had taken Destiny to an amusement park so Devon went straight to the bathroom to take a shower. As the steamy hot but bearable water streamed down the back of his neck, Devon tried to massage his shoulders one at a time to loosen the tension that he was feeling. No matter how hard he tried, he just couldn't stop thinking about the trip that he took with his father and two women. After showering Devon got on his knees and said his prayers and he asked God to forgive and bless him. The next morning he was scheduled to go to the school to get a physical for football, and as he stared at his MVP trophy that sat on his burgundy wooden dresser, he laid on his back with his hands in his head while tears rolled down the sides of his cheeks.

Instead of feeling sorry about himself about his recent road trip, the next day Devon went for his physical exam at the school. When he arrived to the training room there was a school nurse wearing super tight tan pants with a green sweater holding a clipboard. She took his height and weight and told him that she needed to take his blood pressure too.

"Are you Devon," asked the school nurse.

"Yes ma'am, hi how are you?"

"Well aren't you a gentleman, I'm fine thank you. Ok, roll up your sleeve for me."

"Huh, you mean to tell me that I have to get a shot," asked Devon fearfully.

"No silly, I need to take your blood pressure!"

"Oh, good cause I don't do needles!"

"You play football and you're afraid of needles? Aren't you the star quarterback? I've seen you play!"

"Star, the only stars that I know about are in the sky," laughed Devon.

"Well then you must have just fallen because like I said I've seen you play and you my friend are a star!"

"Well thank you nurse uh, what's your name, does that say Maggie?"

"Yes, it's Maggie."

"I hope I'm not out of line but you are a beautiful woman. You can't be that much older than me, because you look young! How old are you?"

"Didn't you mother ever teach you not to ask a woman her age?"

"Yeah, and didn't your father ever teach you that age ain't nothing but a number?"

"What's that supposed to mean superstar?"

"Oh, so now I'm a superstar huh? We've been talking for only five minutes and I've already elevated my status! Imagine if I took you out and spent more time with you!"

"Boy please, I'm old enough to be…"

"To be the beautiful mature woman that I need in my life!"

"Oh, so not only are you flirting with me are you finishing my sentences too?"

"First of all, a person who flirts has no intent therefore I am not flirting at all!"

"You are a trip," laughed Maggie.

"Well if I'm a trip then come and enjoy this vacation."

"I'll admit that you almost had me Devon. I'm not trying to lose my job over no sixteen year old boy. And to answer your question I am twenty. I'm doing this job until I go for my bachelor's degree next fall."

"I knew it! Well I'll be seventeen next week so what's up?"

"Are you serious? You are really trying to get at me aren't you?"

"The way that you are looking into my eyes tells me that I succeeded. Come here…"

As the nurse finished pumping the blood pressure device, she leaned over and began kissing Devon softly on the lips as he gently placed his both of his hands around the top her neck with her ears resting between his thumbs and forefingers. As the two passionately kissed Devon slowly slid his right hand down chest and caressed her left breast.

"Whoa, wait, wait, stop Devon. Oh my God I can't believe that I just did that!"

"What is it Maggie? I thought that you were enjoying me."

"Yeah, that just it, I was!"

"So what's the problem?"

"Look let me just check your blood pressure, and I'll deal with you later. Oh my, look at this!" Maggie discovered that Devon's blood pressure was extremely high especially for a sixteen year old young man.

"Did you run here sweetie," asked Nurse Maggie.

"Yeah a little bit, but I'm sure that's not what has my pressure up beautiful," said Devon.

"No Devon, this is serious! We're going to have to get you checked out! Take about 5 minutes to relax, and then I'll check this again."

"So, it's that high huh?"

"Yes Devon, it is. Just relax hun."

Devon drank some water and waited awhile before he was checked again, and as he sat on a black wooden stool he lustfully stared at Maggie's legs and butt. Her pants fit so perfect on her defined figure as if the legendary Picasso took the time to paint them on her body. In the back of his mind he thought about Paris and how perfect it would be to have her face on Maggie's body. His fantasy came to an immediate standstill when he noticed a pamphlet to his right next to a plastic bucket of cotton swabs. The pamphlet's title read "Are You Safe With Your Sex?"

Instantaneously, Devon was reminded about he almost threw his life away and that he was the reason that two innocent lives never had the chance to come into this world. His stomach knotted up to the point where he had to stand up and take a deep breath.

"Are you ok," asked Maggie.

"Yeah, can we get this over with? I gotta get outta here."

"Yes I agree. Things feel a little awkward for me too. Give me your arm."

Maggie took his blood pressure again, and after settling down he still had the same results. The young nurse explained that the school would now monitor him for high blood pressure, and that he needed to see his primary care physician. Surprisingly Devon wasn't even alarmed by the news, because he had been feeling it in his stomach every single day. Devon had a lot on his mind. Unlike in the past when he would easily express himself, Devon now would keep his negative energy encased in the pit of his stomach. He had only one sanctuary for his sanity and that was the sport of football. Devon felt that football was his only means for keeping his rationality. He truly loved the game more than life itself. He thrived off of the crowd chanting his name. His ego flourished every time that saw his name appear in the newspaper. Football was his world. It was his everything. It was his addiction!

Although Devon's passion for football was extremely elevated, his love for Paris was also high. In spite of Devon's passion for football, the coming out party for his "football prowess" wasn't going as planned. Although Devon had the skill set to be a dominant quarterback, he played in a system that didn't allow his talents to prosper. Each game Devon really struggled and he just wasn't the same player as the year before.

"Devon, where were you? I tried to catch you after the game but those reporters were swarming you," exclaimed Paris.

"Hey Paris, yeah babe they were pretty tough on me. I stunk it up! I feel so restricted out there on the field! I don't know what Coach is doing and the more that I suggest the more he does the opposite! Reporters are saying that I suck; these bums at school keep saying that I suck, and now I'm starting to think that I'm not that good anymore! Maybe they're right. Maybe we won because of the talent that I had around me! This is some bullshit!"

As Devon punched a small dent into the top of his orange metal locker in the hallway next to his homeroom, Paris jumped out of fear because of the aggression that he displayed. Devon was beginning to crumble under the pressures of being a typical teenager as well as trying to maintain the tradition of football greatness at his high school. On top of the peer pressure was the fact that he and Marsha hadn't been seeing eye to eye, and Chippy was too caught up into chasing his "baby mamas" and his kids. Devon had suppressed the beast within him for so long that one day he just couldn't take it anymore.

Fighter

It's so hard to fight especially when you're up against a fighter.
By now you should've figured me out. I'm that burn in your soul,
I am the igniter.
It's no secret anymore. I am a Beast, and I represent so much.
As you bob and weave I merely laugh, because you're easy to touch.
Can't you see that I'm Ignorance? Are you truly that blind?
There's only one way to Escape me. You must elevate your mind!

David V.M. Kennedy

One day Devon was hanging out in Penn Park after school with Bluck and some of his friends, and out of nowhere a big kid named Phil approached him. Phil was what most would call a "man child!" He had a thick mustache and compared to Devon he had the physique of a grown man who had been lifting weights for years! A small group of teenaged boys and girls followed Phil as he approached Devon and Bluck, and Bluck said to Devon,

"Yo, what's up with this? Watch your back!"

"Who is that Bluck? Oh, I think that's Paris's cousin and his crew. Yo, he looks pissed. I wonder who he's coming after."

"Shit it ain't me," said Bluck.

"Well it ain't me. It must be them cats over there on the court!"

"Yo, I don't know Devon; it looks like he's coming our way! Damn, man what did you do now," laughed Bluck.

"Aw, Damn, man, I think you're right he is coming this way! Man, didn't do shit! Just watch my back yo."

"I got you D. You know how we roll!"

As Phil came within 30ft of Devon he yelled,

"Your ass is mine!"

"Yo, I don't even know what you're talking about! I don't even know you like that," exclaimed Devon.

"Well you're about to know my fucking fist," said Phil as he swung a haymaker at Devon's face.

"Yo, what the fuck? How you just gonna swing at me like that? Bruh, chill, I didn't do anything to you!"

"I heard what you said, you faggot," scolded Phil as he swung and missed again.

"Look man, I'm gonna say this one more time. I don't know what you're talking about and you better chill! I already let you swing on me twice! Ain't gonna be no third!"

Devon had no clue as to why this kid approached him in this manner. Phil refused to heed Devon's warning. Phil threw another wild left hook, and Devon bobbed and weaved like the champion boxer he idolized his entire life! Devon retaliated by ducking under the punch as he followed up with a vicious uppercut! Blood began to fill in Phil's mouth as his entourage heckled him as he spit the blood out. Phil's pride was on the line as he unsuccessfully tried to swing at Devon's face. Devon connected with a crushing body blow to Phil's kidney area, and then capped it off with a monstrous right hook to Phil's jaw!

As a crowd of people swarmed around the two brawlers, Phil dropped to the ground and clutched his side while he moaned in agony.

"Stomp dat ass Devon," yelled one of the smaller teens in the crowd.

"Fuck that Devon, chill," commanded Bluck.

In spite of the uproar from a crowd of about forty teens, Devon ceased his attack at the sound of his best friend's words. During the fight Devon's conscious seemed to get the best of him anyway, because he had no reason to fight the kid. He began to feel sorry for Phil, because he was really no match for him.

"Look, man I don't want to fight you," said Devon as he dropped his hands and stepped back away from standing over him.

"Fuck you! The sun was in my face! I'm gonna kick your ass," said Phil as he stumbled trying to get up.

Phil tried to sucker punch Devon as he stood up and Devon continued to dodge his punches with ease.

"Look man, just give up! I don't wanna hurt you anymore," pleaded Devon.

The kid refused to quit and he just kept coming forward. Even though Devon previously felt sorry for the kid, he began to get annoyed and he wanted to stop the fight without hurting Phil. After multiple pleas and warnings to Phil, Devon had enough of not only his persistence but even more of the crowds heckling. Phil's foolish will power drove him to advance slowly but deliberately at Devon again; and instead of swinging at Phil, he spit a ball full of snot directly between his eyes!

"Now I told you to chill the fuck out! If you swing again then I'm really gonna fuck you up!"

"Oh, he punked you Phil, he punked you," said multiple chants from the crowd.

Phil wiped his face which had an embarrassing look on it, and fearfully looked into Devon's eyes. At that moment he knew that he was out matched, but more importantly he saw a look on Devon's face that he had never witnessed before. It was as if the Beast itself had transformed into physical form! Phil turned and walked away as the crowd dispersed, and Bluck walked over to Devon and said,

"You ok bruh?"

"Yeah man, let's get outta here. I knew we shouldn't have come to Penn Park. These south side cats always wanna start trouble. I have no clue what that shit about!"

Devon later discovered that Phil had heard a rumor which was untrue. Phil heard that Devon had been bad mouthing him behind his back. This type of problem was a common ground for the students in this York High School. It seemed that they had nothing better to do with themselves but to start rumors that would eventually cause drama. For every single student that had a positive achievement going on for them, seemed to be one hundred students assigned to bringing that particular person down! This "crab in the barrel" mentality was as if it was Three Mile Island having a meltdown that leaked a poisonous gas of ignorance throughout the city.

Even though Phil later found out that the rumor said was untrue, his apology to Devon was null and void because even though school was out the fight took place in the school zone. The two of them got suspended ten days from school, and instantly they became the center of attention for ridicule amongst their peers! Nobody at York High cared how Phil or Devon felt. The only thing that they worried about was what the next hot topic to discuss. If words were like fresh paint, then the halls of the school the size of a York City block would be decorated in "Guess what I heard?"

Vicious Cycle

Why is it that I can do no right when you can do so wrong?
This Vicious Cycle needs to stop; it's been going on way too long!
I've recognized your existence, so now what am I going to do?
Well my mind is not enslaved like others; therefore I foresee major complications for you!
You are a Beast, but like a ringmaster I'm unprovoked and here to tame.
As you pursue your conflicting interest, I'll establish and elevate my mental as I put your ignorance to shame!

David V.M. Kennedy

Even though Devon did no wrong by defending himself, he now had to face the wrath of his mother! Naturally, he knew that his mom would be furious about the events that took place. Devon walked towards the west end of town over a bridge that crossed a creek named Codorus Creek on Princess St, and all he could think about was how his mother was going to react. He thought to himself,

"She won't trip, because she always taught me to defend myself. She always said that if anyone gets crazy then I need to get crazier! It's all good, and besides she doesn't get home until after 7 O'clock this evening. Yeah, I'm good. My mom will understand!"

As Devon continued his walk towards his home, he noticed that his mother's car was parked outside of his home. His brisk walk turned into a snail's pace. Devon swallowed the saliva in his mouth and took a deep breath as he quickly tried to think how to approach his mother. Devon walked up the noisy wooden steps on the side of the large row home that led to his apartment. As he opened the door Marsha was standing in the living room waiting with her arms crossed. She was still in her all black work attire and the high heels brought her height a little closer to Devon.

"What the heck is your problem boy?! You just can't seem to stop getting into fights," Marsha yelled.

"I didn't do anything wrong! He just came at me, what was I supposed to do, just let him hit me," argued Devon.

"You know what Devon, I am sick of your same excuse! Someone is always coming at you! So I guess you gotta big bulls eye on your back huh," said Marsha sarcastically.

"Did you ever think about turning the other cheek?"

"Turn the other…What the heck am I supposed to do when someone swings on me?! First you used to complain that I was too soft! Stop being scared! Stand up for yourself! You're the one who threw me off the porch in the projects to fight Spoon! I hate this place! I hate York! All of my life I've been picked on and I'm sick of it!"

"You better change your tone of voice before I smack the black off your lip!"

"This is bull mom! I can't walk two steps without someone saying something ignorant! When I get good grades then I'm a nerd! When I win football games then I'm not that good and I really suck! I can't go to my Dad's house, because all they do over there is talk trash! You act like you don't have time to deal with me because you're tied up with Destiny and Ben, I hate this place! I didn't ask to be born! I hate this fucking place!"

"Go to your room," demanded Marsha.

As Devon stormed to his room furious at his mother for misunderstanding, he experienced a rage so intense that it caused the young man to start to cry. Due to the old age philosophy embedded in his head that men aren't supposed to cry, Devon tried to hold back each pulsating emotion. He began to pace his bedroom while he shook with fury looking for something that he could hit without gaining the attention of his mother. Punching the pillow just wasn't enough. It was as if Devon was possessed. He needed to destroy something but he couldn't, therefore all of that craze built up inside had to remain!

Even though Devon seemed obsessed with fury because of his mother's reaction, he was really angry at her for being hypocritical. His entire life he was taught to defend himself, and now that he got put on suspension he was being punished. Devon felt like a yo-yo,

"You drop me, than you pick me up, you drop me, than you pick me up! This is bullshit" he said out loud.

"I didn't ask for this shit! Don't nobody give a fuck about me! I should just take this belt and hang my fucking self! Ugh, why me? Why me God? Fuck that, there ain't a fucking God! God won't make me go through this shit!"

"Ugh, hey Bucky Beaver," he reminisced as he played the taunts of his peers in his head.

"Hey geek, look at the nerdy dork! Look at his teeth! Look at his glasses! His mom thinks she's all that! His Dad has 50 million kids to 50 million women! Devon's a bum! I should just jump out of this fucking window! I should cut my fucking wrist!"

The Lord's Prayer

Our Father, who art in heaven, hallowed be thy name.
Thy kingdom come, thy will be done, on earth as it is in heaven.
Give us this day, our daily bread and forgive us our trespasses as we forgive those who trespass against us.
Lead us not into temptation, but deliver us from evil, for thine is the kingdom, the power and the glory, forever and ever."

In Jesus name

Amen

Devon prayed and asked God for forgiveness, and he eventually calmed down as he cried himself to sleep like a little baby. There is an old cliché that says "time heals all wounds"; therefore if the wound is too deep than there will be a considerable amount of time before it will heal. If a wound is never treated then infection is sure to run its course. After Devon's suspension expired he got ready for his first day back at school. He gently caressed his eyebrow as he stared in the bathroom mirror at the scar above his right eye as he briefly reminisced about his childhood incident...

Contrary to his physical wound that once healed over a short course of time, Devon was unaware of how to treat the injury that he now shared with so many others. "Time heals all wounds". The question is will there be enough time to heal the emotional injury sustained to Devon's ego? After prayer Devon didn't dwell over the argument with his mother and he moved on, but he was about to encounter a blow to his heart so devastating that it would change his life forever.

Devon quickly brushed his teeth returned to school excited that his ten days were up but in order to go back to class he had to get counseling from the assistant principal. As Devon anxiously sat waiting in the principal's office to be seen, he noticed out of the corner of his eye his girlfriend Paris entering the office. Paris made eye contact with Devon and her eyes grew so big that is was as if she had seen Satan himself in front of her! Devon stood up and began to approach her but she tried to act as if she didn't notice him and she started to leave the office.

"Paris!" Devon firmly called.

Paris's natural reaction was to turn her head, and as she did Devon noticed that her neck was covered with red marks on it. The students referred to them as "hickeys or suck marks". Devon had been on punishment for ten days and there was no way possible for him to have done it!

"Oh, ok, it's like that huh," Devon said calmly.

Paris just looked at him with no verbal response, and she scurried out of the office and headed back to class. Inside Devon was boiling like a pot of water on a stove in preparation for hard boiled eggs!

Although Devon was visibly upset, he had to get his anger under control before he went into the assistant principal's office. After his counseling he went to his first class, and as he walked the halls he noticed snickering by some students walking behind him.

"Yo, that's him, Richard Hagman took his girl," said one of the girls in the group.

"I know right, he is so stupid," said another girl loudly as they laughed.

"Excuse me, but do you ladies have something that you wanna say to me to my face?"

"Don't try to play hard with us, Mr. I can't please my woman," snapped the young African- American teen girl.

"Whatever chicken head, you don't know shit about me!"

"Who are you callin' a chicken head? I know you ain't talkin' to me! I'll get my cousin to kick your ass!"

"Whatever, I don't have time for your ignorance," said Devon as he turned down another hall.

"Yeah that's what I thought! You know my cousin will beat dat ass!"

Devon knew how the peers at his school operated. Certain students with low self-esteem would go to great lengths to stir up controversy. As he approached his locker he surprisingly noticed the kid Richard Hagman standing there waiting there for him! Devon was now 6ft tall weighing 150lbs. Richard was about 5ft7 and noticeably smaller than him, and yet he stood in front of Devon's locker smiling, and he said,

"What's up cookie?"

"I'm trying to get to my locker, that's what's up!"

"Well how about I'll just take your locker like I did your bitch?"

Devon looked Richard in the eye and peacefully said,

"Look man, she's all yours I don't want anything to do with her; I've got no beef with you. Now could you please step aside so that I can get into my locker?"

Richard barely moved and Devon opened his locker as Richard stood beside him staring menacingly. As Devon closed his locker and walked to class a teen from Richard's crew belted out,

"Yo, he's a punk! He's scared of you Richard!"

Obviously, Richard mistook Devon's diplomacy for his weakness, because at that moment he yelled at Devon,

"Yo, after school it's on!" Devon ignored the comment because the way he learned was to never fight over a female. As one of his best friends Bluck would say,

"There are plenty more books in the library, all you gotta do is check one out!"

Although Devon heard the subtle threat from Richard, he maintained his composure throughout the day. Students kept harassing him by asking if he was going to fight after school, and he simply replied,

"I'm not fighting over a girl."

As the final bell for the day rang, Devon went outside to meet his friend Mike Dillon whom he walked to school with on a daily basis. Devon's 1st cousin Evan Soriano was on standing on the school steps as he came outside.

"Yo, what up cuz? I see you're off suspension," said Evan.

"Yeah man, that ain't no joke. How's Aunt Nancy doing?"

Before Evan could respond to Devon's question about his mother Nancy he noticed that Richard and a plethora of boys approaching them.

"What's up now punk," Richard said with confidence.

"Yo, I don't know what this is about but ain't nobody gonna jump my cousin," stated Evan.

"Chill cuz I ain't fighting this dude over no broad, come on let's get up outta here."

Devon began to walk home with his friend Mike Dillon who was a pudgy kid who played on the basketball team and Evan as they headed down College Ave towards the west side of York, Pa.

As Devon got around the corner and headed north towards Princess St, he felt a strong push in his back from Richard. Surprisingly to his Evan and his fried Mike, Devon ran!

"Yo, did he just run," asked Mike Dillon.

"Yo, I know my big cousin didn't just do what I thought he did," said Evan.

"Come on man, I know Richard talks a lot of trash but Devon ain't scared of nobody! Let's catch up to him. Yo, Devon wait up!"

As Mike Dillon and Evan chased after Devon, they saw him duck into an alley across the street from the school. Richard followed suit with his entourage of minions behind him. Evan and Mike ran faster to make sure that Devon wouldn't get jumped.

"I told you he was scared," yelled one of Richards buddies.

"Get him Rich," commanded another minion. Richard ran as fast as he could after Devon, but little did he know that Devon was not running because he was afraid, he was just trying to avoid fighting in front of the school! As Richard entered into the alley his Olympic style sprint turned into an immediate halt. It was as if he were a deer caught in headlights on interstate 83 in Pennsylvania! T Devon stood menacingly awaiting like he was a lion ready to pounce on his prey!

"What's up now cookie," yelled Devon.

As soon as Richard got close, Devon swung with a haymaker that was so devastating that it looked as if he spun Richard's entire head around. The punch connected with Richard's eye and he immediately dropped to the ground! Richard's crew was in shock as some of the other school kids went into an uproar. Although he had a group of "tough" guys in his crew, none of Richard's friends dared to jump in the fight because Evan Soriano presence was a reminder that Devon Chance was a Soriano too. He just carried his mother's maiden name. The Soriano were a family not to be reckoned with, and they got their notoriety in the hood for helping to fight for the rights of their people during the riots in York, Pa during the 60s.

Devon's fight with Richard was no match. Once Devon saw that Richard was no challenge he began to feel sorry for him and he stopped the beating and turned to go home. As he walked down a small hill he noticed a young girl behind him yelling,

"I'm telling Slink! It's over for you!"

Slink was a high school dropout who was about 20 yrs. old, and for some peculiar reason he would always hang out in Penn Park right after school when the kids let out. One day Slink decided to form somewhat of a "gang", and it was amusingly obvious that he was copy catting one of the popular movies that was showing at the time. Richard was a prominent figure of Slink's "gang", and word got back to Slink about what happened between him and Devon. Even though Richard wasn't the toughest kid in the "hood", his reputation for being a force to be reckoned with was known throughout the city.

In spite of Richard's infamous notoriety, Devon had a reputation of his own that he felt that he needed to protect. The following day Richard returned to school wearing a pair of dark sunglasses. His eye had been closed shut from Devon's punishing blows to his face. Deep inside Devon felt somewhat remorseful about fighting Richard, because he knew that this kid had no chance of beating him. Regardless of how many boxing matches that he watched or brawls that he encountered, he truly did not like to fight. He just knew how. One lingering question that ritually became rhetorical to Devon was, "why do people always want to test me?"

Although Richard learned his lesson and never messed with him again, Devon still wasn't through fighting this teenage battle that was a precursor to an adolescent war. School was about to let out, and Slink had gathered his gang across the street as usual. Roughly one hundred kids gathered in Penn Park, and as Devon came outside he noticed the bunch staring at him. Even though neighborhood kids in York, Pa chastised each other for "jumping" a person during a fight, Devon recognized that he was outnumbered and he didn't want to risk the chance of seriously getting hurt.

"What's up now cookie," yelled Slink who was a tall lanky young man who stood 6'3.

"Yeah, you little bitch, I told you that I was gonna get Slink on your ass," yelled the young girl who previously warned Devon.

"Yo, Devon what's going on, are you good," asked Devon's Cousin Evan as he came outside the school while walking down the front steps.

"Hey, what's up cuz? Yeah I'm good. I guess these cats got beef with me."

"Yeah big Cuz, I saw Richard's eye! Damn Cuz did you have to do him like that," laughed Evan.

"Yo, I'm just tired of these bums testing me lil Cuz. All of this over a broad! I don't even want her like that. What's done is done."

"Well, let's get up outta here big Cuz, because my mom just bought me these sneakers and I ain't trying to get them messed up fighting these clowns!"

"Man you're killin' me lil Cuz! How many pair of kicks you got? You stay having the freshest sneaks!"

"Cuz, I don't know what it is, but these girls seem to sweat me just for that alone! Ain't like I'm gonna let them wear them so I don't know what the deal is! It's just another weapon in my love armory!"

Devon and Evan avoided confrontation as the two headed west down College Ave while Slink and his "gang" gawked at them. The next day at school Devon was called to the office, because school officials became aware of what was transpiring. It was determined by the assistant principal that Devon, Evan, and a few of their friends had to be released 30 minutes early from school for precautionary measures until things died down. Even though Penn Park looked like it was campus grounds of York High, it was a public park; therefore Slink had every right to stand across the street from the school. After his conversation with the assistant principal, Devon was threatened to be placed in the school's S.T.A.R. program for troubled youth because of his constant fighting. Fortunately for him, the director of the program grew up with his mother and knew him very well; therefore it was his idea to have Devon released early from school until the hype died down.

Even though the park across the street was public, the police were called and Slink was no longer allowed to hang out there after the kids got out of school. This infuriated Slink because hanging out in front of the school with a massive entourage made him look like a "godfather" and this was a way for him to get his recruits. One night Devon went to a party at a place called the Elks. Devon met up with some friends and he also noticed that his cousin Evan was there. It was unfortunate but reality for teenagers to rarely have anything to do in the city of York, and parties like this became their sanctuary. Unfortunately for all, there were always

a few "crabs" that ruined it for the rest of the barrel.

As Devon walked to say hi to his cousin, the vinyl record that the D.J. was playing suddenly scratched as the music shut off.

"Yo, what the fuck," yelled the D.J. into his microphone as a loud ear piercing sound blared through the six foot tall speakers.

Chairs and tables began to fly as the party turned into a fight. While Devon headed to a safe spot he scanned the crowd and noticed that it was one of his teammates who were involved. One of Slink's so called "gang members" belted out, "112 bitches!" as the teenage crowd began to disperse. The fight was broken up by the bouncers inside, but the aftermath carried over outside into the parking lot.

D.F. who had been one of a handful of white teens in the party was initially beside Devon, but he had gotten separated during the melee. As Devon made his way through the crowd towards the back door of the building, he turned and noticed D.F. heading out the front.

"Yo D.F. wait up!"

"Yo, I thought that I lost you Devon? Where's your cousin Evan at? I heard some dude talking like he was gonna do something to him!"

"What, who was it? Do you know who it was?"

"Nah, but if I see him then I'll point him out to you!"

"Yo, D.F. find my little cousin, I gotta make sure he's safe!"

Even though Evan was a tough kid, he was only a freshman, and the kid that wanted to fight him was a senior, who was significantly bigger than Evan. D.F. and Devon made their way to the parking lot and as they approached a swarm of teens, Evan stood brave but petrified in front of the senior kid squared up and ready to fight. Devon sprinted through the crowd not caring who he aggressively bumped into and reached out and grabbed Evan's arm and said,

"Yo! Evan, get over here! Don't worry cuz I got this!"

Evan and Devon were always taught to protect their blood at all cost. As Devon stepped in prepared to fight, someone yelled, "5-O!" At that moment the excited mob of kids quickly dispersed and ran down Maple St. heading east towards Penn Park. As Devon arrived in front of a church that had a big clock tower, he ran back into the kid that was about to fight Evan. The senior was standing with some of his "gang members" as Devon noticed that the people that he ran alongside of after the crowd dispersed were not any of his friends or associates.

"So what's up now pussy," said the senior kid as he stood in front of a group of ten.

"So what, I guess ya'll are gonna try to jump me now? What's up with the fair one?"

"Ain't shit fair in fightin', this is 112 bitch!"

The crew was ready to jump Devon when out of nowhere one of Devon's football teammates who was a 6ft5 245 lbs. kid yelled,

"Fuck this shit, anybody that fucks with Devon has got to fight me! How about that?! Ain't gonna be no jumping around here! I dare one of you motherfuckers to jump him! If they're gonna fight than it's going to be one on one!" None of the "gang" accepted the challenge of going against the word of Devon's teammate, and Devon and the kid were surrounded by a crowd as they formed a large circle. The fight occurred as if it was a scene out of a movie. Although there were so many kids, they formed what seemed to be a perfect circle around the two fighters.

Once again Devon found himself going toe to toe with someone for no valid reason. Knowing that he wouldn't be jumped, Devon electrified the crowd with punishing blows to the kids face. As the crowd became awed by Devon's skill, the sound of cop car sirens blared as the crowd dispersed once again. The kids ran by the park down an alley towards George Street. In the mix of the frenzy Devon lost track of D.F.

Even though D.F. was popular amongst his peers, Devon knew that he wasn't a fighter and being one of a few white kids that was at the party didn't help either! D.F. had run ahead of Devon and as he walked down Lafayette Street, two of Slink's "gang members" approached him and punched him in the face while kicking him to the ground.

"Take that cookie! You ain't black you stupid honky!"

D.F. was pretty popular in school from playing football, but mainly because he was so cool and laid back. He pretty much grew up around African American people, and he was easily accepted in the African American community people because he never portrayed an image of "acting black". D.F. was himself. When he talked amongst his peers with slang or "hipness," it wasn't because he was trying to "act black" but because that was his nature. That was who he was! As Devon walked towards Lafayette Street he heard someone yell,

"Yo, they got D.F!"

Even though Devon couldn't pinpoint D.F's location, he heard the alert that his friend was jumped, and he instantly became enraged.

"I'm sick of this shit! Where the fuck is Slink? His ass is mine!"

Devon walked down the middle of S. George Street which was one of the main streets that ran through York, and he noticed that Slink was in his sight.

He had his entire "gang" with him. Devon knew that he was outnumbered but he did have a few of his football teammates that were hanging out on the block. Devon noticed that on one of the stoops was one of his childhood friends along with Bluck's cousin who was about three years older than Devon.

As Slink and his minions started to walk towards Devon, his heart started to pound rapidly as they came closer. Devon saw a brick within reach, but didn't want to make it obvious that he would try to pick it up due to the fact that Slink was closer to it then he was. Just as Slink stood 30ft away, Devon caught eye contact with Bluck's cousin and his old friend. The two sat on their stoop and gave Devon an exemplary nod of their head to let Devon know that it was about to go down!

"So now what punk," yelled Devon?

"Now what, you can't fight me without those little bitches surrounding you? I'm here by myself, so what's up," he said as he threw his hands up.

As Devon approached Slink, he was intercepted by two of Slink's so called henchmen. Before the two henchmen could even get close to him, Bluck's cousin and Devon's childhood friend swarmed on them like they were two giant killer bees protecting their hive. The two swung punch after punch as the other kids on the block began to run towards the fight. Devon had Slink in a position to battle one on one, and to Devon's surprise Slink sidestepped behind the rest of his entourage and ran like a coward. For the first time in his life, Devon was actually afraid to fight, but like Marsha would always preach,

"If someone wants to act crazy towards you, than you better act crazier towards them!"

Slink was much more mature then Devon, which left him dumbfounded as he went home that night laughing to himself about how Slink ran. He just couldn't believe that after all of that trash talk the great Slink ran like a coward.

Even though Marsha had many philosophies about fighting, she didn't condone violence. As a single mother she had to raise her son the best way that she knew how, and most of her teachings were meant for self-defense. Marsha was an exceptional woman and a great mother to Devon, but one flaw that she did have was listening to others and passing judgment on him before hearing his side of the story. As Devon entered into the house that night, Marsha was waiting in the living room with her arms crossed.

"What were you doing fighting on George Street," asked Marsha.

Intrigued by how his mother even knew about what happened Devon replied,

"Huh?'

"Don't play dumb with me boy," she screamed.

"But mom I…"

"Shut up, I don't wanna hear it, go to your room!"

As Devon headed to his room, he slammed the door with all of his might,

"I'm sick of this! You always think it's my fault!"

Like a ninja in the night carrying his sword, Marsha grabbed her broom out of the kitchen and smack!

"Who the hell you think you talking too," Marsha screamed at the top of her lungs. Devon's reflexes caused him to block the blow with his elbow and a knot instantly appeared on is arm as if someone had stuffed a golf ball inside his skin!

"Ow! C'mon Mom, that hurt, I didn't do anything!"

"Just shut your mouth! I am sick of you! I didn't raise you to be no hooligan, and this is gonna stop or else you are grounded until you turn 18! And I mean that!"

"Well I'll just leave now then, how about that!"

Marsha was fed up with Devon's excuses so she told him that if he didn't want to abide by her rules than he could leave. Devon was so upset that he could care less about what his mom had to say. He threw a bunch clothes into an oversized green army laundry bag and stormed out of the door.

As Devon walked down the rickety steps of his apartment, Marsha came out on the balcony as if she wanted to call for him to come back. Devon looked back at his mother with tears flowing while realizing that the encounter with Slink occurred in front of the shop where his mother got her hair done.

"That's how she found out," he thought to himself.

"I hate York!"

Even though Devon wanted desperately to stop in his tracks and do an "about face," his pride wouldn't allow it. He took his belongings to his friend Mike Dillon's home that had lived around the corner from his grandparent's house. Devon and Mike met at a day camp when they were kids at a place called the Lighthouse which had an inner city youth development program.

Devon had developed a strong relationship with Mike and his mother Ms. Lana Dillon. Mike was a High School All-American in basketball, and his mother was a beautiful Creole woman from New Orleans. As Devon approached the Dillon's home on W. King St, he heard the soothing sound of birds chirping from inside.

Instead of setting his oversized bag of clothes on the large wooden front porch so that he could open the screen door, Devon chose to make an attempt to open it with his hands full. As he reached for the black push button handle, the weight of his bag caused it to abruptly roll off his shoulder as it dropped to the porch floor. Simultaneously when the bag hit the ground the white screen door slammed so hard that it made him jump!

"Michael, is that someone at the door," asked Lana as a loud shriek from her blue parakeet sounded off.

"Huh, I didn't hear anything," yelled Michael from upstairs as he sat playing Nintendo.

Devon could hear the sounds of the birds getting louder as the mother and son communicated. He rang the doorbell and Lana screamed,

"Dagnabbit Michael answer the freakin' door!"

"Aw man, can't you get it? I'm about to beat the boss!"

"If you don't get that dang door I'm gonna show you a real boss and beat that butt!"

Devon rang the doorbell one more time and Mike answered the door with a smile. Mike was a light skinned kid who was one year younger than Devon. He was a pudgy sleepy eyed kid who was known to the girls as "Charm One". Devon and the fellas called him "Charm One" because if there was a circumstance where a young lady would bring one of her girlfriends with her to an outing, then he wasn't gonna just charm one! Devon told Mike what transpired between him and his mom asked,

"Do you think your mom will let me stay awhile?"

"What happened?"

"My mom put me out of the house," said Devon.

"She put you out or did you leave?"

"Let's just say both, "suggested Devon as he tried to end the conversation.

"I don't see why not, she's not going to let you be out on the streets," said Mike.

Devon knew in is heart that he could go home anytime he wanted, but he wanted to prove to his mom that he could make it on his own.

Even though Devon was only sixteen years old, he felt like he had all of the answers to his problems. His main objective was that he wanted his mother to understand him better, but he just wasn't educated enough to express his feelings without the two of them clashing personalities. That evening Ms. Lana came home from work that and said,

"Hey Devon, how's it going baby, what are you doing here so late?"

"I moving in," said Devon.

"You're moving in," laughed Ms. Lana as she almost choked on water that she was drinking from a blue plastic cup.

"Well that is if you don't mind. My mom put me out."

"You're mother put you out? Now Devon I don't know your mom that well but from what I do know about her makes that hard for me to believe!"

"Well it's a long story Ms. Lana. Can I please crash here for a while?"

"Ok, it's late we'll discuss what's going on in the morning," chuckled Ms. Lana.

Ms. Lana had the same bedroom eyes as her son, and was by far one of the coolest adults to ever walk the face of the earth. She had a reputation for helping misunderstood teenagers. She would often say,

"I know how tough it is being a teen; my door will always be open." The next morning Devon woke up to the smell of bacon and eggs. As he entered the kitchen Ms. Lana said,

"Ok, baby what's going on?"

"Everything Ms. Lana, you name it from getting Paris pregnant, getting suspended, my grades, football, and I got into a fight last night," confided Devon.

Devon had been talking to Ms. Lana about his problems on a regular basis and she always found a way to shed light on the situation.

"Listen Devon, I told you before that you need to open up and communicate with your mother. Let her know how you feel inside. You've been getting into trouble but at least you're not out here in the streets like some of these other kids. You're not out here smoking and drinking, wait; you don't smoke or drink, do you?"

"No! I don't mess with that poison," exclaimed Devon.

Even though she always seemed to say the right thing, Devon's problems were now becoming overwhelming to him, and he was starting to think that his life wasn't going to get any better.

"I don't know Ms. Lana, I know I'm not perfect, but I should be doing so much better in life. I mean I was a gifted student, and now look at me. I get average grades. My mom always thinks that the trouble that I got in was always my fault. Ever since Ben came, it just hasn't been the same. Sometimes I feel that she doesn't really care about me and that she only deals with me because she has to. You know if I wasn't born, she probably would have made the Olympics. And there's my Dad who treats me as if I'm a big failure or something. He always has something negative to say about how I don't know how to do "manly" things like he does. He always finds a way to talk down on me in front of my little brothers and sisters, and he won't even call me or come see me. I have to go to him first! Sometimes I just wish that I wasn't born," expressed Devon.

Ms. Lana replied, "Listen Devon, God has put you on this earth for a reason. Stop feeling sorry for yourself. Don't for one moment think that you were an accident, and I need you to realize that no one brought into this world is an accident. It is all a part of God's plan. God blessed man with free will so what you do with life is in your control. One thing that you have to realize about any relationship is the fact that the lines of communication must always remain open. Talk to your parents, let them know exactly how you feel, but show them respect while you're expressing yourself. Do you see that door over there?"

Devon looked with admiration and nodded,

"Yes, I see it."

She continued,

"That door represents reality. You take your behind through that door and don't let reality smack you in the face. Take your little narrow butt back home and talk to your mother! Apologize to her and tell her that you love her. Oh, and about that little girlfriend of yours, I know you still care about her, but you have to just let her go. If you truly love something, set it free, and if it comes back to you than it's yours!"

Devon smiled and gave Ms. Lana a hug as her bird gave a loud chirp while he grabbed his army green duffle bag and walked home to talk to his mother. Even though Ms. Lana gave wise words of encouragement, Devon was still a little uncomfortable talking to his mom, but he did apologize for being disrespectful. Devon told his mother that he was going to try his hardest to improve in school, and he made her a promise.

"Mom, I'm sorry for disrespecting you. Will you please forgive me?"

"Listen Devon, first of all, of course I forgive you. I love you son. You just have to understand that I want nothing but the best for you. All of this trouble that you're getting into is sending you down a path to nowhere! You've gotta buckle down Devon."

"I know Mom but it's just that I feel so much pressure. I hate York!"

"What do you mean you hate York Devon?"

"I hate living here! I hate how the people act around here. Everybody talks about everybody, and they never can say anything positive. I never do anything anyone and yet I've been in so many fights! People keep testing me for no reason and I refuse to just walk away because they will never stop!"

"Devon, do you remember when you were little that I said violence begets more violence?"

"Yes Mom I do; and I also remember you throwing me off of the porch when we lived in the projects because I kept running home afraid to fight."

"Well Devon in two more years you will officially be considered an adult, and all of this fighting will be far worse than suspension from school. It will get you locked up! I need you to promise me that you will try to diffuse these types of situations differently!"

So Many Questions

Who can a man turn to when times are really tough?
Who can he lean on when he feels like he's had enough?
What's a man to do when he feels that no one is there?
What's a man to do if he feels that no one would care?
Where can he turn if he feels that he's lost his soul?
Where can he seek help when he feels that he can't achieve his goal?
When was it written that a grown man can't cry?
When was it pronounced that if at first you don't succeed continue to try?
Why is it so hard for a man to accept and admit that he failed?
Why is it so hard to accept that just like a ship his dreams have sailed?
How can you wonder when the answers are all there?
How is it that you don't see that you need God to help you prepare?
Who? What? Where? When? Why? How?
Prayer is the answer to these questions, so get on your knees and bow.

David V.M. Kennedy

Although Devon promised his mother that he was going to amend his ways, the one thing that he couldn't change was his personality. Ignorance is a beast that dwelled in the city of York, Pa, and the seeds of anger and hostility were implanted by this beast within Devon long before he was conceived. Marsha's wish was for her son to stop getting into confrontations, but the reality remained that he had developed a complex about being deemed inferior. Devon hated to hear being told that he couldn't achieve things, and more importantly he despised those who ridiculed him.

In spite of his pact with his mother, Devon returned to school ready to deal with any repercussion from the brawl that occurred on George Street. He had no intentions of fighting, but he was prepared for the backlash that was almost certain to come. Devon noticed that the guy that he fought by the clock tower came to school with a swollen black eye which was worse than what he did to Richard's eye.

Ordinarily, Devon would feel remorseful but this time he felt vindicated. Devon still couldn't fathom the fact that his best friend D.F. had been jumped during that melee, and when he saw the damage to the kid's eye it reminded him of the pain that D.F. felt. As the two crossed paths in the hallway Devon stared directly into his eyes as if he dared him to say a word!

"Ooo! That's the guy that Devon beat up, look at his eye," chuckled a Spanish teen as she laughed with three African-American teen girls.

"Yo, I wonder if they are gonna fight now, let's follow them!"

"Ain't nobody fightin' nobody, why don't ya'll go sit your chicken headed asses down somewhere," snapped Devon.

"Forget you Devon! You ain't cute neither!"

"What da… What da heck being cute got to do with this? Shut yer ass up!"

Devon continued on to class and he overheard the girls still gossiping behind him as one of the girls stated that she knew who punched D.F. the night of the brawls. Devon knew the guy that they were talking about and before he went into class he met with two of his friends and said,

"Yo, what' s good fellas? Yo, I just found out who hit D.F. I'm about to get that bum, you watch!"

"How'd you find out Devon," asked his friend J.J.

"Special thanks to the can't get fresh crew over there!"

"Boy, you're a fool! Yeah if anybody would know then it sure would be one of them!"

Later that evening Devon and his friends were driving around town like they so often did when Chippy would allow Devon to use the car. Lesser attractive cars or "hoopties" were the fad for the teens during this time, and Devon drove what was known around the way as the "Blue Falcon". After Devon and his friends got tired of cruising around they headed for home. As Devon made a turn by Penn Park, he noticed the guy that hit D.F. walking with the same kid he fought at the clock tower. They started heading down an alley behind the church where the clock tower was and Devon stated to his friends,

"Look! That's the guy that jumped D.F! Yo, I'm about to pull the "Blue Falc" over! I'm gonna to get this bum!"

Even though he promised his mother that he wasn't going to get into any trouble, Devon felt that he had to avenge his best friend. He jumped out of the car by himself and briskly walked towards the two boys. He gave a hard stare to the kid that he fought previously, and the young man put his hands as if to say, "I ain't in this".

"Yo, why you gotta jump my boy," Devon asked the other kid.

"What you talkin' bout cookie? Ain't nobody jumped nobody!"

"Yo, who you callin' a cookie? You tryin' to be hard?"

"Ain't nobody tryin' to be hard. You the one rollin' up on me! You don't know me; I ain't no soft batch cookie like Slink! If you're talkin' bout dat punk ass white boy who thinks he's black then yeah I busted him in his mouth so what?

The kid that hit D.F. responded by grabbing his crotch as if he was tough, and at that moment rage took over and the response that he gave to Devon wasn't what he wanted to see. With one blistering right cross Devon knocked the kid out cold, and he fell against the fence! As the kid bounced off of the fence and fell face first to the alley ground, Devon turned and walked back to his car as if nothing happened.

Even though Devon's antics were premeditated, his two friends just couldn't believe it. His actions were so out of character for him. J.J. who was with him said,

"Yo, I didn't think you were going to do that!"

"That's my boy yo, he would never hurt anybody, and he only hit him because he was white. Now he knows what it feels like to be sucker punched."

"But that wasn't even a sucker punch Devon! You straight up punked him! Yo, I ain't even gonna front, we were scared sitting here! Those two can fight, and even though it would have been three against two, I ain't never fought nobody except for my sister! Hell even she kicks my ass!"

"Hey, it's all good J.J. I knew what I was doing. Those two are punks and they only prey on people that they think that they can beat. This time they've met their match!"

Devon drove his two friends to their home and afterwards he stopped by D.F.'s house so that he could tell him what happened.

"Yo, D.F. what up? I just smashed the dude that jumped you!

"For real, you didn't have to do that man, I'm cool."

"Yeah I did, because if I didn't then the next time that he sees you he might try that bull again! Oh, you best believe if he sees you again that he'll walk the other way!"

"My boy! You didn't bust his grill did you?"

"Man, I was gonna beat the shit out of him, but I felt that he just needed to be knocked da fuck out!"

The two of them laughed and talked about the past events until their sides hurt. Devon felt good inside not because he knocked someone out, but because he defended the "little man". Devon had begun to take it very personal when someone picked on him or someone that he cared about. He carried a personal vendetta against people who bullied others, because this was who he became as a person. Devon displayed a tendency of acting off of his emotions, and this behavior consistently got the best of him.

Since Devon had been teased and chastised since the tiny age of three, his natural reaction was to survive. He learned at an early age that contradictory to common belief, violence was the way! He witnessed his mother being abused more than once. His father was only there for him part time; therefore he really wasn't learning how to become a "real man". He refused to accept his mother's boyfriend as a father figure, therefore he shut down and he didn't communicate with his mother like he once did before. Devon's whole existence was fueled off of violence, anger, and hostility.

On the outside Devon was a sweet, loveable, and respectful young man, but deep within a monster was growing inside. How could he suppress the beast inside of his heart? His heart was broken at the tender age of sixteen. Beauty was supposed to tame the beast not unleash it! Devon was left with a dilemma. When times got tough he felt like he had no one to talk to. He felt like he was all alone and no one would understand where he was coming from. So many questions would often race through his head. Many of his questions were entertained by friends and loved ones but one question that could not be answered was how could he escape the beast within?

Graduation was soon approaching, and Devon's grades simply weren't strong enough anymore to earn a scholarship to college due to his lack of focus. Devon took heed to Ms. Lana's warning and he faced reality but he refused to let it smack him in the face. He still had plans to play college football, but the odds were stacked against him. Devon's first game of his senior year was approaching and he was a little bothered by the fact that he wasn't getting the most repetitions at practice at the quarterback position. Outside of the locker room in front of the coach's office Devon waited to speak with the head coach after their meeting.

"Coach, can I speak with you real quick?"

"Sure Devon, what's up?"

"Coach, what's going on?"

"Uh, nothing what's going on with you," said the balding African American head coach who had a glistening head with black and grey hair on the side.

"Come on Coach don't play me like that! What's going on out there?"

"Whoa, young squirrel! Mind your tone when you address me!"

"Mind my tone? I have no tone. I just wanna know why I'm not the starting Qb. I've been a starter since my sophomore year, and now all of a sudden you're playing that guy? I mean I know that this is your first year as a Head Coach, but you've been here! You know what I can do on the field!"

"First of all Devon, need I remind you that you are ineligible for the first game?"

"Yeah but that's only one game, and I ain't the only one!"

"Yeah but? How about yeah but you are the main one!"

"Ok Coach, but there is no way that we're gonna win with that kid, and you announced him as the starter in the newspaper! So are you saying after I come back that I'm on the bench?"

"Look Devon, you chose to not go to summer school to make up that bad grade! You let your team down, and more importantly you let yourself down!"

"Yeah but Coach, I had a lot going on at home! No one even told me that I had to miss a game until last week! Let's be real about the situation Coach. There is no way that we're gonna win with that guy! This will be my only shot at college! My grades are better now! You can't do this to me Coach!"

"Don't blame me. Blame yourself! You should've thought about your team. There's no I in team!"

"Yeah, and there's no team without me!"

"It's that selfishness that will keep your ass grounded to the bench!"

"Don't talk to me like that!"

"I can talk to you any way I feel. If you don't like it then get the fuck off of my field!"

"What? Man, fuck you! You bald headed sucka!"

"What did you just say to me boy?"

"Boy? I am young man! Boy is what Massa called his slaves!"

"Get your ass out of my stadium! Clean out your locker! You're fucking done!"

"With pleasure, I didn't wanna play for your sorry ass anyway!"

Devon stormed away from the coach and headed towards the entrance to the stadium. As he passed by the snack bar before walking up a small incline to the exit gate that led to a gravel and stone parking area, he thought to himself,

"What have I done? How could disrespect the coach like that? My mom taught me better than that. Oh my God please help me! Now what am I going to do? Football is all that I have left! My God, please help me!"

Selfish Captivation

We've been caught up in our own realm,
and we've been captivated by our selfish ways.
Now is the time to reminisce and reflect upon our glory days.
Times have changed, and it now seems
that society wants our mentality encased.
Let's look back to when a helping hand was
admired and when the needy never felt disgraced.
We've been caught up in our own realm,
and we've been captivated by our selfish ways.
A vicious cycle of Ignorance is upon us. Escape this Beast and enjoy your prosperous days!

David V.M. Kennedy

It was time to take finals before graduation, and Devon needed to pass his honors English literature class in order to graduate. Even though he felt remorseful about arguing with his coach, he never gave the coach an apology and his graduation was quickly approaching with no football scholarship offered to him. Devon's grades were mediocre at best, and in order to walk the stage he had to get a minimum score of an A on his final exam. As the days grew nearer to graduation, Marsha was well aware of her son's situation and in spite of the circumstanced Devon showed no signs of being worried.

"Devon, what are you going to do," asked Marsha in a demanding voice.

"About what," asked Devon dumb-wittedly?

"Don't give me about what, you know what! What are you going to do about that English grade? I can't believe that you are in this predicament. Look how smart you are and yet here we are. You stand here looking at not graduating right in the face."

"Mom, I'm going to graduate," Devon chuckled.

"It's not that serious."

"What, it's not that serious? Have you lost your mind? You need an A on this final or that's it, you're done. You'll then have to go to summer school and not walk the stage! Listen son, even though I received my diploma I didn't get to walk the stage because I didn't have anyone to babysit you."

"Really, you couldn't find one person to watch me while you went to your ceremony?"

"Well at the time your Grandparents were so upset with me that they didn't want anything to do with me. I was going to take you with me but the school would not allow it."

"Why? That would have been cool."

"Not according to them! An 18yr old with a 2yr old son just wasn't happening back then. Anyway Devon I need you to walk that stage. It will mean the world to me. I spoke to your teacher and she said that there was no way that you'll be able to get an A based on the work that you've done. She said that this is going to be the hardest final that she's ever given"

"So she said that huh," Devon chuckled.

"Well I guess I need to prove her wrong huh?"

Even though things were looking grim for Devon's situation, Marsha had confidence in her son, and to prove it to him she went ahead with plans for his graduation party. It was time to take finals and everyone who new and cared about Devon's situation were on pins and needles. Misery loves company, so a few of Devon's peers who already had to attend summer school in order to walk the stage heckled him the next day in school and hoped for his failure.

"Yo Devon, can I get a ride with you to summer school," laughed a heavy-set black kid with a large afro with a pick in the back of it.

"Sure, I'll drop you off since the school is close to downtown where I can get a nice pretty frame for my diploma," snapped Devon.

"Fool you ain't graduating! I just took that teacher's test and nobody in our class got higher than a C! I know that if some of the kids in my class didn't do well then there is no way that you will get an A!"

"Yo, you need to step! You don't know shit about me or what I can do!"

"Uh oh, here comes anger man! Yo, let's get up outta here before Demolition Devon explodes!"

As the teen and his entourage of misfits laughed as they walked to their next class, Devon clenched his fist as he gritted his teeth. The pressure was definitely on and the book "Paradise Lost" by John Milton was the material that was being tested. As Devon walked into the class room he noticed a list of grades posted with no names assigned to them. Three classes were listed and Devon saw one A and only a handful of B's posted. The more Devon stared at the list the more determined and focused he became. The sound of the laughter of his peers rang through his head. The conversation that he had with his mother about the teacher saying that there was no way that he would pass echoed as he stared at her before he took his seat.

Although this final exam was definitely a challenge for the average student, Devon was by no means average. In spite of the fact that he didn't apply himself he was still that gifted child who read books at the tender age of three. Even though Devon didn't show academic progress on paper, he still paid attention in class. One thing that helped Devon earn his gifted title was his ability to remember things that he felt were most important. His mind was like a mental tape recorder that could play back scenes in his livelihood as if they were being displayed on a video monitor.

Devon took the test and after he finished it he walked up to the teacher and handed it to the teacher with a smile. As she accepted it she said,

"Well Mr. Piccolo I guess this is it."

"Well Teach, I guess you're right," Devon replied jokingly.

"So how'd you do? If you have a few minutes I told your mother that I would grade your exam right away to keep her from stressing any longer."

"Well Teach I do have a few minutes, but I can't stay too long because I have to meet my mom so that we can go to the mall to pick out my graduation outfit. Is it okay if you just call her?"

Devon's teacher smiled but in her mind she thought,

"There's no way he could have gotten an A on this!"

After school Devon walked home as he laughed to himself as he imagined how the teacher's face would look after she graded his exam. Devon walked up the noisy wooden steps and as soon as he walked through the door his mother had just hung the phone up.

"That was your teacher," she said.

"Ok, so…"

His mother shook her head and said,

"Umm, Umm, Umm."

"Come on mom, let's go, I know I got an A," Devon said as he tossed his back pack and walked into the kitchen to grab a banana from the fruit basket.

At that moment Marsha's smile went from ear to ear and she said,

"Your teacher called and she just couldn't believe it! You got the second highest grade out of all of her classes! She said there was no way that you could have cheated either, because it was all essay form and she just couldn't believe it!"

Devon responded,

"Mom, just because I didn't do my homework, doesn't mean that I never paid attention. The work was just never interesting so I got discouraged. With everything that was going on from Paris getting pregnant and then with you and I bickering, I just didn't care too much. I did listen in class though, and I mean come on this is me we're talking about!"

Devon and his mom embraced with a hug and she said,

"I can't imagine what's going to happen when you decide to apply yourself."

"I don' know, maybe I'll write a book or something. Yeah, and I can get you that diamond dress that I promised you!"

Devon's accomplishment was pivotal in the betterment of his self-esteem. He knew what he was capable of, and he felt that from this point on he needed to take heed to his mother's advice and begin applying himself. Self-confidence was a vital weapon for Devon to use in his battle against the beast within his heart. He recognized his strengths but more importantly he began to recognize his weaknesses. Chippy often expressed that a man must learn from their mistakes and this was advice that his son was living up to.

Graduation came and Devon walked the stage gracefully as he accepted his diploma. Marsha and his Stepfather Ben sat proudly as he raised his hands in triumph while the flashes from the cameras went off. As Devon took his seat he peered into the crowd to see where Chippy was sitting. Name after name was called and while each student received their diplomas he got a little antsy, because he couldn't find where his father was sitting. As the principal announced the graduating class, hats navy blue caps flew up in the air and then rained to the ground. Devon picked up one of the caps and slowly walked towards Ben and Marsha.

"Congratulations son," said Ben.

"Thanks Ben."

"Smile Devon, why the long face," asked Marsha.

"Huh, oh, no long face here. Hey did you guys see where my Dad sat?"

"Oh God, here we go. Ben you deal with this, I'm going to use the restroom."

"Deal with what? What is she talking about Ben?"

"Devon, come on let's take a walk son."

"There's no need to walk Ben. He didn't come did he?"

"No, he didn't come and you know how your Dad is," proclaimed Marsha as she returned from the restroom.

Even though Chippy wasn't the social type, Devon thought for sure he was going to attend his graduation. It seemed that whenever Devon would be let down by his father, than his mother always state "You know how your dad is!" Devon was often baffled by Chippy's behavior. For as long as he could remember his father never attended any of his sporting or school events. He knew that his father loved him, but sometimes it just didn't seem like it. Every time Devon would invite his father somewhere he would end up getting disappointed because he didn't come. Marsha didn't make it any better, because she would constantly belittle Chippy in front of Devon in spite of knowing how much he looked up to his father.

Chippy continuously let his son down, and regardless of the fact Devon still felt the need to seek him on a regular basis in order to spend quality time with him. Throughout his teenage years there was a void missing that continued to eat at him daily. Devon was struggling with his identity and what it took to become a man. He was always known as a football player, but after his fallout with his coach this distinctiveness and his dreams were becoming harsh realities.

After graduating and watching his friends go off to college to pursue their goals, Devon felt like he was stuck. He put so much emphasis into making it in football, but yet he lacked the grades as well as the assistance from his coach which could have helped him play college ball. He was always taught that men don't cry. In spite of this, Devon felt that all he managed to do lately was cry. He needed someone to talk to other than his friends. He needed to hear a different voice other than his mother. Ms. Lana's wisdom rang into his hears as he sat in his room on his bed with his back leaned up against his cherry oak headboard. All he could hear was her voice playing over and over in his head.

"Don't let that door of reality smack you in the face! Don't let that door of reality smack you in the face! Don't let that door of reality smack you in the face!"

The reality was that Devon needed his father. The reality was that he was a teenage young man about to join the adult world, and he was not prepared. He gathered himself by grabbing one of his T shirts that was hanging from the bed post, and he wiped the tears and snot from his face. As he tossed the shirt onto the floor it slid into the corner with enough force that it pushed a pile of clothes up against the wall. He rubbed his hand across his chin and noticed that the boyish hairs on his face were now getting thicker, and he went into the bathroom to look in the mirror.

Even though he noticed that he needed to shave, another harsh reality was the fact that he didn't know how. Ben had a smooth baby face, therefore he would simply get his mustache trimmed up at the barbershop so Devon never witnessed him shaving. He had no clue what to do. Marsha bought him razor weeks prior as she raved about how he needed to "take that crap off of his face." Devon stared in the mirror. He couldn't believe that he was growing a full beard. As he stared longer what he really couldn't believe was how much he looked like his father.

Ignorance had taken its toll on Devon. The simplest task of grooming was unknown how to do. Ignorance is a beast, and the beast could do nothing but laugh as Devon stared into space. He clenched his fist and spoke out loud,

"Look at me, I can't even fucking shave! I can't believe that I don't know how to shave! Where da fuck are you when I need you Chippy, huh? Where the hell are you? Yeah, um hmm, I know where you are! You're at Paula's house with her kids, or better yet at Mahogany's with her kids, or no wait at my sister's houses with their moms! You ain't fucking here, damn it! You ain't fucking here!!! You were never here!"

As he yelled at the top of his lungs he threw his razor up against the bathroom wall and punched the mirror over the sink! The glass shattered with a crashing sound as pieces fell to the floor while splashing into the toilet a few feet to the right. As he stood panting as if he just finished doing a full day of football practice, he stared at his fist that was covered in blood. A large shard of glass rested at his foot as he reached down to pick it up. He gripped the glass so hard that the palm of his hand began to bleed more than his knuckles. He placed the sharpest edge of the glass up to his neck and said out loud,

"How about this Chippy and Marsha, how would you like it if I give you both your wish? Let's just say that I end this shit right now! Neither one of you gives a shit about me! I was mistake nothing but a fucking mistake right? I can take all of your misery away now so how about that?"

As he slowly pressed the glass harder into his neck, a tiny drop of blood began to trickle down his atom's apple. He pulled the glass away and placed it on top of the inside of his wrist and Bang! A loud crash occurred outside the house at the intersection of Linden and Belvedere which was visible outside of his bathroom window. The noise was so loud that it startled him as the glass fell from his hand and crashed to the floor dispersing tiny pieces of glass all over the bathroom floor. Devon looked out the window and saw a woman screaming frantically for help!

Even though his hand had blood on it Devon quickly grabbed a wet wash cloth and wiped his neck and hand. He sprinted out of the bathroom and ran a few feet down the hall that led to the side door to his home. He busted through the door and grabbed the wooden handle of the rails of the wooden staircase made the same distinctive noise but louder as he skipped down the entire flight of stairs in three bounds.

"Please help me, please help me," screamed a distraught Hispanic lady as she clutched her face with her bloody hands.

"Are you okay, are you hurt," asked Devon as he looked to see if she was physically harmed.

"Ayuda por favor! Mi bebe necesita ayuda! Oh, dios ayuda por favor a mi bebe!"

"Ma'am I'm sorry, but I don't speak Spanish! Please calm down, is it your baby?"

"Si, me baby please help me!"

As Devon looked towards the intersection he heard the sound of a little boy faintly sighing for help. Flames burst from the front of a small white car that was flipped over with the hood caving in on the rear passenger side. As the flames began to spread Devon heard the little boys sigh turn into a desperate plea.

"Oh my God, hang on kid! It's ok, stop screaming and listen to me! Can you move your arm?"

"Yes but my leg is stuck," yelled the Hispanic kid who looked to be around 8yrs old.

"Oh, shoot I see what it is kid! It's your shoe stuck between the seat and the arm rest! I think that I can reach your foot so I'm going to untie your shoe, and I want you to try and wiggle your leg out! Can you move your leg?"

"I think so," cried the kid.

"Listen kid, you can't think you gotta do it, and the fire is getting close so you have to! Now move your leg!"

"Ouch, hit hurts, I can't!"

"You can do it kid! What's your favorite sport? You look like you play football."

"I do I love football."

"Me too kid, now I'm a quarterback and right now we need a touchdown and you are the only one strong enough to break through the line and score! Let's go, ready, set, hut!"

At the sound of Devon's commanding football cadence the little boy wiggled his leg free and Devon pulled him from the engulfing flames as the sound of fire trucks came racing down the street. Devon picked the little boy up and raced away from the car as a loud explosion went off as the two fell into the grass in Devon's front yard. The firemen eventually got the blaze under control and after a short while all that remained was a charred car frame. The Hispanic lady clenched her son and wept as she kissed Devon on the cheek and said,

"Gracias mister, thank you!"

"That was a brave and unselfish thing that you did son. You are a hero and you saved that kid's life. God sent that kid an angel today," stated a fireman as he shook Devon's hand.

Although Devon was thankful that the little boy was okay, he felt like he was far from a hero. He stood and looked at the charred vehicle and he thought about the generous words of the fireman. The fireman called him unselfish and an angel sent from God, but contrary to his kind words the angels sent by God was the Hispanic lady and her son. That car accident stopped what could have been the most selfish act of all. God used that car accident that left the little boy and his mother unscathed to keep Devon from doing the unthinkable. Ignorance is a beast that lies within all of our lives.

Ignorance prevented Devon knowing how to cope with the everyday pressures of life. The door of Reality has closed, and it smacked him right in the face; but Knowledge is definitely a key that can be used to unlock reality and allow him to embrace his world of dreams. Ignorance has overwhelmed Devon from the time of his birth. God, faith, and family are needed for him in order to function with a stable lifestyle. Faith and spirituality is a vital weapon that can be used to destroy this Ignorance which is known as the beast within. Education plays a major role in defeating the beast as well as long as one does not become selfish by withholding the knowledge that they have attained. In order to battle, one must know how to fight, and in order to fight each one must teach one, and this will eliminate the chokehold that Ignorance has upon us.

UNITY

In order to have unification that means you have to unite!
It seems that it is easier to unify when there's drama pertaining to a fight.
U-N-I-T-Y
Unity Needs Intelligence To Yield.
It doesn't take rocket science to be an expert in this field.
And to yield means that you must produce,
Therefore U-N-I-T-Y can't remain this separate or loose.
Now it the time for UNITY and like this we must come together!
U-N-I-T-Y let's come closer and UNITY will be forever!

David V.M. Kennedy

One day Devon came home from the barbershop and found a large manila envelope lying on the kitchen table. Thinking nothing of the envelope he decided to make a sandwich that his sister Destiny often referred to as "jelly bread" which was a PB&J without the peanut butter. As he stood over the kitchen counter spreading the jelly he noticed that the sink was full of dishes, and his mother was about to come home from work. His daily ritual was to make sure that the kitchen was cleaned before his mother came home so he quickly finished making his sandwich and placed it on the table on top of the envelope.

"Dang it, I got jelly on this envelope! What the heck is this anyway? It's from a military academy in Philly, why are they sending me this?"

"Devon, I'm home," yelled Marsha as she walked through the front door as and tossed her purse on the living room couch.

"Hey mom, I'm in the kitchen!"

"You better have it cleaned, I know that!"

"Uh, that's what I'm about to do!"

"Boy, what did I tell you about your chores?"

"Mom, I got you, but I started reading this mail sent to me, check it out!"

"What is it? Military school, why are they sending you this?"

"It looks like they want me to play football and they're offering a scholarship! It's just a prep school for one year but it says that they are willing to pay!"

"Hmm, let me see that. Yeah, you're right it looks like they want you. When is the last time that you saw your Dad? You should go show him."

Even though Devon wasn't offered a scholarship to a college, he was very excited about the military academy in spite of knowing what going there would entail. He heard about junior colleges that had football programs, but he had no knowledge of where any of them were located or how to go about getting into one. Devon kissed his mother on the cheek and raced out the door to head to find Chippy. As he went down the steps that led from the side of his oversized apartment that was the top half of a colonial style three story home, he thought to himself,

"Man, I wish that I had one of the big cellular phones that just came out! I'd could call my Dad and let him know that I'm close so that he could pick me up. I really don't feel like walking this far. Man, forget that I'm gonna ask my mom for her car!"

Devon hurried into the house, and he asked his mother if he could borrow her car. She told him to bring it back before she went to work the next morning, and he darted back out of the house with a huge smile on his face and thought to himself,

"Yeah, looks like I need to make a pit stop to Michelle's house! I know she better let me get with that tonight! If not then it looks like Chippy's kid needs to pull out his "Chippy charm" and head up to the Penn Park and holler at the honeys! It'll be a smorgasbord of freaks up there tonight you best believe that!"

Although Devon thought about going to an old girlfriend's house, he decided to stop by his dad's house first, because he knew that his father would drop some knowledge on how to approach the girls. Since Mahogany and four of his brothers lived closer to his old girlfriend he thought that he would check to see if Chippy was there first in order to save himself an extra trip if Chippy was there. Mahogany stated that she hadn't seen Chippy for a few weeks and that they had just got into a big argument and he never returned. Before he went to Paula's house he hung out with his four little brothers and played football in the street as they watched out for cars.

Eventually Devon caught up with Chippy at Paula's house and as he opened the door to her house one of his younger brothers Cain opened the door.

"Hey it's Buckzilla guys! Devon you're a bum, you don't got no job, and Dad said he ain't giving you no money!"

"Shut up Cain, you don't got no English. Who's your English teacher?"

"Mrs. Johnson and I know her full name too! Mrs. Kristin Johnson, so now!"

"Well that bitch needs to get fired, because she's dumb as hell and she ain't teaching you shit! Back up Satan, you're stealing my joy," said Devon as he pushed his brother Cain hard onto a big pillowed couch.

"Yo, Dad what up? Check this out! I think that I might wanna go here!"

"Hey Slick, long time no see. Whatcha got? Hmm, military school huh, yeah you need to get disciplined, but a military school? I done told you about that military stuff! No black man should join any type of military. They'll try to brainwash you, and this school will do the same to get you to join. They'll break you down and reprogram you."

"Come on Dad, that's not true," laughed Devon.

"Like hell it ain't son! They prey on the weak and turn them in to human robots!"

"Now you're losing it Pops! It just takes a special person to be a soldier. We owe them our livelihood for protecting our freedom!"

"I see that I raised you to stand firm in your beliefs. I like that young buck! Just realize the truth of the matter though. If you would ever decide to join the military, then you would want to go in as an officer. Don't be fooled son; the less that a person is educated the easier it is for them to throw on the frontlines. I'll go ahead and pay for this how much do I need to fork out?"

Although Chippy was willing to pay for his school, Devon explained to him that the military school was going to give him a scholarship for 12,000 dollars for the one school year. The year was 1991 and Devon was now 18 years old and determined to make it in life. Once he accepted the offer he received a welcome packet in the mail explaining everything that he needed to have for enrollment. He was so anxious and motivated to get out of York, Pa that it didn't dawn on him that he was going to be going to a military school!

"Well mom, this is it," Devon said.

"Yeah baby it's a new beginning for you, are you ready," she said proudly.

"I guess now I have no choice, and I am a little nervous but I'll be ok."

"I guess this is it then," Marsha sighed.

"Go grab your things and let's head out."

"Ok, is my dad going, he could at least do that," said Devon.

"Actually, he is and I didn't think anything of it, but Ben suggested that just the three of us go up there."

"Wow, that was what I was kind of hoping for, and that's nothing against Ben."

"He figured that Devon, and he understands."

"I swear Mom it seems that Ben's timing is always on point! You better keep that guy," Devon laughed.

Devon was ecstatic, and he enjoyed every minute of their drive to Valley Forge, Pa which was about a two hour drive from York. Even though the drive wasn't long it still felt like it took an eternity to get there. Devon began to bite his nails as his nervousness began to take over. As the former couple drove down interstate 76 Chippy looked over to Marsha and said,

"Listen, I want to thank you for raising our son the way that you did. I know that I have my own issues, and I haven't been the greatest father in the world, but I want you to know that I really want to see our son become a better man than I ever could have been. You worked very hard, and from this point on I want to step up and take it from here."

"Chippy I just earned a whole new respect for you. I want you to know that I don't blame you for anything. Let's just face it and Devon you and I already had this discussion, we were just too young. We were ignorant to a lot of life situations, and we were just dumb teens who thought that we had everything figured out. You had a rough life not knowing your parents, and mine was just as tough knowing a mother who wanted nothing to do with me. It's sad Chippy, and it's a vicious cycle of behavior that has affected our son throughout his young life."

Devon sat in the back seat of his Dad's classic Dodge Challenger, and swallowed every word with a cheesy grin on his face.

"You know something you're absolutely right Marsha. I'm going to make sure that the vicious cycle ends. Our son will get educated, and whether or not he earns a scholarship I'm going to pay for him to get through college."

The three arrived on campus at the academy and Devon noticed a group of boys in formation ready to march.

"I forgot that there ain't no girls at this place," he said shockingly.

"Yeah your behind was so concerned about football, and you didn't even once think about that," laughed Marsha.

"Good, you'll stay focused, and I told you that a black man has no business in this type of environment! Besides, you're a Soriano and when challenged we'll try, but while we do we intend to multiply! You sure won't be multiplying here," laughed Chippy.

"Ha, ha that's very funny Dad. I got this!"

Devon grabbed his bags, and he and his family went to the main office to check him in. As he gave his name to the registrar's office he began to second guess and wondered if he could really handle an all boy school. Even though there were no girls at the school, his minor dilemma was soon to become the least of his worries. A tall white gentleman a buzz cut and very broad shoulders came into the lobby decorated with an excessive amount of medals. The man in the uniform looked intimidating to Devon as he shook his hand and said,

"Hi, my name is Sergeant Buster, I'm afraid that we have a small problem."

"Hi, I'm big Devon, what's the problem sir?"

"Well sir there seems to have been a mistake with your son's scholarship. If you'd please step into my office then we can see if we can work something out."

"Sir, I'm Marsha, does this mean that our son can't come here?"

"No Ma'am, not at all. I'm sure we'll be able to work this out. Here have a seat, and can I offer you some water?"

"No, we want to get to the bottom of this," exclaimed Chippy.

The sergeant explained to Devon and his family that there had been a mistake and they didn't have a scholarship to give to him. They could only offer to pay 25% of the cost. Although Chippy agreed to pay for his education, he didn't have the amount of money that the academy wanted at the present time. Marsha became furious and said,

"So why in God's name did you wait until we drove way down here to tell us?"

"Now Ma'am calm down please, it was a simple human error. It looks like we do not have enough funds to offer your son a full scholarship but if you can pay this portion then we'll cover the rest."

"Calm down, this is my son's life that your messing with here!"

"Marsha, don't waste your time on this asshole. Devon grab your things and let's get out of here," Chippy said calmly.

Shocked and confused Devon grabbed his belongings and headed with his mother to the car as Chippy stayed in the office while the door closed.

"Look here Buster…"

"Uh, that's Sgt. Buster sir."

"Look here motherfucker, you lost that respect from me a few minutes ago! You had me bring my fucking family down here when you knew all along that you had no intentions on giving my son a scholarship! You could've fucking called us! Now I have to explain to my son how much of an asshole you and your organization represent! You know what, Fuck you Buster! Fuck you and your fucking family, and I hope that your loved ones will feel the type of dejection that my son feels at this moment!"

Chippy walked out of the office and peacefully walked through the lobby towards the exit. Sgt. Buster sat at his desk flabbergasted at what just occurred. Naturally Devon was devastated. The drive home was somber. Devon didn't speak one word for the entire two hour trip, and when he got home he went straight to his room. He dropped his luggage in the corner of his room and he opened the closet door and sat with his back against the closet wall with clothes draped over his head while his legs stretched out of the closet. Tears began to pour out of his eyes uncontrollably as mucous dripped from his nose onto the clothes that covered his face as they hung from the rack.

"What am I going to do now," he sobbed.

"God please help me, I have nothing! God I beg you, please, please, please. I have nothing God please!"

Devon sat in his room for hours as he cried until his eyes swelled and his head began to hurt. His mother tried to lighten the mood by ordering food, and he refused to even come out to eat his favorite food which was pizza. Like a baby Devon cried himself to sleep, and the next morning he refused to come out of his room again other than to use the restroom. Depression had set in, and he thought that his life was over, because unlike the ambitious peers that he surrounded himself with the only thing that he could think of was to find a job and hope for the best.

Devon was crushed that his dream of going to college to play football was shattered, but he was more devastated because he felt that all who said that he would never make it seemed to be proven right. He had given up, but what he failed to realize was what his mother had told him his entire life. She always said to him, "The Lord works in mysterious ways!" After three days he had finally decided to come out of his room, and after not bathing for three days he made it a point to get washed up and go to the barber shop for a haircut. As Devon walked to the shop, he couldn't help but daydream about his bleak future. As he looked at the row houses peering over the trashy streets some were boarded and some had "crack heads" passing through them. He couldn't help but think, "I've gotta get out of here, I just can't take this place anymore!"

Since Devon had a strong belief in God, he decided to pray more and to stop feeling sorry for himself. He restored his faith, and he believed that things would get better. On his way to the barbershop he passed by his ex-girlfriend Paris who was sitting on her stoop in front of her house.

"Hi Devon," she said enthusiastically.

Devon walked right past her as if she didn't exist without acknowledging her presence by not uttering a word. He thought to himself,

"God please send me a woman who is faithful, and if you don't mind let her be an athletic woman who enjoys sports!"

Devon laughed to himself as he entered into the barbershop. As he sat in the shop awaiting his turn to get in the chair, he heard a deep but high pitched a voice say, "D?" Devon looked up and saw his mother's 1st cousin Carl Weaver entering into the barbershop. Carl was ten years older than Devon, and he had a smooth dark chocolate complexion. He was dressed as if he just came from a fashion show, and his overall persona had success written all over it.

"What's up boy," asked Carl.

"What's up cuz, nothing," Devon replied.

"Are you still playing football? I heard how good you were!"

Devon's head dropped at the sound of the question as if he was ashamed to answer truthfully.

"Well, not anymore. I just came from a military school and they played me with the scholarship offer."

"Why don't you go to a junior college?"

"Well, they don't have any around here, and I don't think that I'll qualify to get in with my GPA."

"Boy you don't need to qualify to get into no Juco! You graduated right?"

"Of course, I graduated. I thought that you needed to qualify shit I didn't know."

"Of course you have to take placement test, but I'm sure you won't need to take remedial classes, because you're too smart for that."

"I wish I was smart. If I was that smart then I'd be somewhere."

"Man quit feeling sorry for yourself! Shit happens, but that doesn't mean you're a dummy. Ain't no dummies in this family! Well, what are you going to do?"

"What do you mean? I guess I'll try to find a job or something. To be honest cuz, I don't know."

"I'm going back to Phoenix in a few days, do you want to go?"

"Phoenix, Arizona, what's out there?"

"Aw man, you'll love it! It's way bigger than York and there is plenty to do out there; besides they have plenty of Jucos that you can enroll in. Scout sign kids left and right from there, and I know you'll tear it up out there! So what's up, do you wanna go?"

"Heck yeah, I don't have anything else to do!"

"Ok, I'm leaving in three days so if you're serious I'll talk to your mom about it," Carl said excitedly.

"Alright cool cuz, I'll go right home and tell her after I get this fresh one!"

Although Devon knew that he had a short amount of time to prepare for departure, he spent no time contemplating the offer and he seized the opportunity. After he got his haircut he ran the entire way home to tell his mom the exciting news.

"Mom, I'm going to Phoenix!"

"What are you talking about Devon?"

"I just saw your cousin, well our cousin Carl in the barbershop, and he said that I can move to Phoenix with him!"

Devon explained to Marsha that he spoke to their cousin Carl, and that he wanted to go back to Arizona with him so that he could go to junior college to play football. Marsha heard the excitement in her baby now turned man's voice. His face said it all. He went from a depressed 18yr old boy to an enlightened ambitious man, and even though she didn't agree with the idea she didn't want to see her son the way that he was a few days ago; therefore she gave her son full support on his decision. Later that evening Marsha spoke to Carl, and he explained to her that he was going back to Phoenix for a while until he had to return to medical school in Nevada. He told her that their Aunt who already lived in Phoenix agreed to let Devon stay with her while he went to school.

Devon's prayers had been answered and his life was beginning to take a turn for the better. He only had three days to get prepared to embrace the biggest decision of his young life. After packing his clothes he made his round of visits to his friends and family to give his love and to say good bye. Three days seemed like three minutes as time flied, and it was now time for Devon to leave. His father had agreed to pay for his airplane ticket as well as the rental car that he and Carl were going to use to drive to Indiana to visit Carl's mother before they headed to Phoenix. Devon was packed and ready to make the drive to Indiana when he noticed that his mother was nowhere around.

"Ma!" he yelled.

There was no answer but Devon knew that she was still in the house, because she wouldn't just leave before he could say goodbye. "Mom!" he shouted louder.

"I'm up here," Marsha said weeping.

Devon ran up the stairs to his mother's room and he found his mother crying as she sat at the foot of her bed.

"Mom, are you ok?" "

"No, I'm not. Don't go Devon," she pleaded.

Devon looked into his mother's eyes and her eyelashes looked as if two black rose petals were floating on top of two miniature ponds. Devon couldn't hold back his tears as he reached for his mother's arms. For the first time since Devon's birth, Marsha didn't feel as if she was holding her baby. She was now being held by her son who was now a grown man, and as Devon wiped the tears from his mother's face he said,

"I love you mom, but this is something that I have to do. If I stay in York then I will become nothing."

"Devon York is what you make it son. There is nothing wrong with living here."

"You're absolutely right Mom. York isn't a bad place to live, but for me at this moment it is. Mentally I am too caught up in dwelling on the ignorance that has surrounded me for so long. All of my friends have moved on to newer and better things and it seems that now I constantly come across people who are miserable and want nothing more than to bring the next man down. Right now I'm at a point in my life that I just can't handle the constant pressure of negativity. I have to seek out a new path to travel in order for me to walk down the golden road of prosperity. Please don't cry. I need you to be happy when I walk out of that door. Can you do that for me?"

"Of course I can son. I am so proud of you! My baby has become a man," she said with a big smile.

At that precise moment, all of Marsha's uncertainties had been relinquished. This defining moment of Devon's manhood gave her the confidence that her once baby boy was going to be alright in the tough world that he was about to face. With just shining moment and hug, her son had reassured this former 15yr old teenaged mother that her 18 years of sacrifice had paid off! This defining moment had wiped away all of the previous heartache that the two had endured. Marsha placed both of her hands on Devon's shoulders and said,

"I love you Devon. Jesus is the answer and through him all things are possible. No man will ever be able to close the door that God has opened for you!"

A man's gotta do

In order for man to do what a man's gotta do,
then there are things that need to be done.
In order for a man to do what a man's gotta do,
he must always be there for his son.
A man's gotta do what a man's gotta do,
therefore step up and stake your claim.
Now's the time men, to do what you gotta do,
Cause if you don't then it's you we must blame.

David V.M. Kennedy

Carl arrived at Devon's house, and he reassured Marsha that everything was going to be alright, and that she had nothing to worry about.

"Listen cuz, this will be the best for Devon. It will make him a man," Carl reiterated.

"I know Carl, but it's just so far. What if something bad happens? What if he decides to stay out there? Devon don't go out there making any babies! You already slipped up once!"

"Mom! Come on Ma, you just put my business all out there!"

"It's ok lil cuz, things happen. So where's your little one? Did your girl have the baby yet?"

"No, and she never will have the baby, or babies I should say," Devon said shamefully.

"Oh, I see, well I'm not gonna comment on that touchy situation. Let's just get you up outta here so that you can better your life!"

Even though Marsha knew that her son would be ok, it was still hard for her to let go, because for a while Devon was all she had and now her baby was leaving the flock. Devon kissed his mother goodbye and she gave him a worry free hug as the two men got into the car, and headed for their journey west. Devon was full of excitement, because other than a few trips along the east coast he had never been anywhere. Other than the trip to football camp upstate New York, this was the first time he had gone this far alone.

Carl and Devon drove to Hammond, Indiana which took the two approximately nine hours to arrive.

"Boy, we did good time," Carl said happily.

"Yeah, that car was floatin," exclaimed Devon.

"Look D, we're only gonna stay here for a few days so that I can see my mom and then off to Phoenix we go!"

"Cool cuz, so what are the dime pieces like up here?"

"Dang lil cuz, we just got here and you're already concerned with the ladies!"

Although Hammond wasn't the most exciting place in the world, the change of scenery for Devon made him feel like it was a vacation resort. Devon was adventurous by nature therefore he didn't hesitate getting outside to try and make new friends. Carl had an abundance of friends and relatives in Hammond as well as nearby Gary, Indiana and whenever he went to visit them Devon would go too. He was amazed as he admired the loving response that Carl received from his peers. It seemed that every person they visited made them feel as if they were celebrities returning home after a moment on the big screen! Carl immediately became a role model to Devon. He admired his style and charismatic charm, and the two had bonded like they were two explorers ready to take on the new world.

In spite of only being in Indiana for a week, Devon had already felt that he was becoming successful in life. He was now away from the ghetto of York, Pa, and once again he had a plan to achieve his goal of going to college. Carl was a master at motivating Devon, and he would often tell beguiling stories about his experiences in Phoenix. It seemed to Devon that his meeting with Carl was divine intervention, and he often said to himself,

"Wow, what if I wouldn't have gone to the barbershop? Would I still be stuck in York? This all feels like a dream!"

Once again his mother's wisdom was proven to him. The Lord does work in mysterious ways, and this was a revelation to Devon which made his faith grow stronger. As each day passed his confidence suppressed any fears or doubts that he previously had. He realized that the "real world" would be challenging, but for now with a little help and knowledge from his family the beast within was tamed. Pure will power and determination went into Devon's repertoire of weapons that were needed to alleviate the distractions of ignorance, and with this armor he was ready to conquer his new territory of self-worth.

Carl had finished his visit with his mother, and the duo now packed their belongings as they headed to the airport in Chicago, Illinois. Even though Devon had traveled on a plane before, he was a little nervous but not really afraid to fly. His philosophy was, "If we go down, than God's just calling me home." Carl and Devon went to the counter to check their bags in and Carl noticed that his black planner was missing.

"D, did you see my planner?"

"No, didn't you have it over there where we were sitting?

"Aw, man! I did, and I set it right on that seat, and now it's gone!"

"What was in there, money?"

"My money and our tickets, shit!"

"Now what," asked Devon?

Although Carl had his bankcard taken as well, he assured Devon that he would handle the dilemma, and reassured him by saying that he had nothing to worry about. Carl called his girlfriend in Phoenix and had her purchase tickets for the two of them to get there. The two men sat a few hours while Carl's girlfriend took care of their reservations, and while they laughed at Carl's bonehead mistake; Devon couldn't help being impressed at how Carl maintained his composure as he handled the situation without panicking.

In spite of Carl's mishap, Devon short experience away from home was admirable simply because he actually got a chance to spend quality time with a family member who was handling grown man responsibilities. Although Ben married Marsha, Devon's initial resentment towards him deterred and type of man to man bonding. Carl was only ten years older than Devon, and to see him dress like he was important and to witness the attention that he commanded was soothing for his ego.

Even though Carl had a thorough approach to daily living, he spent the entire flight beating himself up about the tickets, and he had a different version of the story each time he told it. Devon laughed until his side hurt, and before he knew it they were landing in Phoenix, Az. As he peered out of the airplane window, he noticed how dry everything looked and also how flat the land was.

"Wow, this looks nothing like Pennsylvania, where are the trees," asked Devon.

"Man this is the desert; you're not going to see a lot of greenery!"

"Hell, I can see that, with all these cactus and what not!"

Carl had previously explained to Devon that he was going back to Nevada to go to school very soon, so he would only be able to spend a limited amount of time with him. As the two went to claim their luggage Devon noticed that Carl was spending a considerable amount of time on the pay phone. He hung up the phone, and walked towards Devon noticeably upset.

"What's the deal cuz?"

"Man let's go, I'll tell you on the way," Carl said as the two of them loaded their bags in the trunk of his 1990 silver Volvo.

"You alright man," inquired Devon as he watched Carl angrily throwing the luggage into the trunk.

"Look man you can't stay with our aunt," Carl said bluntly.

"Why can't I stay?"

"I don't know man; apparently her husband doesn't want you there. You know that she's married to some old white dude right? I don't think that he likes black people."

"That doesn't make sense cuz. Why would he marry her if he didn't like black people?"

"Man, I don't know, but I know he always treats me and my brothers some type of way. I can't explain it. Let's go!"

"Wow, you think they would have told me that I couldn't stay before I got here! Now what the hell am I supposed to do?" Devon was supposed to stay with his great aunt who he hadn't seen since he was a little kid, and since he barely knew her he really didn't know how or even if he should respond directly to her.

Even though Devon was puzzled and confused, Carl remained poise and said,

"Look here D, don't sweat this. We're family and we're going to take care of each other. I've been staying with my brother Paul in Tempe which borders Phoenix. You'll just have to stay with us. It's gonna be tight because he only lives in a small studio apartment, but we can make it work."

"Ok cuz that sounds good. I mean hey we grew up in the projects, and we're from York, so there is no bad situation that we can't overcome!"

Unaware to exactly how small a studio apartment was Devon's face practically hit the floor when he walked through Paul's door. Paul greeted him with a smile from ear to ear and he was very excited because he hadn't seen Devon since he was a little boy living in the projects. When Devon was younger he would often go to his great aunt Wanda's house who was Paul and Carl's mother, and they would baby sit him often while his mother would work. Devon recalled how Carl and his younger brother would playfully beat him up while trying to get him tough. Paul would always be the one to save Devon from the "beat downs"!

Devon greeted Paul with a hug, and although he was happy to see his cousin, his spirits were a bit dampened by the size of the apartment. As he stepped through the door he took three steps, and there was a couch sitting in front of a divider wall. Four steps to the left was a small kitchen, and on the other side of the wall a bed, two small dressers, a closet, and a bathroom! Devon looked at his cousin Paul who was 6ft 4 about 200lbs as well as Carl who was 6ft 2 220, and then he thought to himself,

"I'm 6ft 2 180lbs, so how in the hell are we going to live here?"

"It's good to see you little cuz," said Paul.

"Man, you too, it's been a long time," stated Devon.

"Well Devon, you Carl and I are family so I'm here for you and we'll come up with something okay?"

"Alright cuz, that's what family is all about," exclaimed Devon.

The three significantly large men were now going to live in a studio apartment and although it was tight quarters, they were prepared overcome adversity due to the simple fact that they grew up in York, Pa. York had a lot of drama in the small community, the one thing that the true "Yorkers" in that time period knew how to do was fight! By not having the "finer things in life" Devon and his family were able to improvise and make the best of what they did have.

Although Paul had to make a drastic adjustment to his living conditions, he accepted Devon with no qualms and gave him no time limits to leave. Devon immediately recognized the sacrifices that his cousins made for him and rather than gripe and complain he once again encaged the beast within and refocused his energy towards his goal. Time passed on and Carl eventually left for Nevada, and Devon was now enrolled in Phoenix Community College. He had met with the head football coach and the coach had set him up with an apartment where he stayed with two other roommates. The coach explained how financial aid worked and the way that he explained to Devon led him to believe that he would get enough money to pay for his living conditions. Devon was ignorant to the whole college football experience; therefore he became a victim of the business aspect of the game.

Even though the coach arranged an apartment for Devon, he misled him into thinking that financial aid was like a scholarship. Devon received financial aid but it wasn't close to the amount necessary for paying for an apartment. He was now stuck in an apartment with two roommates who were also misled into thinking that the room and board would be covered by the financial aid. Neither of them had a job, or transportation, therefore going to school and working for a living was going to be a difficult task!

Devon was only 18yrs old and he had never been away this far from his family. Carl left for Nevada, and Paul was miles away in Tempe. He was angry and confused about what to do. Phoenix was so big and the streets were so long that it was almost impossible for him to go to school and work without transportation. The public transportation was available, but it would take up too much time to allow Devon to work, go to school, and play football.

The pressures of not having a comfortable living condition became too much. Devon would go days while eating only one meal per day, and sometimes none at all because he didn't have enough money to eat with. It got so bad for Devon that he actually got into a fight with one of his roommates for eating a steak of his. Even though growing up and York, Pa provided Devon with a strong will, he eventually came to a breaking point.

One day Devon came home to find his belongings trashed and at that point he became furious!

"I can't take this anymore," he yelled.

"This is too much! I need help. Every time I call home my Mom claims that she has no money! My Dad said that he was going to help me, but he only sent a little bit of money and it is so hard to even get in touch with him! I don't even know what to do!"

At that moment Devon packed his belongings and stored them in his closet while he left for his Cousin Paul's house. Bubbling with fury, he began to walk from his apartment which was located on 27th avenue and camelback all the way to Tempe which was on 48th street and Baseline road. This was approximately 15 miles of walking, and out of habit of being able to walk across town in York, Pa he didn't even think twice before doing it. He left in the early morning, and he did a combination of walking and jogging in order for him to get there as quickly as possible. Paul was at work so there was no way that he could get a ride, and he had no money left for a bus or taxi.

Devon was a survivor and the enraged fury fueled each step as he got closer to his destination. He picked oranges off trees along the way to pacify his thirst and hunger. He noticed that it would be getting dark soon, and although he was close to arriving to Paul's house his feet were starting to hurt and he was starting to get dehydrated from walking through the desert in October. Devon stopped at a pay phone and made a collect call with some loose change that he still had to Paul. Paul drove a few miles and picked him up, and he was simply amazed at how far Devon had walked.

"What in the world were you thinking," asked Paul.

"I've been fighting with my roommates, and they tried to steal money from me. I haven't been eating, and I really need to get out of there," proclaimed Devon.

"I see, well let's go back and get your things. Are they still there? Do I need to call for reinforcements?"

"No, they went with some girls so I doubt that they will be back for a while. Thanks cuz."

"No sweat lil cuz, that's what family's all about. Just know that you have to learn how to depend on yourself now. You're young but it's time for you to grow up real fast!"

"Yeah you're right. I'm just so ignorant to so many things cuz. And I thought that I was smart!"

"Just because you don't know certain things doesn't mean that you aren't smart Devon. Becoming a man means learning from your mistakes and experiences. You'll be fine. Just keep educating yourself."

Paul took Devon back to the apartment to gather his belongings, and afterwards the two of them drove back to Tempe. Even though Paul wasn't going to let his cousin live in disarray, he still wasn't in a position to have Devon live with him permanently. Devon explained to Paul that his father Chippy said that he would pay for him to go to school, but he only would send money occasionally and it wasn't much to survive off of. Paul allowed Devon to finish his 1st semester of school while living there, and it eventually came to the point that Devon had no choice but to call home to his mother for a plane ticket back home.

In spite of finishing his 1st college semester with a decent grade point average, Devon still felt like a failure because he had to return home for the summer. Marsha was elated to have him home, but she was very unhappy about the turn of events that occurred.

"What in the heck went on out there Devon?"

"It's a long story Mom. It was rough but you taught me well, so I was able to handle."

"Well I gave my Aunt a piece of my mind, and you can best believe that!"

"I bet you did," laughed Devon.

"You're darn right I did! Anyway I have another Aunt who just moved out there and she said that you can stay with her for as long as you want."

"She doesn't have a husband does she? If she does then I'll pass!"

"No, she's by herself and she'll look out for you."

"That's cool, and that way I can get a job without having to worry about any bills yet. I'll kick in some money to her once I get things going."

"I'm proud of you son. Keep fighting the fight and you'll achieve anything that you set your mind too! I don't really want you to go back, but a man's gotta do what a man's gotta do."

The year was 1992 and the fall semester was ready to begin. Devon moved into a one bedroom apartment with his Aunt Sharon who let him sleep on the couch in the living room. Even though his objective was to play football, he didn't trust the coach anymore, so he decided to try a different school. In the meantime he had to live; therefore he decided to go to the corner store to pick up a newspaper in order to look for a job. In high school Devon did telemarketing and he noticed an ad that had the title Next Data now hiring posted on a bus stop. Devon smiled and took the ad to be an omen, because he felt that this would be his next job. Excited Devon went to Next Data to apply for the position. His fluency in reading impressed the hiring manager, and he was told that he could begin work the following day. He felt good after having the interview because he loved when someone complimented him on his intelligence.

Devon woke up the next morning and asked his aunt if he could borrow the car for work. He hopped into a mustard yellow Monte Carlo and drove off to his job. As Devon pulled into the parking lot he noticed a strange green looking Honda Accord parked crooked in the last open space.

"What freaking idiot parked this piece of junk? Why in the heck did they take up two spaces? This stupid idiot, shit now there aren't any spots left, and

I'll have to go way the heck across the street to park! Fuck, now I'm gonna be late!"

He finally found a parking space and as he walked into the training room the trainer announced jokingly,

"Well look who's late on the first day!"

"I'm sorry sir, but someone took up two spots in the parking lot and the rest were full. I had to park way across the street!"

"It's ok sir, you're only two minutes late, and I was just joking with the class that people will be shocked when they try to find parking around here. You're fine, have a seat."

As the crowd erupted in laughter, Devon noticed a young woman who had a smooth caramel complexion which was topped off with an angelic smile that stood out amongst the crowd. Her skin looked as if the world's largest candy producer personally used her skin for his secret candy recipe.

In spite of the roar of laughter, Devon was numbed by the young woman's beauty. He was mesmerized by her sensual smile, and although he didn't want to stare he couldn't help but try to make eye contact. The training class began and Devon had to literally snap himself out of his hypnotic mind set and focus on the material being taught. The class was instructed to read a script out loud, and Devon saw this moment as an opportunity to impress the young woman. As the other guys in the room stumbled across their words, Devon noticed the young woman shaking her head as if to say, "Boy these guys are dumb." It was now Devon's turn to read and he flowed through the words as if he already had the script memorized. He noticed out of the corner of his eye that the young woman hung on to every word that came from his mouth, and even when he was finished he noticed that she kept staring at him. It was at that moment that he decided that he was going to approach her once the opportunity presented itself.

As the class resumed, Devon rehearsed in his mind what he might say to the young lady when he got the chance. Even though he was confident that she noticed his fluid style of reading, he was unsure what type of man she'd be attracted to, because she really didn't say much during the class. The trainer of the class issued a break, and Devon sat in his chair anxiously waiting to see what the young woman's physique looked like. Devon was trying not to be too obvious so he engaged in a conversation with another fellow classmate who was a male significantly large in stature.

The young woman walked by the two gentlemen as they were talking and the large young man said,

"Damn, she's fine! I gots to get with that!"

"Yeah right, what you gots to do is get better English," joked Devon.

"Whatever bro, she's bad and I know that I can pull that!"

As soon as Devon heard this ridiculous comment he thought to himself,

"Yeah right, maybe if you were 10 Philly cheese steaks lighter!"

Devon began to walk down the hall towards the steps to make his move and strike a conversation with the young lady. As she walked down the stairs, he couldn't help but notice the woman's bulging calf muscles. She wore a red cotton half turtleneck looking shirt with a red mini skirt and black stockings. Her outfit looked as if it was stitched to perfection clinging to every voluptuous curve of her well defined body. He wasn't looking his best because he hadn't had a haircut in two weeks, but he knew he had the savoir faire to make his move.

Even though Devon rehearsed what he wanted to say, he knew that the best game was no game at all. He decided that he was just going to be himself and go for broke. He approached the young woman and said,

"Excuse me Ms.; can I get your name?"

"Datmug, and you?"

"Datmug, what kind of name is Datmug, African?"

"Dat mug on your shoulders looked real goofy when you came in late for work," laughed the young woman.

"Ok, Ms. Thang you got jokes!"

Laughing the young woman said,

"My name is Lala Jenkins, what's yours?"

"I'm Devon, Devon Chance how are you this fine evening?"

"Ok, Mr. Chance, I like that name Devon Chance."

"Oh you do huh; well you know what they say."

"And what is that?"

"Everyone needs a Chance!"

"Ha-ha, that's real cute Devon Chance!"

Devon instantly felt a mutual physical attraction and as he continued conversing, the big bodied young man that he was talking to earlier came over to them and loudly said,

"What's up my people?"

Devon looked at the young man with a facial expression that said,

"Will you get your ass out of here?"

The large obnoxious man continued talking until he began to dominate the conversation with his loud abrasive behavior, and he had a laugh that made Devon cringe on the inside every time he heard it.

Break time was over and the group headed back to the room to continue training. Despite speaking only a few words, Devon was certain that Lala was "feeling him". As he walked up the stairs the large abrasive man said to him,

"Yo, did you see her cousin? She's the light skinned chick who looks mixed, and you should holla at her!"

"Yeah, she's cute but I like Lala."

"Lala, oh so is that her name? Whatever dude, that's me! I'm gonna get with that!"

"Man, get the fuck outta here! You didn't even know her name!"

"Bro why don't you holla at her cousin? She ain't your type!"

"Look here big man you're cock blocking, and where I come from, we call that 'captain save a ho'! Stop saving G!"

"G, why did you call me G bro?"

"Huh, nothing forget about it. It's an east coast thing!"

Devon laughed to himself for the remainder of the class as he watched the abrasive young man try to impress Lala throughout the training. He then figured that after all of the obnoxious guy's antics that she probably wouldn't want to be bothered. The class ended and Devon was the first to leave for the parking lot. As Devon walked down the stairs to the door he heard,

"Devon, wait for me!"

"Oh, hey Lala what's up?"

"I was wondering if you would be kind and walk me to my car."

"Sure I don't mind at all, and hopefully you didn't have to park as far as I did. Some idiot in a green Honda Accord parked all crooked and took up two parking spots! I mean talk about selfish!"

"Really, well you know that they say that dorks are very attracted to idiots," said Lala as she smiled and opened the door to the Honda Accord that Devon was referring to. He stood flabbergasted and embarrassed as Lala blew him a kiss and drove off towards the parking lot exit. Devon stood and watched as if he had his feet stuck in the cement. After she drove out of sight, he could only laugh at himself, because he knew in his heart that he was about to start dating the woman that he prayed for. Lala had looks, a sense of humor, and a charming personality. Judging by her physical stature Devon assumed that she was involved in sports, and although he didn't believe in love at first sight, he knew that this was definitely the type of woman that he could fall for.

Devon and Lala continued to work at Next Data and they continued to flirt with each other on a daily basis. He was amazed at how wonderful her personality was and how it coincided with his. One day he invited Lala over to his house to have dinner.

"Hey Lala, would you like to come over so that I can make you some of my delicious fried chicken?"

"Are you asking me on a date?"

"No, I'm asking you to come over for some chicken."

"Oh really, and is that all that you want me to come over for?"

"Yeah, but if I didn't know any better than I'd think that you want to come over for a little more."

"And if I did then exactly what would a little more be?"

"It'd be Kool-Aid of course," laughed Devon.

Later that evening Lala agreed to meet with Devon at the mall by her house since he was going there anyway to purchase a tie for work. Devon purchased his tie and sat in his car waiting for Lala's arrival, but an hour had passed by and there was no sign of her. He began to wonder why she wasn't there yet so he decided to go to a pay phone and call her house.

"Hello, may I speak to Lala?"

"Who's this," asked a demanding voice.

"This is Devon, who is this?"

"This is Louis, and she ain't here!" Click!

The phone immediately hung up, and Devon instantly thought that maybe Lala didn't show up because she had a boyfriend, but then he thought,

"If she had a man, then why would she give me her home phone number?"

He looked at his watch and figured that he would give her another thirty minutes to come. Thirty minutes passed by with no sight of Lala, and Devon starting getting upset,

"I know this chick didn't stand me up! She seemed like she was feeling me! I know that wasn't her man on the phone, it just couldn't have been! She seems too good of a woman to play me like that!"

Even though Devon had suspicion about Lala having a boyfriend, he was to the point now that he didn't care for waiting anymore and he remembered seeing her address written on some paperwork at work. He decided to drive over to her house he said to himself,

"I can't go out like this, if she's trying to play me than she's dealing with the wrong person!"

Devon pulled into Lala's apartment complex, and he got out of the car and headed to her door. When he knocked on the door a man stood about 6ft tall with a slender athletic build, but he looked like working out was more important to him than brushing his teeth!"

"Is Lala here?"

"She ain't here," said the man who Devon recognized his voice as Louis from the phone conversation about an hour ago. Louis gave him an evil look as he slammed the door in Devon's face. Devon couldn't react because he was stunned at how fast and hard the door slammed in front of him.

Although Devon appeared to be desperate, he didn't want to make a scene so he walked away feeling dejected. He had just started to get to know Lala and he felt that they really had a connection. He decided to drive home as he tried to forget about the situation happening, and he figured that it would be her loss and not his. On his way home Devon got a little more frustrated because he had to sit in traffic for at a light around the corner from Lala's apartment because of a car accident. He said to himself,

"Boy, I just can't catch a break tonight!"

He got home and decided to call it a night, and right when he was preparing to get into the shower, the phone rang.

"Hello," he said.

"Devon, it's me Lala."

"Yo, how the fuck you gonna play me, I thought we had something! What did your boyfriend tell you that I came over?"

"No weird butt, that was my brother," she said laughing hysterically.

"Sure he was. Who do I look like, Tommy Tucker, the neighborhood sucka?"

"Boy you got a million of em' don't you Devon! I was in a car accident when I was on my way to see you!"

"Car accident, are you okay?"

"Yeah I'm okay but I did get rear ended. My neck is a little sore."

"Yo, I'm sorry for snapping at you, but I thought that you tried to play me."

"I wouldn't do that to you Devon. I really like you."

"I really like you to Lala. Why don't you come over and let me take care of that neck for you. Do you need me to pick you up?"

Despite the fact that Devon briefly knew Lala, he knew that she was special and he was already starting to catch feelings for her. After he picked her up from her apartment the two of them laughed the night away about the incident, and Devon couldn't help but think,

"I'm so glad that I didn't act a fool. I probably would have gotten my behind kicked and I would have lost my girl!"

Devon and Lala began to date each other, and they started to spend a considerable amount of time with one another. He not only found the woman of his dreams but he also found a new best friend. He had eventually saved enough money that allowed him to move out of his Aunt's house into a small apartment of his own. Every day for three months straight Devon spent time with Lala, and he suddenly felt that he was falling in love. He was the happiest man alive until one day the two of them discovered that Next Data was going out of business; therefore they were going to be out of a job. Devon was already living check to check, and his aunt had moved back to Pennsylvania, therefore he didn't have a vehicle anymore.

Even though Devon was falling in love, he barely knew Lala and he had no family living in Arizona other than Paul and the Aunt that didn't allow him to stay with her because of her husband. He spent a considerable amount of time trying to find a job to no avail.

"Hello Lala, hey babe, how are you?"

"Good boo, how are you?"

"I'm not good Lala. I'm not good at all."

"What's wrong Devon?"

"I'm about to get evicted, and I can't find a job anywhere! I don't have any more money except for enough to get a plane ticket back to Pennsylvania.

"Devon, I Love You. I know it's only been three months, but we've spent so much time together, and I really don't want to lose you!"

"You know what, I love you too Lala, but I have no money or family to help me out, and I don't know what to do. I'm only 19 and until I get done with college I'm not going to be able to find a decent job!"

"Well maybe you can stay here with me and my two brothers!"

"Lala you're crazy! I know Louis can't stand me as it is ever since that day that you got in that accident. First impression is a lasting impression, and he hasn't been impressed with me since."

"I know my brothers, and they are always looking to help people out. My oldest brother especially will do it because he likes the fact that you're all into football. Let me ask them and see what they say. It will only be temporary, and then we can get our own place together."

In spite of the fact that the young couple's relationship was in its infancy stage, Lala's brothers had agreed to let Devon move in. At first he was a little reluctant to move in and not because he only knew them for three months, but because he was somewhat embarrassed that he couldn't get any help from his own family. Where was Chippy's promise? He often wondered why he had to pull teeth whenever he called home for help.

He noticed how supportive Lala's family was for her, and how they even took in someone who just started dating their baby sister. Even though he was shocked, Devon was truly thankful for the hospitality, but the more that he thought about the struggles he endured trying to survive the more that his conscious began to tug at his insecurities. He constantly said to himself,

"What is it about my family? It's almost like they want to see me fail! Every time I call home for help they seem to give me the same tired line that they had to struggle so I need to learn how to struggle. Why should I have to struggle just because my parents struggled? Why don't they want it to be an easier road for me? This is pure ignorance! Each one is supposed to teach one not each one defeat one!"

Instead of conceding to the ignorant thoughts that filled his head, Devon snubbed the beast within, and he became motivated to prove that he could make it on his own.

He accepted Lala's invitation to live with her brothers, and even though he was very appreciative towards them he still felt uncomfortable about living there. Devon couldn't seem to get over the anger of having to rely on total strangers for help. He often pondered about why his father wasn't there for him the way he said that he would be, and he was somewhat disturbed that his mother and stepfather only contributed on occasions. He was still significantly young and new to the "real world" and although he grew up as a gifted child, he was still ignorant to a variety of life's obstacles.

Devon was at a point in life where he understood that things wouldn't be easy for him, but he often felt that they shouldn't have to be as hard as they were either. When things would go bad he just couldn't stop uttering his infamous phrase,

"What did I do to deserve this? I just want to be able to go to college and play football. I've noticed that other families help each other as much as they can, but for some reason mine seems to want the next person to struggle! Forget this; I'll make it on my own. I don't need them!"

Devon had been rejected by his great aunt's husband, lived with two grown men in a studio apartment, and is now living with a young woman and her three brothers; yet he still maintained his focus as he aspired to earn a scholarship playing football. Even though he was now somewhat stable and motivated more than ever, he was unaware of how difficult the road ahead was about to become. Devon was now living in Mesa, Arizona and since the coach at his former school was untrustworthy, he decided to enroll into Mesa Community College where he was going to try to "walk on" the football team.

Lala and Devon eventually moved out and got their own apartment and Devon completed a semester of school at Mesa Community College. One day he and Lala decided to visit back to Devon's home in York, Pa. Devon was very excited about Lala meeting his family, but what Devon didn't realize was that they were technically traveling back not as a couple but as a trio. Lala was in her first trimester of pregnancy. Although she wasn't 100% sure about being pregnant, she had a strong feeling that she conceived and since she was unsure of how Devon would react she decided to wait until their return from York to take a pregnancy test.

Delicious Cycle

My intentions were to lead you throughout this voyage as I enlighten you
even though our journey is not complete.
Our world has been worsened by internal causes
that have reciprocated a sweet yet bitter treat.
Ignorance has consumed us to the point where we can now taste it in the air.
This beast within us continues to cook a delicatessen
that we must no longer share!
Regardless of your belief you have been blessed
spiritually with a wonderful unique gift.
I've embraced my blessings. That cycle that was once vicious taste so
delicious especially now that I'm able to uplift!

David V.M. Kennedy

When the young couple arrived in York, Pa Devon introduced his new girlfriend to his mother, and Marsha set aside her motherly instincts of "losing" her son. Lala was very respectful to Marsha, and Devon's mother was pleased to see that he was happy even though she thought that he was too young to have a steady girlfriend. Even though Lala was already pregnant, Marsha pulled Devon to the side clearly stated,

"Listen boy; don't be way out there making any babies!"

"Come on Mom, I'm grown now," laughed Devon.

"Look, I'm only 37 and you are 21. Do I look like I want to be a grand mom?"

"Well hey, no disrespect but you didn't look like you wanted to be a mom 21yrs ago either."

"Yeah but if I…"

"If you what? What were you gonna say? Huh, I'm not stupid. I know what you were gonna say! I'm outta here!"

"Devon wait, I didn't mean anything!"

"You didn't have to say it Mom! I know that you regret having me as a teenager! I've been nothing but a thorn in your side since. Where's Lala? We're going to my Dad's house!"

Little did Marsha know but the damage was already done. Even though the young couple was unaware that they were about to be blessed with a child, Lala was pregnant.

"Lala, Lala, let's go Lala!"

"Hey, why are you yelling? What's wrong Devon?"

"Just get in the car! We're going to my Dad's house!"

Devon and Lala drove off in his old car "The Blue Falcon" down Conewago Ave towards Parkway Blvd. Devon was visibly upset and Lala tried to calm him down before asking what was wrong again.

"Hey, isn't that the football field where you played as a little boy?"

"What? Oh yeah, that's Boys Club field."

"Yeah, your mom was just telling me how she was the loudest mouth out there cheering you on. I bet that was exciting for you!"

"Yeah, it was real exciting," he said sarcastically.

"Devon what is wrong?"

"Do you want the truth or do you want me to make something up?"

"You know I want the truth, silly!"

"I'm a fucking accident that's what! She cheered on that field, because she had to not because she wanted to! Hell I'm going to visit a father who never even saw me play on that fucking field! Fuck! That explains why I had to struggle so much. They could've been helping me more. Shit you don't see white kids struggling like this. Their parents go above and beyond to make them comfortable. Why do black parents make their kids struggle just because they had to struggle when they were young? I can't help that I was born, so why am I being punished for it? I feel like once I reached a certain age that both of my parents felt like they were done parenting or something! I mean look at you. You're on point. You knew how to balance bills. You understood credit. You just knew things that I should have but didn't! It seems like every white person our age that I met in Phoenix had things or knew how to get them! I don't know shit, and that's because I ain't shit. I'm a bum. I'm an accident. My life shouldn't have occurred!"

"Are you done," Lala smiled.

"What?"

"Are you done talking stupid?"

"So now I'm stupid?"

"If you are the ranting words that you just spoke then yes! Devon, you have to believe that you were placed on this earth for a reason! Do you believe in God?"

"That's a dumb question, you know I do."

"Ok then, are you saying that God makes accidents? Our God doesn't make mistakes Devon. You were blessed with a purpose and it is your responsibility to find what that purpose is. Your Mom and Dad aren't perfect, but they did the best that they could raising you and look what you've become. Think about their upbringing Devon. You told me that they both were adopted and that they had a rough life. Add up everything that happened to them, and still here you are about to play college football so that you can earn a degree to better yourself. Stop feeling sorry for yourself Devon. Your mother loves you, and so does your father. They just have different ways of expressing it."

Devon drove the rest of the way to Chippy's house in silence, and he was blown away and amazed by Lala's wisdom. As they got to Chippy and Paula's townhouse in a complex next to a bowling alley, Devon noticed eight of his brothers playing football in the parking lot in front of the home.

"Devon, what's up big bro," said Chippy's second to the youngest child Carter.

"What's up Mr. Carteer?"

"Yo, why do you always say my name like that?"

"It's from a TV show little brother don't sweat it. Let me see them hands!"

"Devon you're a bum! Dad said he ain't giving you any money," yelled Devon's annoying brother Cain.

"Man, shut the hell up Cain! Is that all you do is talk trash? You're a bum!"

"No you're a bum and that's why Dad said that you don't like to work. He said that you're like Aunt Sarah. You're a con artist!"

"Yo, I'm gonna punch you in your freakin' head you little piece of shit!"

"If you touch me I'll tell Dad!"

Devon's visit home was reality check as to why he was so anxious to leave York, Pa. To him seemed that no matter what he tried to do with his life that there was always someone there to either criticize or call him names. Since Devon experienced this type of behavior since he could remember, the most minor words of criticism would set him off. He would get so emotional and anger would build inside of him as quick as two eyes could blink. It was piercing to Devon's ears to hear his little brother Cain talk bad about him, because Cain knew what to say to get under his skin.

"Dad just bought me a new bike too so you can forget getting any money for school you bum!"

"Boy, I swear I gonna punch you right in the face when I catch you!"

"Who is that? I know that ain't your girlfriend Devon, because you're gay!"

"Fuck you Cain!"

"Aw, I'm telling my mom that you cussed at me!"

"I don't give a shit, you little spawn from Satan! Lala let's get out of here! I'm ready to go back to Az. These people got issues!"

Even though Devon wanted Lala to meet Chippy and spend some time with him, Cain got under his skin so bad that he was ready to cut his entire trip short and go back to Arizona. Devon decided to take Lala to a small petting zoo and get some ice cream so that he could calm down at a place on the eastern side of York. On their way back in town Devon wanted to show her where he grew up in the projects.

"This is called Parkway projects, and I used to live right here on the corner."

"Oh, wow, I always imagined that the projects would be trashy and run down," said Lala in amazement.

"Yeah, I'm sure a lot of people think that. Some cities they are, but here in York we take pride in ourselves. York is not a bad place to live as long as you can elevate your mind above the ignorant mentality that some people have."

"So Devon, tell me why do you always say that you hate York, Pa so much, but yet you seem to love it here where you grew up?"

"It's not that I literally hate it here. It's just the fact that there seems to be a conscious that engulfs a vast majority of the people in this city. York is not the biggest place in the world, therefore people know a lot about each other. Not only that there used to be a time when the old heads used to get their groove on so bad that they didn't always tell kids who their real fathers were. This is a problem, because many people here are related to one another without even knowing it and especially in the black community. People here seem to have the mentality that they need to talk bad about the next person and wish them the worst. I think that it's because those types of people are just miserable, and as the old saying goes misery loves company."

"Yeah but Devon you have that everywhere. There are always going to be people that hate on you for no specific reason due to the fact that they are just jealous."

"You're absolutely right Lala, but the problem with York is the fact that it is so small and people here love to gossip. It's as if they are drug addicts that need a fix of negativity. They act as if this community doesn't have an identity or something. I mean New York is the "Big Red Apple" and Philadelphia is the city of brotherly love. Baltimore is America's charm city and what is York?"

"That's a good question, so what is York?"

"York is America Lala! This small city has a lot of history. A major part of this country was born here. It is known as one of the nation's first capitals. People don't even know that the Articles of Confederation were drafted here, and that is why York claims to be the first capital of the United States. They should be proud! The Article of Confederations was the first legal documents to acknowledge the colonies as the United States of America! Do you get what I'm saying Lala? United is a key word here! So my point is that York has an identity, therefore people should have more pride in themselves, and they should embrace the fact that it all started here. People need to open up the lines of communications, and become more united!"

"I agree with you but that's easier said than done."

"No it's not Lala. There needs to be what is called a paradigm shift here in York, Pa."

"I heard of that in one of my business classes but I didn't quite understand it."

"Well think of it as a pattern of how people think. The mental pattern of how many think here is equivalent to the crab in the barrel mentality. If someone is trying to succeed or get out of the barrel, then you have the other crabs clinging on trying to pull that person back in."

"I see where you're going so what exactly is a paradigm shift going to do?"

"Well Lala, the paradigm shift is a change in the pattern of thinking. It won't just happen overnight. There needs to be something major. There needs to be a revolution. There needs to be multiple occurrences of positive thought patterns displayed on a regular basis. People need to shift their mental thought process and way of thinking. For example, like me people need to stop saying that they hate York. We need to ask ourselves why so we hate York, and then we need to make a collective effort on improving on the things that makes us hate living here. There needs to be a unified metamorphosis with the conscious of the city of York, Pennsylvania. We need to believe whether we still live here or not that we are descendants of people who started this country. If we are able to shift the paradigm to where people are more positive and unified throughout the community and then change for the common good will occur."

"I agree Devon, but you will always have those 'crabs in the barrel' that will continue to hate no matter what."

"Exactly Lala and a perfect example of a paradigm shift is to now look at that crab that is clinging, and see it as not pulling the other crab back into the barrel, but see it as holding on to the crab because it receiving help to get out of the barrel!"

"Devon you are a genius! I love you so much!"

"That's what she said," laughed Devon.

"Very funny Devon, that was very funny!"

As the couple laughed Devon drove past a basketball court at Jefferson school that was an abandoned school that sat adjacent to the projects.

"Whoa, there goes my cousin Omar! Yo, O what's up cuz?"

"What's up Devon? When did you get back? How's Arizona?"

"It's all good. I like it and all but it's just so different. It's clean I know that! Especially compared to here, there's hardly any trash on the streets!"

"Cool, are you still playing football? You're getting' fat boy!"

"Yeah, oh this is my lady Lala, and she's the reason why I'm getting a gut!"

"I don't tell you eat so much, so don't blame me!"

"Anyway yeah, I'm about to train hard and try at it again. What are you doing with yourself?"

"I just finished running the Penn Relays for a Juco in Maryland but they don't have a football program."

"Yo, why don't you come back with us? We just got our on crib, and I know you and I can tear it up out there!"

"I don't know Devon, I have a daughter now and I need to take care of her."

"Now Omar you know that if you don't take care of yourself first then you can't provide to your baby girl like you need!"

"When are you going back? I'm ready to bounce anyway, because these folks around here just don't get it! They're fucking miserable!"

Even though Devon and Lala just started to get on their feet, Devon was always willing to help out any family the best way that he could and Lala had the same compassion for family as well. Devon told Omar that he and Lala were leaving in the next few days and that it would be okay for him to room with them since they had a big two bedroom apartment. Omar agreed to give Phoenix a try and the trio eventually flew back to Arizona together.

Even though the ambitious trio had plans for being successful in Arizona, Devon received a shocking surprise one morning in the bathroom.

"Lala are you okay? What are you doing up so early? Gross, are you okay babe? What did you just throw up, last night's dinner?"

"I think I'm pregnant Devon!"

"I know you just didn't say the P word!"

"I gotta be! I haven't had my period in lord only knows when, and I've been throwing up a few times! You're mad aren't you? You're probably gonna leave me like the men did to the other women in my family huh?"

"No, but I should leave you for making that dumb ass statement! The way that I've been feeling lately, I need a son! It will just motivate me more!"

"Who says that it will be a boy?"

"God says because he knows that I'm not prepared to have a girl yet! If you're pregnant then it will be a boy. Besides, I told you before that if it happened then happened. We could have used birth control, but we didn't so I guess it was meant to be."

"If you say so Devon, but my mom and dad are going to be pissed!"

"Yeah my mom will be too, but we're grown so they'll get over it. My dad will be happy! He's wanted me to have kids since I could bust one!"

As foreseen, both Devon's Mom and Lala's parents were initially unhappy about the situation, but they eventually accepted the blessing. Devon was now motivated more than ever to play football. He took his passion for the game to another level because he now had a sense of urgency to get educated in order to provide for his soon to be child. Even Omar couldn't believe the desire that Devon displayed during their workout sessions. Devon felt a new beginning on life, and he refused to let anything or anyone stop him from achieving his goals.

Although Devon had the desire, determination and dedication, he still wasn't fully equipped to battle the ignorance that he was about to withstand. Omar and Devon attended tryouts for the Mesa Community College football team, and Devon was in the best shape of his life. He was spectacular on the field, and it appeared that he Omar was creating a buzz amongst their new teammates that the kids from Pennsylvania were who they needed to win a championship. Throughout the practices Devon was often complimented by members of the team on how good of a quarterback that he was and how fast Omar was. Devon and Omar brought a different attitude and style of football to the locals, and the two of them were the highlights of every practice.

In spite of their peers overall approval, Devon was in for a rude awakening when the cut list was posted after tryouts. Devon and Omar were so confident that they made the team that they already made plans to go to the mall to buy team colored cleats and accessories for their uniforms. Even though the two cousins had high praise from teammates, Omar's name was the only name of the duo that made it! Devon stared at the list in disbelief while Omar appeared to be more upset than he was as they analyzed the list.

"Yo Devon, what the fuck yo? This is some bullshit! Yo, you was killin' it out there kid!"

"I don't know O, I thought that I did good out there too. I need to go talk to that coach, because the Qb coach acted like he loved me!"

"Yo, this is mad whack cuz. Everybody out there was on your jock! I can't believe this shit!"

Devon and Omar walked to the coach's office for an explanation as to why he didn't make the team.

"Coach Cornbaugh what's going on, is that list right?"

"Huh, what are you talking about?"

"The roster for the team is up, and I don't see my name on there."

"Are you sure? Did your check again?"

"Well actually no, I only looked once. I'll go look again."

Devon and Omar walked about fifty yards back to the locker room and noticed that the list had been taken down already.

"Yo O, I know this coach ain't tryin' to play me!"

"Man I hope not. Maybe they needed to add your name on and didn't bring it back over yet. Why else would he ask if you checked again?"

"Yeah that's a good point cuz. Let's go back and see what he says."

"What the f…" said Omar.

"Can you believe this shit Omar? The door is locked!"

"Yo, here he comes Devon; he's walking with some of the team."

"Coach Cornbaugh, hey the list is gone! Look kid you're not on the team okay? Good luck to you!"

"Good luck to me, what do you mean that I'm not on the team? Why did you tell me to go check the list again? How did I not make the team? Weren't you watching out there? I was almost flawless!"

"You're just not a quarterback son, have a good day!"

"Come on coach, be real! I was the best out there and you know it!"

"Look kid, you wouldn't have been a starter for this school and you probably would have been third of fourth on the depth chart anyway."

"You've got to be kidding me! Everyone loved how I played! What the hell were you looking at out there?"

"Don't sass me kid, and besides you're not a quarterback, your just a thrower, and as far as I'm concerned your too stupid to play that position!"

The sounds of these harsh comments hit Devon's ears like a submarine missile exploding into a ship at sea! He was furious, and inside the beast within began to rage! Devon clinched his fist tightly and his first impulse was to strike, but then he took a deep breath, swallowed his pride, and walked out of the office. Omar was outside of the office waiting for him, and he was able to ear every word that was said between the two. As soon as Devon walked outside, he dropped to one knee and began to weep. Omar reached down and snatched Devon by the shirt and said,

"Get your ass up cuz; don't let no punk ass bigot get you down. Everyone out there knows that you were the best Q.B."

"What the fuck Omar," Devon cried.

"Yo, get up man. Don't let him have the pleasure of seeing you upset! Fuck that dude! Let's get out of here."

With that said Devon rose to his feet and wiped away his tears and the two of them headed for home with Omar saying sarcastically,

"I wish I would play for that bum, fuck that coach Devon! Let's bounce."

Even though Omar and Devon felt that the whole incident was racially motivated, Devon didn't want to believe it, but he decided to make a complaint with the Dean of Students. He walked into the Dean's office and before he could introduce himself the Dean already knew who he was. The Dean said,

"Hey Devon, everyone's telling me that you're the man out there on the field!"

"Well apparently the coach doesn't think so, I got cut!"

"You got cut? Now that's hard to believe because I came to practice to watch you, and I came because I heard a lot about you!"

"Well I did, and I don't understand it!"

"Let me talk to the coach Devon so that I can find out what's going on."

The next day Devon was called into the office and the Dean said,

"Listen son, I don't know any other way to tell you this but to tell you the truth. This is a Mormon school, and if they can help it they won't have a black quarterback leading their team."

"You're joking right? In 1995 you mean to tell me that they told you that?"

"Yeah son, I'm sorry."

Although Devon had an idea that the decision for him to be cut was racially motivated, he was still shocked at how the situation came to be. In spite of being hurt by the comment from the coach, he was somewhat pleased because the Dean was honest and straight forward by telling him the truth. Devon continued to take classes, but decided to transfer back to Phoenix College because the coach there had been fired. Omar decided to go back home due to the fact that he missed his daughter and girlfriend. Devon tried to talk him in to staying, but he told he said that he was too homesick and that he might come back another time. Devon continued to work and Lala gave birth to a healthy baby boy. He was now a proud father, and he was now at a major crossroad in his life. He wondered to himself, "Now what, if I don't get an education I won't be able to give my son the life that I know he deserves."

Despite being a young father with no real financial stability, Devon knew that the only way to take care of his family was to get a college education. He continued to go to school part time while he worked and after his son was one year old, he decided to try to play football again. Lala knew how hard Devon worked at pursuing his dream, and she wanted him to make it more than anyone, but she sensed that he was giving up.

"Babe, are you okay?"

"Huh, yeah I'm fine. Why do you ask?"

"Well I see that Phoenix College is having open tryouts for walk-ons, and I haven't seen you training as hard. You're getting a little tummy there buddy," she joked.

"Ha-ha, I wonder why. Thanks to you Ms. Black Mexican! All we eat is Mexican food and I've been chilling on the couch after school and work. I don't have time to work out with us having the baby now."

"Devon, listen to me. Quit the damn job and go achieve your goal!"

"Did you say quit? Yeah right, your family and mine already think that I'm a bum who is just chasing childish unrealistic dreams! I ain't trying to hear that shit anymore!"

"I could care less what they think Devon. I believe in you, and I don't care what it takes. We've been together for a while now and I know you. You need to finish what you've started or else you will be miserable for the rest of your life! Don't stop playing until you want to stop. Don't let the so called powers at be deter you from your dream. Make your dream a reality. I thought that you were a Yorker!"

"No, I'm a true Yorker, get it right!"

"Well then get your pudgy behind off of the couch and go up to that school!"

Even though Lala began to feel the pressure from her family that Devon wasn't much of a man because he never kept a job for a long time and that he was just chasing childish unrealistic dreams, she was convinced that he was going to do something special, because she believed that together they could overcome anything. Devon was catching heat from both his and her family and he told Lala,

"I guarantee to you that I will get a full scholarship!"

"I know you will Devon; let's do this!"

"Boy, get your hand off of my butt and get out of here!"

Devon was now 21yrs old and he weighed 233 pounds. He decided to try walking on at Phoenix College one more time, so he stopped by the practice field during spring session. He walked onto the field and he approached a man who appeared to be an assistant coach.

"Hey Coach, my name is Devon Chance, and I was wondering if I could try out for your team?"

The coach took a look at Devon from head to toe and said,

"Sure, what position do you play, Linebacker?"

"No sir, I play QB."

The coach chuckled and yelled toward the head coach,

"Hey Coach! I got a quarterback for ya!"

The Head Coach looked at Devon as he laughed and said,

"What are you talking about, that Defensive Tackle standing next to you?! The biggest Qb I've ever seen in the NFL was no more than 200lbs! I think Montana is only 195!"

Devon was not at all amused by the jokes that the coaches were making and he felt that they were having a little too much fun at his expense. He grabbed a football that was in the center of the field resting on the goal line and dropped to both of his knees and yelled to another player,

"Yo, go deep!"

"Ok, I got you! You're on your knees though do you want me to jog?"

"No, run a deep 9 route as fast as you can!"

The kid took off running down field with amazing quickness and explosion as Devon launched a perfect spiral that traveled 55 yards in the air as it landed into the player's hands perfectly while he was in stride.

As Devon stood on his feet another assistant coach came walking on the field and said,

"Whoa, boy you gotta rocket arm! How much do you weigh?"

"I weigh 233lbs sir, but I just started running. I can drop this weight with the quickness. It's just water weight!"

The Head Coach looked at Devon as he laughed and said,

"Yeah, you have an arm but anybody can throw a football! I bet you can't even move! Yeah, come back when you're slim and trim and we'll give you a shot."

The assistant said, "Look, don't listen to that. Look at me and listen. Dawg this is Phoenix, Arizona. They ain't ready for no black quarterback. I'm the offensive coordinator so check it out; if you can get down to 220lbs then you can play for me."

"Consider it done, and Coach I'm not coming to sit the bench!"

"Son, I gotta feeling that you are planning on way more than just making the team! Do what you gotta do and I'll see you soon!"

After the encouraging words from the assistant coach Devon worked out obsessively because he felt like this was his only and final opportunity. He worked out religiously with a former world class sprinter who had train him by running a quarter mile up a mountain every other day. Devon came back into training camp in the best shape of his life weighing 215lbs and he was determined to not let anything or anyone stop him from being the starting quarterback for Phoenix College. When training camp was over Devon was announced to be the starting quarterback of Phoenix Community College.

Even though he went on to set numerous school records, during the season his coach would constantly take him out of the game to replace him with the backup quarterback.

"Coach Milton, why does he keep taking me out of the game," Devon asked the assistant who gave him a chance.

"I don't know man, we've been arguing about that all season! Just keep doing your thing. You're here to move on to a four year school more than you are to win so don't sweat it.

In spite of often being benched, Devon went on to make the junior college all American team and recruiters were contacting him every day.

"What am I you secretary? You had another recruiter call," said Lala as Devon came home from a practice.

"Yes you are, and a damn sexy one too! Come here beautiful!"

"Quiet Devon, you're going to wake the baby."

"No, when I get through with you, then you're gonna wake the baby!"

Devon was elated about all of the attention that he was receiving, and it was evident to Lala that he was a new man around the house.

Although Devon had all American honors, his recruiting process was not smooth at all. He later found out that his coach was telling recruiters that he was ineligible to play division one football, and that he would not be eligible until the following year. He couldn't understand what the coach's motives were, and at first he thought that it was racially motivated, but he immediately dismissed that notion because the coach's entire staff was African American!

"Why would this man say that I'm ineligible Lala?"

"Maybe he wants you to play for him next year. Can't you leave Juco after this summer?"

"You might be right. Do you think that he would really try to shaft me for that? I mean the more players that he sends to college the better he looks."

"It's college, but it's also a business Devon. You gotta realize that."

Lala's logic made a considerable amount of sense to Devon, and he became infuriated at the thought of the coach being unethical. Devon got fed up with being screwed by his coach with the D1 schools recruiting him and he took liberty of signing with a smaller school that was on the division two level. One day Devon was walking to class and the Head Coach passed by.

"Devon, where were you on Wednesday? The University of New Mexico was here looking for you!"

"I went back east to visit my mother. She was sick. I had no clue that they were coming. Why didn't you tell me?"

"Well, they were here!"

"Wait, that's it? Is that all you have to say?"

"I'll see if they still want you. Go to class and learn something!"

"Wait a fucking minute! Who do you think that you're talking to Coach? Oh, by the way I spoke to Missouri yesterday. Do you care to explain why you told them that I'm ineligible?"

"I don't know what you're talking about! If you keep this tone then you'll sit the bench next season!"

"Fuck you! I'm going to be a starter at Clark Atlanta University next season!"

Devon stormed off, and he was now at a point in his life where he didn't trust anyone who was Caucasian holding an authoritative position. The beast allowed Devon's mind to become shallow, and he decided to sign with a historical black university for the simple fact that it was a predominant black college thinking that he would never get the kind of treatment that he got from the two colleges in Arizona. Arizona already had the reputation of being a racist state due to them not recognizing the Dr. Martin Luther King Holiday as a national holiday. This fact in addition to the treatment that Devon received, change his perspective on how white people acted.

Even though Devon had Italian roots as well as many white friends including D.F. who was one of his best friends, he was still hypocritical by categorizing white people. He often tried to justify his ignorance by using somewhat of a disclaimer by considering the "man" another word for the "corporate world white people". Devon signed his letter of intent to go to Clark Atlanta University, and he moved to Atlanta, Georgia while Lala stayed in Phoenix with her mother so that she could have help raising their son. Even though Devon achieved his ultimate goal of getting a full scholarship, until later in life he felt that he settled for less.

He knew that he was one of the best quarterbacks in the country and the stats proved that he was. Regardless of the fact that he had an opportunity to earn a degree, Devon still felt that he had something to prove. Before Devon went to Clark Atlanta University ignorance began to consume his heart. The beast within Devon was now at its strongest, and anger fueled with passion was like an anchor that was attached to his heart. He had been oppressed his entire young life, and he now adopted a "me against the world mentality".

Devon thought that he was treated unfair simply because of his skin tone, and although his mother raised him to be "color conscious" and not color blind, he still felt that he wouldn't have these type of discriminations at a black school. Before Devon enrolled into classes he had a long talk with the coach that recruited him, and he told his new coach about his experiences the coach responded by saying,

"Listen son, in today's world green is the only color that matters. I guarantee you one thing though; by you attending this historical black university your life is going to change. Mark my words. This school is going to make you a man!"

The Promise

I'll never give up; because if I do then I give up the ones beside me.
I'll never give up; because if I do then I give up
on the ones that believe in me.
I the person next to me gets down, I'll pick them up, and they the same.
I'll never give up; I'll believe in the cause, I'll fight to the end.
I will win.
This I promise.

After enrolling into Clark Atlanta University in Atlanta, Georgia, Devon was on cloud nine because his dreams were coming true. He remembered lying in his bed while he was young living in the projects wishing that he could play football and travel to other places to play. He often wished that he could be on a team that would wear the same traveling attire as they flew on planes and traveled on buses. For a young kid living in the projects who was raised by a teenage mother, these simple achievable goals for most were a long shot for Devon. Although h thought that going to a black college would be a perfect situation, it wasn't.

Devon knew that he had the ability to play on practically any team that he wanted, but he chose this particular university because of their academic reputation. While being recruited he was told that his school would be like attending a black Ivy League School. Devon wanted to major in sports medicine and he bought in to the recruiter's pitch that they had an excellent sports medicine program. He showed his athletic prowess on the football field as expected. Midway through the season his team was undefeated and it was evident that he had helped to put this tiny unknown school back on the map. His name appeared all over the largest newspaper in Atlanta and like the fable Midas everything that he touched turned to gold.

Devon's team went on to win the divisional championship, and he gained notoriety within the city of Atlanta. Even though he experienced an unblemished start to his college football career, his dream world was about to collapse.

"Coach, Coach, wait up!"

"Hey Devon, how's my Qb doing?"

"Whew, one second, let me catch my breath! Coach I tried to register for class, and they said that my major wasn't offered here and that I would have to transfer to Georgia State."

"Really, are you sure? I thought that you wanted to major in sports medicine. We have that."

"No coach, they only have allied health and it is only a two year program. I want to be an athletic trainer and she said in order to do that then I have to transfer! I can't do that while I'm on this football scholarship!"

"You're right, you can't. I am so sorry Devon. When I checked they said that they had sports medicine. I should have looked into it more."

Naturally the coach played dumb to the situation, and he apologized to Devon for any misunderstanding. Devon had no other alternative but to transfer his classes into the health and physical education field. Reluctant to major in health and physical education, Devon did so even though he objected to the physical education portion of the degree. He enjoyed the health classes because some were what he would have taken if he did sports medicine.

In spite of having to settle for a major that he didn't want, Devon went on to have a successful college football career by achieving MVP honors as well as setting school records. Although he had his entire education paid for, he still felt the pressures from Lala's family that he wasn't taking care of his responsibility by raising their son. Although he was on a full scholarship, he decided to take out a couple of student loans in order to help support his son. His thinking was that he could silence his critics by providing a substantial amount of money every now and then. Time passed and Devon began to miss Lala and their son so bad that he decided that he would get an apartment going into his last semester of school. The cost of living was not as high in Georgia as it was in Arizona; therefore he felt that it wouldn't be difficult for his family to live.

Devon was about to complete his final season of college football. The pressure of hearing that he wasn't taking care of his son became too much to bare, and even though he knew that moving his family closer to him would be self-motivating, his coaches completely disagreed. They didn't like his decision, because they felt that it would be a distraction. One day Devon was in his dorm room and he received a phone call from Marsha.

"Hello," said Devon.

"Boy, what are you doing," asked Marsha in a very demanding tone.

"Well hi Mom, I'm studying right now."

"Don't play dumb with me Devon Soriano Piccolo Chance! Why are you moving that girl down there?"

"What are you talking about?"

"Don't make me fly down there Devon!"

"Come on Mom, really? No disrespect but I'm grown!"

"Well your coach called me and he said that you don't need to bring your family, because he doesn't want you being distracted!"

"Mom relax, I got this!"

Although Marsha agreed with the coach that this would be a distraction, Devon could care less. He was a grown man and his decision was his own. He thought to himself,

"Why in the world did he call my mom? I am a grown ass man! All of my life my parents would talk around me. I am so sick of people talking around me and not through me! All he had to do was come and talk to me. My Mom and Dad used to do the same thing. They never came to me!"

Devon had developed a communication complex, because while growing up within a broken home, he often experienced his mother discussing matters about him to his father while he wasn't around. Stories often got misconstrued because Devon was never able to tell his side. It always seemed that his parents already had preconceived notions about the situations that he would experience on a daily basis. Instead of Devon expressing himself completely to his mother, he chose to hold his anger in, and this rage was nutritious for the hunger that the beast within craved. Devon decided to ignore his coach and mother, and he moved Lala and their son to Atlanta to be by his side.

Despite what his coaches thought about his decision, Devon continued to play as if he had no worries in the world. He proved both his mother and the coach wrong by taking his team to the national championship. He used the doubt that was cast into his mind by the coach as an inspiration to succeed. Even though he gained accolades in football, his achievements weren't gratifying because he wasn't doing it to satisfy himself, he was basically trying to say to the coach and his mother that he was right and they were wrong. Devon had enough money from his student loans to support Lala, and their son throughout the football season and they rented an apartment in the southwestern part of Atlanta better known as the "Swats". Lala took on a part time job working at a local video store, and after football ended Devon got a job with a trucking company delivering various supplies throughout Georgia.

Although Devon did extremely well in football, he didn't get noticed by the Major Football League which offered the best players millions of dollars to play football. Devon did get noticed by another league which played their games during the spring. He was offered a contract for $80,000 to play the upcoming season. Even though the money was substantial, he wanted to finish school and earn his degree. Amazingly Lala was able to land a career oriented job in Kennesaw, Georgia therefore she told Devon,

"Look that money will be there. Finish what you started, we'll be fine."

"Yeah but it's 80 G's for only a few months of football, now that's good cheddar!"

"I know but God forbid, if you get hurt, that cheddar becomes molded quickly!"

"Babe you always know what to say don't you?"

"That's because you always know what to do, now bring your handsome behind over here!"

Even though Lala convinced Devon to look at the big picture, she was unable to foresee what was about to happen. He returned home from school ranting and raving as he walked through the door.

"Those bastards, I can't believe those ignorant bastards did this!"

"What's wrong with you," asked Lala.

"They cut my scholarship! Those bastards cut my scholarship!"

"What do you mean?"

"My scholarship was for $19,000 per semester, and now they say that I only have $800! This is bullshit!"

"So why don't you go to your Coach and the financial aid department?"

"I did that, and I just keep getting the run around! Besides, the stupid financial aid department is being investigated for fraud by the FBI. I'm through with this school and I'm signing that contract! Black folks are just as scandalous! I don't give a shit what color you are. Money is the root of all evil, and this place dug that root right out of the ground!"

Instead of thinking things through ignorance prevailed. Devon allowed the beast within to make his decisions for him. He signed the football contract, because he felt betrayed by his coach and the school. He let his emotions get to him to the point where he didn't even bother to formally withdraw from his classes or say good bye to his coaches or teammates. In the midst of Devon's newfound chaos Lala became pregnant with her second child.

Even though Lala had a stable job, her pregnancy would cause her to eventually miss work, and neither of them had family to help with the kids. Devon now felt even more pressure to make money in order to support his family. He had two months before it was time to report to training camp and one day he received a phone call from his eighteen year old brother.

"Chyeah! Big bro, what's up?"

"Brother," said Devon that was an inside joke in a voice that sounded like he was out of breath.

"Chyeah, what's up Robo Buck?"

"Ah, so you got jokes huh?"

"Chyeah! You're teeth are so big that when you sneeze you put a hole in your chest!"

"Oh so you tryna blow me? Yo, you're teeth are so crooked that when you smile it looks like your tongue's in jail! Take that little brother! So what's up with you?"

"Yo, I just got that scholarship to the Art Institute of Atlanta! Only problem though is that they pay for everything but room and board. Can you help your little brother out?"

"Come on Carter now you're asking stupid questions! Of course I'll help you. That's a little drive from my crib but we can make it work."

"That's what I'm talking bout big brother! Shout out to Chippy's kids! Everybody knows that you need a Chance in your life!"

"Speaking of Chippy how is Dad anyway?"

"All you know, he's the same old Dad. He and Mom still go at it. She put him out again."

"Let me guess, he's back at Mahogany's with our other four brothers huh?"

"Nah, I think he's at our sister's mom's house this time in Spring Grove, Pa."

"Yo, Dad is a pimp. How does he do it? Better yet, how do they keep letting him back?"

"I don't know Devon. Hell I thought that I nice up in the bedroom! Oh, ah, Chippy long stroke!"

"Boy, you are a clown! You know I just got this football deal so I'm coming home for a minute before I report to camp so you can fly back with me."

Devon rarely got a chance to visit his family in Pennsylvania due to the fact that he didn't have the finances to do so while trying to go to school. When he did travel he would always get money sent from Chippy so that he could fly. Even though Devon wasn't financially stable yet, he still wanted to help Carter get out of the ghetto so that he could try to help him see different things other than the inner city of York, Pa. Before heading off to play pro football, Devon felt that he needed to go home to York, Pa in order to humble himself. Being home gave him a sense of purpose. He felt like a rock star when he returned, because of the love and attention that he received from his loved ones.

In spite of the fact that Devon tried so desperately to leave York, Pennsylvania, he always yearned to go home. For decades the anthem of his hometown was, "I got to get away from York!" Devon adopted this statement as his own personal agenda and although he remained focused and motivated it wasn't York, Pa that he needed to get away from. Devon needed to escape the beast within York, Pennsylvania which was ignorance. The everyday conversations of the community can become overwhelming if it is constant drama and negativity. One can pull a crab out of a barrel, but one needs to realize that they can use that same crab to place back into the barrel in order to pull another crab out.

Devon was famous for saying, "If you try to pull a crab out of a barrel of many, than there is always one trying to pull you back in!" He recognized that this particular philosophy was not only the mentality in the city of York, but it was a mentality of people in general and particularly within the African American community across the country. Even though Devon was able to educate himself he was still learning how to cope with ignorance. Devon was able to leave the ghetto and pursue his goals, but the difficulty of suppressing the beast called ignorance grew immensely. In order for Devon to continue his quest for peace and tranquility, he needed the support of a stable family.

Even though Devon came from a "dysfunctional family, he still had the love and nourishment from most of its members. One definition of family is a group of people connected by a common ancestor. Every family started with a father and a mother. Traditionally the father is the spinal cord of the family, and regardless to what one may think the father is supposed to be the family's strength and wisdom. The African American community is losing its strength! Our fathers are being destroyed by lust, ignorance, and being uneducated! Devon looked up to his father as if he were God himself. He felt that Chippy was everything because he was very intelligent, suave, strong and mentally tough. Even though his father had his mistakes, he still managed to teach Devon not to follow the ignorant path that he laid.

Although Chippy was wise and had courage, his flaws tended to dominate the relationship between he and Devon. While Devon was visiting back home he went to see Chippy at a new house that he bought due to Paula kicking him out again. All of his brothers and sisters were there and all 12 of Chippy's kids were under the same roof for the first time. Devon loved to spend time with his other brothers and sisters and Chippy soaked up moment by staying up with them late at night before going to work the following day.

Even though Chippy enjoyed the camaraderie of his children, he worked long hours therefore he fell asleep in his bedroom. While Chippy was asleep the guys were in the room clowning around having a good time. Devon's brothers were teenagers and they often "cut on each other" or "played the dozens". Devon normally didn't like to participate mainly because he wasn't really that good at snapping back. Although the game was intended for fun, this particular day the joy turned sour.

"Yo, your mom's teeth are so bad that she got pulled over for not having dental insurance," said one of Devon's twin brothers.

"Ah, yo, your mom is so black that she bleeds smoke, chyeah," said the other twin.

"Man you guys are some clowns," laughed Devon.

After the jokes and laughter Chippy awoke from his sleep and Devon asked his father,

"Dad, can I have some money for our trip back to Atlanta?"

"Boy when are you going to be a man and stop asking me for money?"

"Yeah, Devon's a bum," yelled Devon's Brother Cain.

"Yo, shut up Cain, before I punch you in your head!"

"Hey, leave your little brother alone."

"Yo, I'm tired of him Dad! Every time I come home he always tries to start something!"

"Who are you yelling at boy?"

"I ain't yelling at nobody. I'm just sick of him, and you always defend him no matter what he does!"

"You know what Devon, you remind me of my sister Sarah. You're always asking for money. She's always trying to con me out of money for something."

"What are you talking about? I'm not a con artist. I just asked for a little help that's all. I mean you said that you were going to help me with college and you only sent money a few times!"

"I told you Devon, you're just a bum! That's all you do is ask Dad for money! You need a job. You ain't never had no job!"

"Shut up you worthless piece of shit! I can't stand you right now," snapped Devon.

"Hey! I said leave your brother alone Devon. You're bigger than him. He doesn't know any better."

"Dad, he's fifteen years old! He knows what he's trying to do! He ain't nothing but a little instigator!"

Cain had a way of instigating to the point where it would get under people's skin. He was a master at manipulation. He knew what to say, when to say, and how to say things to provoke the emotions people the way that he deemed fit. In Chippy's eyes Cain could do no wrong.

"Devon, why don't you ask your mom and her husband for money? They've got money!"

"Yeah Devon, stop being a bum and ask your mom," laughed Cain.

"I swear, Cain one of these days I'm gonna break your jaw!"

"Dad said that your mom is fake anyway! She ain't got no money! Yeah Devon, your mom's so broke she can't even pay attention! Yeah she's so stupid that she failed a drug test! She's so black that lightening bugs follow her in the day time!"

"Yo, why don't you shut the fuck up Cain?! Don't talk about my mom like that! I'm sick of your little bitch ass!"

"Boy quit acting all sensitive about your mom," said Chippy.

"He doesn't need to be saying all of that right now! I ain't got time for no childish games! He better show me and my mom some respect and I don't care how young he is! If he wants to talk shit like a man then he better be able to deal with the consequences!"

"What did I tell you about being sensitive? Your mom ain't nobody, that bitch has probably got her head stuck up in the clouds somewhere!"

Despite the fact that Chippy was Devon's father, the beast within took over the atmosphere. At that precise moment Devon began to lose respect for his father, and he said,

"Hey man, don't call my mom that!"

"Oh, so what are you trying to be tough? Your mom ain't all that, I used to beat that bitch back in the day, she needs to take her fucking head out of the clouds!"

At that precise moment Devon experienced a flashback of images that traveled at the speed of light as they raced through his mind. He had an image in his mind that was so quick yet vivid of his mother being beaten by the hands of Chippy along with another vision of his stepfather Marcus throwing her across the living room. Instantaneously, Devon exploded as if a beast literally emerged from within him and said,

"Yo man, don't fucking talk about my mom like that!"

"Excuse me, who the fuck do you think you're talking too?"

"You heard what the fuck I said! Don't fucking talk about my Mom like that!"

"Oh, so what, you wanna get something off your chest?"

"Yo, you ain't gonna fucking disrespect my mom like that, I know that much!"

Chippy and Devon began shoving one another as they grasped each other's arms as if they were about to sumo wrestle. Devon's brother Carter jumped in between them so that they wouldn't exchange punches, and Devon and Chippy stood staring intensely into one another's eyes. Devon tried to hold back his tears but he couldn't control them, and he let go of Chippy's shirt and turned to walk out of the front door.

He began to walk as the tears of pain dropped as they seemed to be leaving his somber path. His tears didn't reflect the anguish of the confrontation with his father, but instead they flowed as if he had witnessed the death of his father. Chippy lived about 10 miles from the city, and Devon walked for three miles until he came to a phone booth. For each step Devon took another tear streamed down his face. He could not stop crying. It felt as if he had a dagger lodged in his heart and he couldn't get it removed. He called his mother's house and his sister Destiny answered the phone.

"Hello?"

"Where's mom," Devon whimpered as snot dripped onto the phone.

"She's not here, oh my God what's wrong with you Devon?"

His crying intensified.

"Oh my God Devon will you please stop? What is wrong with you," asked Destiny as she began to weep.

"Just come get me," cried Devon.

Confused about what was going on Destiny called her cousin to come pick her up and the two of them drove to a gas station where Devon was located. When they arrived Devon was standing there still weeping as if he were in physical pain. Destiny said,

"Devon, talk to me! What is wrong with you?"

Devon said nothing as he got into the car. He put his head in his hands and he cried the entire ride back to his mother's house. Marsha, Lala, and Devon's son were at the mall shopping and when Destiny and Devon got home she grabbed the phone to call their mother.

"Mom, there is something wrong with Devon, he has been crying continuously like he is in pain, and he won't tell me what is wrong," cried Destiny.

"Put him on the phone," demanded Marsha

Devon grabbed the phone while he still continued to cry and said,

"Hello?"

"What's wrong with you Devon, asked Marsha"

"I hate HIM! I hate HIM!"

Devon dropped the phone and sat on the floor as he curled up into a corner in the fetal position while wept some more. Marsha rushed home to find her son who was in his mid-20s lying on the floor as if he was that three year old kid from hope alley crying like someone stole his favorite red ball. She held her son close to her bosom caressing his soft wavy hair repeating,

"It's ok baby, its ok! It's ok baby, ok!"

"Why," he cried over and over again.

"Devon, it's okay just please baby calm down. Mom can't help if I don't know what happened. Calm down and tell me okay?"

After soothing her son for fifteen minutes Marsha asked Devon what happened, and he went into detail about what occurred.

"Now Devon what you Dad said was wrong, but he still is your father. You know very well to honor thy father and thy mother."

"He called you the B word and bragged about beating on you! I'm supposed to honor that?! I saw visions in my head as if a vivid memory was unlocked! It was so real! I saw him beating you over and over again. I knew you guys used to argue, but I never remembered that!"

"Listen Devon, if I'm not worried about it anymore then you shouldn't be either. We were young son. Your father didn't know any better."

"How could you say that, Mom? He knew very well what he was doing. I'm sick of him and my brothers calling me a bum too! He's the one that said that he was going to help me pay for college. What if I didn't earn my scholarship? It's not like he came to any of my games anyway! He doesn't care about me! He ain't no man!"

Devon gathered himself and wiped the tears from his face as he blew his nose into tissue that was on the mantle over the fireplace. Marsha somewhat justified Chippy's behavior by saying,

"Look Devon, your Dad doesn't know any better. First of all he doesn't even know you. Think about it son, was he here every day of your life? Did he go to the store to fetch for the calamine lotion when you got the chicken pox? Was he there when you made the all-star team your first year ever playing baseball? When none of your friends could come outside to play, did he throw the football with you in the front yard?"

"No, and that's my point! He didn't, you did."

"Exactly son, he wasn't there, so he doesn't really know you as a person. He only knows the part of you that he briefly saw throughout your life. You basically know your father as the guy who you occasionally reached out to for money. The two of you didn't spend the quality time that a father and son should spend with each other. He knows you as the son that always comes around for money. The rest is hearsay. He only goes off of what others tell him about you! Listen son, we were babies ourselves when we had you. Truthfully, we just weren't ready to be parents."

"Yeah I get it, I was an accident so please don't remind me."

"No, Devon God intended on you being here. No child born into this world is an accident. Did we plan it? No, but you best believe you were sent to me as a gift from God! You have made me the strong woman that I am, and you've brought countless smiles across my face! Pick your head up my young king. You have many gifts from God that you need to share. I love you, and so does your father. He just didn't have the foundation that I had with your grandparents; therefore I don't think he really knows how to love you like he should."

Even though Devon was still a little bitter inside, he raised his chin and went to the bathroom to wash his face. As he finished washing his face he slowly pulled the wash cloth from over his eye, and he looked into the mirror and noticed the scar from the former stitches above his right eye socket. As he looked at the scar he saw a constant reminder of how his life had been since day one. The scar above his eye told his whole life story. As he rubbed his finger over the scar he realized how close he came to having permanent damage to his eye. This scar was more than just a physical wound. This scar was a constant reminder of the struggle that he had been through since the time that he could remember.

Even though Marsha stated that Chippy loved Devon, it was his scar that told otherwise. Devon recalled Chippy's first reaction to his scar as getting into a fight with his mother. For now the beast known as Ignorance has consumed Devon's heart and he refused to forgive his father. As he continued to stare into the mirror he slowly and gently rubbed his scar as if he could make it go away.

He remembered exactly how it happened as if it were yesterday. Little Devon was running for his dear life from a kid six years older than him. As he reminisced about the incident he stared a little closer into the mirror as if he could literally see this beast called Ignorance being born. Jealousy was the beast's mother. Hatred was the beast's father. Together Jealousy and Hatred married each other in a small city called York, Pa where they lived on the streets of Hostility.

When jealousy and hatred are intertwined inside of a hostile environment, anger is certain to be born. Educators say that a child's personality is developed from birth to age five. Children's minds are like tiny sponges that soak up this water that we call life. As an adult we need to recognize how much our children pattern our thoughts and behavior. Regardless of your belief, the fact remains that human beings are only able to procreate by the sperm of a man and the egg of a woman. I believe that this is God's will; therefore no matter what your sexuality is you cannot argue that a father figure is not needed, because nature intended it to be that way.

As healthy human beings develop into adulthood their behaviors will change, but their personality will remain the same. The human brain is like a computer. If viruses are constantly being inputted then similar to a computer a person's mind is destined to crash. Devon needed his Father. He needed the constant guidance and wisdom from a man in order to help him cope with the everyday pressures of life.

Devon couldn't rid the traumatizing events of his life from the hard drive in his brain, and by not having his Father on a regular basis this caused him to develop a complex. Devon became Chippy. Like his father who unfortunately lost his own father, Devon developed a chip on his shoulder due to a void that couldn't be filled. Marsha said it best, and that was Chippy just didn't know any better. Chippy didn't know any better, because he was caught within a vicious cycle of behavior that became a choke hold on the citizens of York, Pennsylvania.

Even though Devon physically left York, he still carried his traumatic experiences with him. What enabled him to overcome many of his hardships was his belief in God, and the support of his loved ones. While staring at the mirror Devon has learned how the beast was born. He recognized the beast strengths as well as its weaknesses. After a few years Devon was able to mend the deteriorated relationship with Chippy. In spite of their relationship not being the same as it was when Devon was living with Chippy as a child, Devon realized that communication was a key component for the two of them. As time passed Chippy opened up to Devon more than he ever did before and for the first time in his life he held his son and said,

"I love you Devon!"

Although Chippy and Devon shared love on multiple occasions, Devon still encountered a dilemma with his younger brother Cain. Chippy warned Cain that there are just some things that a brother shouldn't do especially when dealing with a person like Devon. Devon stopped the vicious cycle by raising his two children in one household with the same woman who he had them to, but a problem that still remained was the battle that was about to occur between he and his brother. Cain was about to learn a valuable lesson. He was about to learn the hard way that he shouldn't have jeopardized Devon's daughter's life. Cain was about to feel Devon's wrath, because unlike Devon Cain's heart was impure. It was unfortunate for Cain, but one way or another Devon was going to eliminate the ignorance between them. With no uncertainty Devon was destined to prove that he no longer wanted to be part of a vicious cycle. Cain was severely about to realize that Devon had escaped the beast within.

LIGHT SWITCH
PRESS